CRITICAL NARRATIVE AS PEDAGOGY

Available from Bloomsbury:

Series Editors: Shirley R. Steinberg and Ana Maria Araujo Freire
On Critical Pedagogy, Henry A. Giroux
Echoes from Freire for a Critically Engaged Pedagogy, Peter Mayo
Critical Pedagogy for Social Justice, John Smyth
Teaching as the Practice of Wisdom, David G. Smith

CRITICAL NARRATIVE AS PEDAGOGY

IVOR GOODSON AND SCHERTO GILL

B L O O M S B U R Y
NEW YORK • LONDON • NEW DELHI • SYDNEY

Bloomsbury Academic
An imprint of Bloomsbury Publishing Inc

1385 Broadway	50 Bedford Square
New York	London
NY 10018	WC1B 3DP
USA	UK

www.bloomsbury.com

Bloomsbury is a registered trade mark of Bloomsbury Publishing Plc

First published 2014

© Ivor Goodson and Scherto Gill, 2014

No responsibility for loss caused to any individual or organization acting on or refraining from action as a result of the material in this publication can be accepted by Bloomsbury or the authors.

Library of Congress Cataloging-in-Publication Data
Goodson, Ivor, author.
Critical narrative as pedagogy / Ivor Goodson and
Scherto Gill. – 1st published 2014.
p. cm. – (Critical pedagogy today)
Includes bibliographical references.
ISBN 978-1-62356-382-0 (hardback) – ISBN 978-1-62356-352-3 (pbk.)
1. Critical pedagogy. 2. Autobiography. I. Gill, Scherto, author. II. Title.
LC196.G66 2014
370.11'5–dc23
2013045201

ISBN: HB: 978-1-6235-6382-0
PB: 978-1-6235-6352-3
e-PDF: 978-1-6235-6689-0
e-Pub: 978-1-6235-6540-4

Typeset by Integra Software Services Pvt. Ltd
Printed and bound in United States of America

Contents

Acknowledgements

This book is the fruit of conversations with many people who have helped us at different stages of developing the key ideas that formed the bedrock of the theories and pedagogical strategies.

We are most grateful to the Guerrand-Hermès Foundation for Peace for its generously hosting Ivor as a Research Fellow during which time Ivor and Scherto have begun to collaborate on this series of work focusing on narrative, learning and pedagogy.

We truly appreciate all the administrative and editorial support provided by the Foundation's staff, in particular, Heather Stoner and Laura Hobson.

We are also thankful to Elizabeth Brigg, whose consistent and reliable support to Ivor's writing and to the final organization of the manuscripts were invaluable.

We would like to acknowledge those who were involved in the book's production for their dedication to bring the book to completion.

Our deepest gratitude goes to the individuals whose stories and narrative processes have featured in the case studies in the book, some of whom are kept anonymous, and others are known. It has indeed been such a privilege to be part of these courageous individuals' narrative journeys of inner exploration and dialogic investigation. Their stories are as transformative for themselves as for us, as listeners, interlocutors and researchers.

We couldn't find any better way to honour their generous gift other than by sharing it with others in the world.

Introduction

Ivor Goodson and Scherto Gill

In this book, we explore the potential of using narrative work in developing learning and pedagogic strategies. We have both been involved in this educational endeavour for many years and have just begun to set out our ideas in a series of essays and books.

In some ways, this book provides a pedagogic companion piece to our earlier work on 'narrative pedagogy' (Goodson and Gill, 2011). In these books, we are concerned with investigating the potential of narrative and life history work for pedagogy and learning. We argued in *Narrative Pedagogy* that although there was widespread evidence of a 'turn to narrative', the importance of the 'pedagogic encounter', taking place in research settings and in everyday situations, had largely been disregarded. We were therefore focusing on the social forms of narrative work and, in particular, its place in encounters, conversations and wider social group interactions. In striving to understand the part that social relationships play in these contexts, we were able to explore what we have called 'narrative learning' (Goodson et al., 2010), and the pedagogical strategies that are salient in facilitating such learning. The previous work on Narrative Learning and Narrative Pedagogy has provided an important set of foundations for our explorations of critical pedagogy.

Following on from our previous work, this book introduces another dimension to our understanding of narrative pedagogy, namely criticality. In view of the burgeoning fields and literature on critical thinking and critical theory, we have become increasingly

1

interested in how narrative can locate critical engagement in both autobiographical reflection and group-based learning. Central to our own inquiry is to perceive narrative as profoundly humanizing, particularly when facilitated by empathetic listening, critical distance and caring analysis. Such narrative processes can lead to transformation and reconciliation.

Both concepts (transformation and reconciliation) are key to learning. In this book learning is perceived, in the broadest sense, to refer to the process that enables us to 'become more fully human' (Freire, 1996, p. 37). Indeed, Freire's vision for learning has inspired us to look into questions about human becoming in the context of narrative, critical reflection and dialogue. In our way of understanding it, transformation and reconciliation are evident as two connected human endeavours. Transformation here refers to the renewed self-awareness and understanding of our relationship with our fellow human beings and our social world as well as our action within it, and reconciliation is about being able to come to terms with past experience and meaning, life journeys, one's purpose in the world, present and future direction and action. Thus in the dialogic nature of narrative reflection, learning is at once critical and holistic. That is to say, without the critical distance, narrative can easily become self-fulfilling prophecy, or romantic or merely self-indulgent, whereas without holistic context, any criticism can seem sour, flat or antagonistic.

Another connected and important concept we introduce in this book is the notion of 're-storying', often allied to 're-selfing' (Goodson, 2013), which we argue is fundamentally connected to the social imagination and to collective transformative action. In re-storying, individuals revise their courses of action and anticipate a new life – a life of healing and reconciliation, a life of direction with integrity, meaning and purpose. Indeed, through engaging in critical narrative, learning is an act of developing a 'deeper social story and meaning' (Lederach, 2005). Such a vision of learning is compelling both in affluent societies struggling to provide an educational experience aimed at enabling wellbeing for all and in conflict-ridden and divided societies striving for peaceful relationships.

The book therefore comprises three parts. In Part One, Scherto introduces the reader to the field of 'critical narrative' and reviews a wide range of trans-disciplinary literature that addresses relevant questions about narrative, critical reflection and identity. We have a particular interest in works that look into narrative meaning-making and questions concerning ethics and morality embedded within narratives. The aim is to pave the way towards developing a tentative theoretical framework through which we could understand better the working of critical narrative in diverse settings – individual (auto)biographical reflection and group-based interpersonal interaction.

In Part Two, Ivor focuses on the personal and individual arena of narrative activity. We argue that 'ancestral voices' and 'autobiographical memory' need to be re-evaluated and revisited as sites of narrative construction and critical reflection. The potential for pedagogic leverage in these sites is, we maintain, considerable. We also scrutinize the processes whereby people develop integrative life themes in their narrative construction and review the processes of developing 'theories of context'. Here we highlight that learning takes place when individuals critically engage with their life histories and place these lived stories and experiences within broader contexts. This is where the personal converges with the socio-political.

Part Three is a significant extension from our *Narrative Pedagogy* book, as Scherto concentrates her investigation on the interpersonal dimension of critical narrative work. The chapters demonstrate with force and poignancy the humanizing effect of narrative and how critical narrative as pedagogy can lead to transformation and reconciliation. A range of settings of dialogic encounters was carefully selected to illustrate the pedagogical potential explored in the book to beyond formal learning situations, including informal peace-building education endeavour in post-conflict and divided societies, adult lifelong learning through critical narrative as part of the restorative justice and forgiveness programmes provided in some UK prisons, and teachers' professional learning within the higher educational settings.

Together the narrative case studies in Part Two and Part Three make a compelling argument that critical narrative as pedagogy can offer learning as a pathway to human flourishing and so enable each person to pursue a fulfilling life. As we explained, what links the three parts of our book is a concern to explore the potential of narratives and narrative analysis in reconfiguring our individual perceptions of oneself in a web of relationships, and indeed in social imagination. We deliberately sequence our move from Part Two to Part Three as a journey from individual reflexivity to social interrogation. We believe that in both settings, the individual and the social are sites of renegotiation and reconstitution as a route to reconciliation in the broadest sense. This reconciliation may take place at the level of the individual as reconciliation within the self, socially as reconciliation with others, or reconciliation with matters at a systemic level. It is difficult to envisage social or collective reconciliation without the accompanying individual reconciliation.

AN OUTLINE OF THE BOOK

The first part of the book has three chapters; each aims to contribute to a grounded understanding of critical narrative as pedagogy.

In Chapter 1, Scherto explores and develops a trans-disciplinary conceptual map of the field of critical narrative. Our particular concern is to clarify the concept of learning and launch an inquiry into the different aspects involved in narrative learning. In this book, we follow many humanistic thinkers to conceive learning as pathways to human becoming and pursuing a flourishing life. Our exploration of the theoretical landscape thus considers moral, social and pedagogical aspects whilst taking a view of these in the context of human agency and action.

In Chapter 2, Scherto continues to review how criticality has been, and is, conceptualized in current literature. The work of Paulo Freire and John Dewey provides us with valuable guidelines in this quest for an understanding of criticality. There is considerable common ground between these two foundational writers in their emphasis on the dialogic aspects of critical pedagogy. Our concern here is to reframe the critical in narrative learning, which is salient in demystifying the often highly politicized societal narrative. In this way, a narrative approach to learning can help the individuals to reintegrate core human values into our day-to-day being and action. This in turn presents an opportunity to place more conventional sociologically oriented and politically focused debates on critical thinking next to a more humanistic conception of criticality.

The third chapter of Part One begins the process of exploring how life narratives can be pathways to making and remaking of ourselves in the process of making history (Freire, 1994), towards an ethical life, with one another. The major concern of this chapter is developing a conceptual framework for critical narrative. In doing so, we point out that the critical narrative pathway is a creative and formative journey where learners consolidate who we are as individuals and communities, where we find our voice, our place in the world and the story that we inhabit and belong, the stories that we truly are and where we continue to engage in social action.

Thus the three chapters in Part One serve to develop a conceptual map for establishing the role of critical narrative as a reflective process and an active ingredient in this ongoing exploration of the meaning and purpose of our lives. Critically engaging with moral and social purposes is both an individual and an inextricably social and collective act.

Part Two of this book looks more closely at autobiography as a site for critical narrative and dialogic learning. Following the introductory chapters, we determined that it was important to provide a 'feel' for narrative data and allow the readers to experience the 'personal flesh' of narrative work. Hence, the chapters in Parts Two and Three provide a broad range of exemplary narratives as case studies to offer an illustration of diverse forms of narrative inquiry.

In Chapter 4, Ivor focuses on an area of narrative inquiry that has been largely neglected in life history studies, what we call 'ancestral voices'. In the world of positivist and objectivist study, this neglect would of itself be unsurprising, but this is also the trend to be perceived as we move our social world online. Nonetheless, our work in investigating narrative pedagogy and narrative learning has highlighted the continuing power and salience of 'ancestral voices'. Therefore, this chapter deliberately employs a range of the author's personal data.

Likewise in Chapter 5, the transcripts of a series of original conversations are included to show the process of developing autobiographical memory, which is conceptualized as a major site for learning and critical pedagogy. It is conceived as a place where we present and reconstruct our knowledge of the world. Moreover, it is in a site of ongoing construction and modification, as Giddens (1991, p. 72) says: '(t)he autobiography is a corrective intervention into the past'. The autobiographical memory is the prime site for understanding our personal sense of memory, morality and purpose. Only recently has this richness of personal meaning-making been recognized by social scientists in general and/or by social pedagogues in particular. Thus autobiographical memory provides a platform for social investigation and provides key opportunities for reflexivity and learning.

In the next chapter, Ivor further examines how people develop overarching life themes in personal narratives. We show how this works in two modes – first in the act of internal reflection where a major life theme serves to unify and integrate the ongoing construction of the personality in one's life story; second the major life theme also acts to align the internal account with the external presentation of the life story to others. In developing our life themes it is often the case that the stimulus of such narrative activity is a social barrier, a critical event or personal trauma. In dealing with these issues the narrator seeks to critically distance himself/herself from, or so to speak to 'dis-embed' from, the psychic dilemma with which he/she is confronted. One strategy for doing so is to develop a 'theory of context', which allows us to deal with and situate the personal challenge within a wider societal trauma or transition, thus reconstructing as a tactic for reconciliation, reflexive compromise or resolution.

Part Three of the book intends to illustrate the working of critical narrative as pedagogy in three different settings. Although the contexts and the narrative processes are different, nevertheless these case studies provide powerful support to the pedagogical framework developed in the first part of the book.

In Chapter 7, Scherto reflects on the narrative and storying processes of two ex-combatants (a Christian and a Muslim) who fought in opposition during the Lebanese civil war (1975–1990). The focus of the chapter is on exploring what happens when two people come together to listen to each other's narratives, even when such narratives are about conflict with, hatred of and pain caused by the other. This case study illustrates the working of narrative as humanization – it is the common humanity within us that compels us to listen empathetically, to show compassion, to forgive and to reach out to the Other in order to move towards a new moral imperative. The humanity embedded in the narrative of suffering and pain and our responsibility for the inhumanity of violence can in turn serve as the basis for constructing a 'we'-consciousness, from where solidarity and affectionate connections can be established between people and communities. The narrative space thus forges a path from personal reconstruction towards social reconciliation. This chapter opens up a host of questions regarding the potential of critical narrative and reciprocal listening in peace-building as well as raises issues regarding the ethics of narrative learning in post-conflict settings.

Chapter 8 examines how narratives and storytelling serve to promote human values such as empathy, compassion, forgiveness, respect, dignity and responsibility. The context is a Restorative Justice (RJ) course for offenders as part of the Lifelong Learning programmes launched in some of the English prisons. The case study aims to illustrate that listening and storytelling can allow the victim and the offender to enter a safe space where it is possible for them to deconstruct notions such as 'injury', 'pain', 'grief' and 'suffering' as well as 'anger', 'aggression', 'violence' and 'crime'. By re-storying, the programme further provides the participants with an opportunity to reconstruct a sense of self and reclaim respect for oneself and the other – a starting point for healing and transformation. Furthermore, in this case study, empathy, forgiveness and other values promoted by RJ are critically examined in the current prison context in order to re-imagine a justice system that can truly restore human dignity and re-pair the broken relationships on many levels.

In the final chapter of this book, Scherto reflects on teachers' biographical learning in higher education to illustrate narrative learning as a process of enacting critical pedagogy through whole-person engagement. The case study further demonstrates that, when teachers/educators explore their personal narratives as a group, each of the participants becomes more reflective and reflexive about their own experience of learning. We stress the importance of reconstructing one's experience within broader social political context that allows us to actively dissociate our stories from inherited 'scripts' and 'patterns' and assumptions and to then reconstruct our understanding of self, other, the world and social actions. We argue that such deeper forms of reflexivity can engender the critical distance necessary to re-engage with one's purpose as an educator and teacher through self-understanding and self-awareness, thus leading on to profound questioning of critical issues and concepts in educational practice, and the institutional and socio-political contexts of such practice.

In proposing a compelling conceptual framework to underpin critical narrative as pedagogy, and by problematizing key themes emerging in practice, the three parts of the book hope to create a space for more scholarly exploration on the potential of narrative learning and critical pedagogy, and to invoke more rigorous evaluations and constructive critiques on the role of narrative in fostering learning, becoming and transformation.

We invite educational thinkers, researchers, practitioners, policymakers and NGO workers to join us in further examining questions emerging from this book and identifying innovative approaches and pedagogic strategies in narrative practices in order that it may present novel ways to meet challenges confronting the learning enterprises in the twenty-first century.

TOWARDS A THEORY OF CRITICAL
NARRATIVE AS PEDAGOGY

CHAPTER 1

Mapping the Field
of Critical Narrative

Scherto Gill

The world is remote and alien enough to effect the necessary separation of ourselves from ourselves, but it contains at the same time all the exit points and threads of the return to oneself, for becoming acquainted with it and for finding oneself again, but oneself according to the truly universal essence of spirit.

–Hans Georg Gadamer, *Truth and Methods*, 1975

INTRODUCTION

Consider any map. It can be taken as a representation of the contours and features of a landscape. If we wish to embark on a journey, a map can provide us with points of reference to real phenomena and help guide our way along the chosen route. In this first chapter, we broadly explore and map out the field of critical narrative. We will observe a set of landscape references by which we can develop our understanding of the pathways to pedagogy and learning.

The map is to serve the purpose of journeys. The journey of this book is a quest and the focus of the quest is to understand more deeply two important concepts: narrative learning and critical narrative as pedagogy. In using the term 'learning', we are borrowing from thinkers such as Paulo Freire and Carl Rogers, and referring to the processes that allow us to be and to become more fully human. What this means will gradually unfold as we share the insights developed through our conversations and exchanges with different interlocutors, including authors of books and articles that we have read, the individuals who participated in our projects and others. Following this thought, each conversation or exchange we had was not only a journey through 'terrains' already known but also a journey to discover new ones. Thus in our inquiry into how learning takes place and how humanity flourishes in each of us within a civilized society, we have included (not exclusively) the following lenses.

First, we have associated a set of features that connect with meaning and the nature of human life. Sources of selfhood like evaluation, moral sensibility, purpose and deriving meaning from moral action in the world; we take these to be primary determinants of our identity. It is necessary, therefore, within this *moral view of the landscape*, that there is an internal characterization or apprehension of what may be the good, or of what counts as significant for how we ought to live our lives. So within this feature set there are inherently questions and responses, all concerning the identification of such qualities as meaning, goodness, morality, dignity and integrity.

The second set of features encompasses indications of those external forces and influences that contribute to individuals' sense of themselves. These are social features relating, for example, to political dynamics, education, social institutions, cultural norms and traditions, religion and other sociological phenomena in contemporary society. These may appear to be effectively constraining influences on our expression of selfhood and of being and acting in any given society. So in contrasting this with the moral view of the sources of the self, within this *social view of the landscape*, we are interested in investigating questions in terms of how a society cultivates or hinders human becoming and flourishing.

Third, as persons are also agents who can make choices (to a certain extent) in life, so as to follow their own pathways and not merely react to what life has thrown in front of them, we are particularly interested in people's narratives, which illustrate their individual journeys and lived experiences, and the choices they made in life's transitions and crossroads. Within this *narrative view*, there are memories, stories, myths, 'life-dreams' and other accounts.

Last, we regard all of the foregoing features in the domain of agency. What we recognize here, within this *autonomous view* of the landscape, is that we are not passive recipients but actors in, for example, the production of culture, construction of meaning, cultivation of ways of being and identification of paths of future social actions. However, although we acknowledge the 'inescapable structural requirements of human agency (Taylor, 1989, p. 52)', at the same time, we also believe in humanity's unyielding aspiration for the good. So the final view concerns how these different landscapes intercept and overlap in the process of human becoming.

So in essence the approach we have taken in this book, namely critical narrative as pedagogy, is the quest for an understanding of learning and human becoming through these perspectives and lenses. Our critical approach is not just directed at, as Paulo Freire has put it, 'naming the world' (Freire, 1996), but is to strive for 'naming the self', and in doing so, knowing our narrative. Learning is therefore about cultivating qualities and virtues[1] that are progressive, creative and life-enhancing. Emergent qualities manifest in our human civilization, feeding back as the framework supporting our being and acting in the world.

---

[1] In *Nicomachean Ethics*, Aristotle advanced his famous doctrine of the mean, according to which the virtues are a mean between two extremes, which constitute vices. This is not the same as advocating moderation. The virtues have a corrective aspect. For example, one person might lack generosity whereas another might be over-generous in the sense of neglecting himself or herself. The virtue of generosity is a mean because it is a corrective to these two extremes.

LEARNING AS BEING AND BECOMING FULLY HUMAN

The concept of learning is seldom clearly defined, since people generally assume they know what it means. Therefore, most learning theories focus on how learning takes place, are about activities or factors contributing to learning, or concern attitudes, relationships and power dynamics within an educative process that are conducive or obstructive to learning.

Neither is it the case that a roomful of theorists and pedagogues would agree on a common definition of learning. In the context of schooling, for example, learning refers to acquiring something through a process of study. Even within the definition of acquisition, educators are not always in agreement about what is it that is to be acquired – some focus on information and facts, others on imparting knowledge and yet others on helping students acquire certain skills.

As we have argued elsewhere (Gill and Thomson, 2012), this definition of learning is just too narrow. If learning in practice is about the acquisition of knowledge, information and employable skills, this is implicitly promoting a culture where people are treated as economic objects, and learning as a means towards an instrumental end, ultimately in the service of fulfilling the growth potential of the state. So it is with a process of learning designed to fill our minds with mental objects. This would not of itself promote the qualities or virtues of being human.

Thus we take as our starting point the imperative that learning should be primarily about being and becoming a more fulfilled human. This acknowledges our potential, accommodates our aspirations and works with us in striving to be more complete. Education is regarded as the most significant way to transform the person and the world around us (Freire, 1996). This is essentially a radical rewriting of the orthodox understanding of learning.

A similar conception of learning was discussed by Carl Rogers in his book entitled *On Becoming a Person*, where he explored not only the conditions that allow each of us to become a person, but also the question of what it means to become a person. Although written from a therapist's point of view, his ideas have currency outside the realm of counselling or the therapy room. According to Rogers, being and becoming a person include cultivating such qualities as self-awareness, self-esteem, flexibility and respect for self and others. In Rogers' words, the individual will thus be

> better integrated ... become more similar to the person he would like to be, be more self-directing and self-confident, become more of a unique and more self-expressive person, be more understanding, more accepting of others. (Rogers, 1961, p. 38)

So becoming fully human is about returning to and reaffirming one's humanity and the humanity of others. Writing in a context where people were finding themselves blocked off from the pursuit of their 'historical and ontological vocation' of becoming more fully human due to oppression or injustice, Freire (1996) refers to the endeavour of education as a kind of mutual-humanization, where social struggle for meaning and becoming involves the return to, and affirmation of, humanity.

Freire considers this a starting point for liberation from oppression – a rejection of the idea that one is good-for-nothing, a rejection of self-deprecation. In other words, in order to pursue or regain our humanity, we must cease to be objects or cogs in a machine. To accept being treated as objects is to alienate us from our volition to be human according to our nature.

Indeed, Freire's conception of learning is about living out the qualities or virtues of being human. As such, education is a process of cultivating human qualities and fostering virtues for one's own wellbeing, which is connected to the wellbeing of others and the goodness of the world at large. This integration of one's values and beliefs into one's actions and way of being is termed 'praxis' by Freire.

Furthermore, in learning as becoming human, Freire highlights the interconnectedness between persons and the world. He says that the significant issue is not persons *in* the world, but rather persons *with* others and *with* the world. Freire rejects the passivity of being human, according to which 'the person is not a conscious being; he or she is rather the processor of a consciousness: an empty "mind" passively open to the reception of deposits of reality from the world outside' (Freire, 1996, p. 56). In contrast, becoming human implies our striving for the *'emergence* of consciousness and *critical intervention* in reality' (Freire, 1996, p. 62). Thus to become human, we must reject any suggestion implicit or explicit that 'man is abstract, isolated, independent, and unattached to the world', and that 'the world exists as a reality apart from people' (Freire, 1996, p. 62). Drawing on Sartre (*La conscience et le monde sont dormés d'un même coup*), Freire passionately argues that '*I* cannot exist without a *non-I*. In turn, the *not-I* depends on that existence. The world which brings consciousness into existence becomes the world of that consciousness' (Freire, 1996, p. 63). The essence of being human in the world is to be consciously aware of our existence in the world with which and in which we find ourselves. Human being is not only in fellowship and solidarity with one another, but also in the world and with the world in order to transform the world and humans being in it.

The notion of becoming more fully human is obviously very important, especially when we conceive learning as just that. Bringing together both Rogers' and Freire's thoughts, the idea of learning is no longer based exclusively on autonomous action, rationality and self-conscious cognitive states. It also includes important aspects of the human condition, such as respect, dignity, friendship/fellowship, solidarity, actions and other noble qualities that count as being human.

In addition, being human embraces psychological, social and most importantly moral experiences, and it is to this aspect we now turn.

SOURCES OF THE SELF AND MORAL ONTOLOGY

There is a strong connection between one's identity and the notion of the good. Charles Taylor claims that it is impossible to define the self without reference to moral goods, which are essential in determining one's place and purpose in the world. These constitute human dignity. Here is his most quoted definition of identity:

> My identity is defined by the commitments and identifications which provide the frame or horizon within which I can try to determine from case to case what is good, or valuable, or what ought to be done, or what I endorse or oppose. In other words, it is the horizon within which I am capable of taking a stand. (Taylor, 1989, p. 27)

In fact, Taylor refers to this framework as our moral and spiritual intuition and thus makes the problem of identity more than a social or political construct or a psychological state of achieved self-concept, as we shall discuss later. The notion of the self is embedded in an inner locus that has been placed within the intertwined realms of the moral and the spiritual. Taylor introduces the notion of 'strong evaluation' in our understanding of our moral self; this involves an ongoing reflection and discrimination of 'right or wrong, better or worse, higher or lower, which are not rendered valid by our own desires, inclinations, or choices, but rather stand independent of these and offer standards by which they can be judged' (Taylor, 1989, p. 4).

Taylor's bold claim above (that there are moral standards, values or principles independent of people's individualized desires, wants and intentions, as they represent standards by which our desires and choices are judged) may not be immediately acceptable for some, especially those who hold a postmodern perspective on the impossibility of any kind of values and moral standards that are normative. We will discuss the sources of self in light of a postmodern conception shortly. Yet, it is widely accepted that moral values do offer structure and direction to our lives, and that they are not merely unique to the individual. Conceiving values in this way can help us correct errors and make the best sense of life, as Taylor would advise, by 'not only offering the best, most realistic orientation about the good but also allowing us best to understand and make sense of the actions and feelings of ourselves and others' (Taylor, 1989, p. 56). Taylor himself refers to these values as 'hypergoods', which form the framework for human moral and aesthetic judgements and decisions. Equally, hypergoods allow us to understand what constitutes human dignity and to equip ourselves with such capacities in order to make strong evaluations in relation to what we do and how we are in the world.

Thus value has ontological status, and is embedded in humans' innate awareness and natural tendency towards the good, which ultimately allows us to develop both moral sensibility and moral responsibility.

Giving morality an ontological status allows Taylor to articulate our deepest moral and spiritual intuitions and instincts, and to extrapolate our 'ineradicable sense that human life is to be respected, as our mode of access to the world in which ontological claims are discernible and can be rationally argued about and sifted' (Taylor, 1989, p. 8). Moral values underpin what we respect and care about, and determine why we aspire to certain modes of life, actions and responses more than others.

Broadly, Taylor approaches moral ontology from three 'axes': in addition to respect for others, respect for human life, rights, autonomy and similar moral concerns – a truly strong evaluation, as Taylor has illustrated, must also include the notion of a full life, by asking ourselves a set of questions:

about how I am going to live my life which touch on the issue of what kind of life is worth living, or what kind of life would fulfil the promise implicit in my particular talents, or the demands incumbent on someone with my endowment, or of what constitutes a rich, meaningful life – as against one concerned with secondary matters or trivia. (Taylor, 1989, p. 14)

Respect for others and a worthwhile life are further placed alongside the notion of dignity, which Taylor defines as 'the characteristics by which we think of ourselves as commanding (or failing to command) the respect of those around us' (Taylor, 1989, p. 15). Taylor claims that the three broad axes exist in almost all cultures, despite the differences in how they are conceived, emphasized or applied to underpin human life.

Frameworks such as this can be problematic in today's world. Taylor himself is aware of the variations and objections to his proposed framework, against which his entire book argues succinctly. He says 'the goods that command our awe must also function in some sense as standards for us' (Taylor, 1989, p. 20); thus we will all live with the guidance of a certain moral compass.

Taylor illustrates the complexity of identifying the moral sources by pointing out three principal domains that provide a grounding of moral standards: the theistic, the naturalism of disengaged reason and Romantic expressionism. He also suggests that when the 'original unity of the theistic horizon has been shattered, and the sources can now be found on diverse frontiers, including our own powers and nature' (Taylor, 1989, p. 496); this does not mean that these moral sources are no longer applicable in a modern world, only that they continue to influence people's moral dispositions and moral outlook in a more overlapping rather than isolated way.

One of the questions that confront people in the twenty-first century is concerned with the sources of our morality. Taylor raises two additional issues, one of which is connected to the conflict we are facing in the overtly instrumental mode of life that people are dragged towards, where 'the solid, lasting, often expressive objects which served us in the past are being set aside for the quick, shoddy, replaceable commodities with which we now surround ourselves' (Taylor, 1989, p. 501). The result of this is that we are to be cut off from sources of meaning and moral depth. The second issue is the fragmented mode of existence where humans are alienated from a sense of coherence, and communities are divided due to individuals merely superficially playing partial roles rather than having a deeper sense of belonging. Thus Taylor himself laments a loss of 'resonance, depth, or richness in our human surroundings; both in the things we use and in the ties which bind us to others' (Taylor, 1989, p. 501).

As we indicated earlier, having any kind of moral standard independent of an individual's subjective wants, desires and inclinations is regarded as impossible by some postmodernists. They maintain that any claim to truth and unity destroys differences and plurality. Postmodernists insist on dismantling any coherence, in a loose play of values and meanings. In this way, the fragmentation and multiplicity may make meaning impossible, as any understanding is perceived as a mere discourse from a particular angle at a particular moment within a particular sociocultural and political context. The acknowledgement that all voices, all viewpoints and all interpretations are valid is to deny any judgement and meaning. We cannot help but pause and ask: whilst there are multiple voices all of which are supposed to be valid, how could one develop a coherent voice that reasons and articulates and guides one's direction in life?

It is no exaggeration to suggest that this postmodern 'playfulness' can risk making existence meaningless. When a person's identity is stripped of its coherence, continuity and wholeness, it can become a cluster of loosely bound social roles and shifting positions that, without integrity-seeking, are always subject to further deconstruction. Thus it is difficult to imagine that such a decentred being can really exist in the actual world – acting with this lack of footing.

In this case, can a postmodern self be responsible for any actions? When there is no coherent notion of the good, where one's sense of selfhood is opted into fragmentation and self-alienation, then we cannot help but ask bluntly: what is the point of life, if any at all? We will return to this towards the end of the chapter.

In this moral landscape as we have seen so far, to be a person is to be able to answer questions about one's life's purpose, the direction in which we are heading and what commands our love and respect, and so forth. By drawing upon the insights emerging from Charles Taylor's inquiries, we are sharing his recognition of the significant moral dimension of our personhood and how it motivates our processes of being and becoming more fully human.

SELF IN A WEB OF EXPERIENCES AND RELATIONSHIPS

Many would refute the idea that morality is normatively claimed and universally acceptable. They would argue, although not to such an extent as the postmodernists would do, negating meaning completely, that values and moral aspirations are culturally diverse and socially constructed. Take the perennial 'what is the purpose of my life?' question as an example. We will receive a myriad of answers depending on whom you want to talk to. There are answers such as the following: to serve God; to prepare for the afterlife; to answer a calling; to embark on a journey of life and embrace all that I encounter; to make positive contributions to the wellbeing of others; to fight for equality; to live life fully in accordance with my gifts and talents; to self-actualize and become who I really am; to satisfy all my needs and experience all that I desire. Perhaps some people will say they want to be high achievers with wealth, status, power and so forth. More frequently, people claim that what one individual finds meaningful and important in life can be very different from that of another individual. They claim that to be a person lies more in the experiences one has had and the web of relationships to which one is connected. Indeed, our sense of self fundamentally lies in the way we experience the phenomenological world on a day-to-day basis.

From a sociological perspective, our purpose is determined not only by our nature and dispositions and our moral choices made as an exercise of free will, but also by the patterns of social change and cultural and institutional practices that have shaped our values. Thus sociology's primary concern is how social and political processes impact humans' identities and thereby their moral order.

We justly ask here if this may contradict Taylor's claim on people's metaphysical intuition described above. We will return to this point later.

To address the psychological, social, cultural and political dimensions of the self, we need to start with an account of how our identity or selfhood evolves and develops over our life course and how such a web of experiences comes into play in that process. Erik Erikson used ego 'identity' to define the self. He writes that identity is never 'established' as an achievement, or a static unchangeable thing. Instead, identity is a 'forever to-be-revised sense of reality of the Self within social reality' (Erikson, 1968, p. 211). Erikson characterizes the process of evolving human identity through our life course and points out that each stage is accompanied by a pronounced conflict or crisis. From early childhood, to adolescence and adulthood, different 'issues' may confront the individual and thus become the drive that serves to renew our identity. These issues or key transitions in the course of one's life can include puberty, romantic relationships, leaving home for the first time, finding one's work and first job, falling in love and getting married, parenthood, the death of one's parents, relationships and divorce, unemployment, serious illness, the death of one's partner or spouse, retirement and the confrontation of mortality.

According to Erikson, the way one masters or deals with the pressing issue at a particular time of one's life, such as an adolescent going through an 'identity crisis', can affect one's ability to cope with diverse identity issues later in life.

Identity allows a person to maintain a sense of sameness and continuity that is not readily given to the individual by society or simply a maturational phenomenon as one gets older. In the Eriksonian view, identity must be developed through sustained individual effort. Failing to address those more pronounced 'issues' at the relevant life stages may result in role diffusion, alienation and a sense of isolation and confusion. Becoming oneself involves the establishment of a meaningful self-concept in which one's past, present and future are brought together to form a unified whole. The life history of individuals and their ongoing personal journeys interact and intersect with the social histories of places and spaces. This becomes a reciprocal process where individuals' identities, life's journeys and activities, and the stories of society support each other's regeneration and development.

In addition to the web of experiences, Erikson's identity theory also places the development and growth of the person within a web of relationships. The individual's effort to overcome the key psychological issues presented to us at different stages of one's life becomes the key struggle in becoming a person. In this way, the sources of one's self originate from our self-awareness, psychological health and, above all, our relationships with the significant others present at different times of our life.

These in turn will impact our personality and choice of work, the way we engage with others and society at large and how we seek meaning. Relationships as sources of self are not limited to people, such as families, friends and others in the community; the web of relationships can also be extended to include how we relate ourselves to social history, ethnicity, culture, education, social institutions, political regimes, religion, spiritual tradition and practices and so forth.

We can see that this is not a purely psychoanalytic view about identity, used to discern a psychosocial self from its moral dimension. Rather, it is an unfolding process where a person moves from childhood and adolescence to adulthood, becoming an autonomous agent and gradually developing awareness of his or her route in relation to the foregoing account of the inherent sense of the good. Although the orientation towards the good arises from diverse sources of one's self, which are complex and multiple, nevertheless it is not independent of the interaction between an 'inner' sense of morality and an 'outer' one that is socially, culturally and historically situated.

The moral landscape, as we described in the previous section, can support a sociological perspective of selfhood in that it is through our experiences that we negotiate value, meaning and purpose. Thus any account of human personhood that conceives identity separately from one's moral intuition and social experience is inadequate or flawed.

Let us revisit Taylor's (1989) claims that our personhood is constituted in and through the taking of moral stances. What is considered to be good may not be the same for everyone, but there must be 'hypergood' to guide one's decisions and actions. Sociology can contribute to this idea by making explicit how individuals navigate the complexity within which one can take a (moral) stance. So the claim that a person's moral orientation is highly contextualized is not to object to any normative claim of the good, but rather to stress the importance of locating our moral self within a phenomenological world with all its complexities.

Furthermore, Taylor also concurs that becoming a person requires the presence of a web of relations:

> one cannot be a self on one's own. I am a self only in relation to certain interlocutors: in one way in relation to those conversation partners who were essential to my achieving self-definition; in another in relation to those who are now

crucial to my continuing grasp of language of self-under-standing – and of course, these classes may overlap. (Taylor, 1989, p. 36)

Thus apart from one's moral framework and spiritual intuition, Taylor introduces the second defining element of our identity – what he calls a 'defining community'. This second dimension of our identity is lived in social and historical particulars, such as the literature, philosophy, religious teaching and great conversations taking place along one's life's journeys. Taylor uses an example of American culture encouraging youths to pursue independence and self-reliance to illustrate the:

> transcendental embedding of independence in interlocution. Each young person may take up a stance which is authentically his or her own; but the very possibility of this is enframed in a social understanding of great temporal depth, in fact, in a tradition. (Taylor, 1989, p. 39)

Taylor concludes that a self exists within 'webs of interlocution'. The community of interlocutors is an important source of our identity. It is so important that in many conflict situations, when a group of people are threatened by another group, the individuals can temporarily put aside their individual identities and focus only on their collective identity. Large-group identities can be the result of myths and realities with common beginnings, historical continuities, geographical realities and other shared linguistic, societal, religious and cultural factors (Volkan, 2006). So the community of interlocutors plays a key role in the formation of our values and our sense of the good. It forms the basis of who we are and what we love and consider as meaningful, and which direction we are heading in life.

Indeed, as Erikson and others have pointed out, the sources of identity also include the following two elements that are overlapping: (a) a web or community of interlocutors that provides us with certain practices, values and the object of our love, and (b) the journeys we have travelled and the rich experiences encountered en route through our life. This journey allows us to build and expand the web of interlocutors, and participate in activities through which we learn to appreciate and consolidate a sense of goodness, negotiate meaning and make choices at life's different junctions and transitions.

Let's pause for a moment and reflect on the social landscape for exploring selfhood. So far, we have discussed that our personhood within the context of social and political complexity does not necessarily negate a prevailing moral vision that gives rise to meaning and purpose in life. In fact, only by addressing moral questions such as dignity, goodness and what is just can sociologists take into account other concerns including power, class, gender, ethnicity and so forth.

Furthermore, a postmodern view that shifting contexts lead to changing power relations, discourses and individuals performing their roles and their 'identities' (i.e. how they are identified by others at a particular situation) differently can mean that it is an endless task to deconstruct individual identities. Therefore, we have equally challenged the notion of a postmodern self, about whom it is impossible to imagine how he or she can act coherently.

Finally, an investigation into the social landscape of personhood has allowed us to address a primary issue in social critique. Seeing people's identity as situated within a web of experience is crucial to uncovering the kind of social institutional cultures, political systems and economic models that result in people being disempowered, and in their inability to become persons such as they are.[2] Paulo Freire sees the social critique as a process whereby people dialogue and collaborate in order to 'name the world' – to

---

[2] See Carl Rogers' (1969) interpretation of Kierkegaard's idea on human becoming. Rogers uses the very phrase: to become who you really are.

identify and transform those norms, cultures, systems and relationships that have led to people becoming alienated from themselves. Further critique leads onward in social transformation.

SELF AS A NARRATIVE QUEST FOR MEANING

Perpetual human action dealing with the problem of existence, and the tension between the finitude of human existence and our own awareness of human spirit as infinite, has led us to pose ourselves some 'immortal questions' (Noddings, 2003). These can include 'what is the meaning of life?', 'why is justice important?', 'what kind of person should I become?' and so on. Many existentialists maintain that these questions are not best answered by resolving or dissolving the problem through pure logical analysis, in the same way that we deal with a mathematical question, or even through a detached approach as if addressing cause–effect questions as we do in natural sciences.

One way to launch inquiry into these questions is through a hermeneutical approach, which aims to understand the problem by looking at its various aspects, historical conditions and ramifications, what it means for a person to have a certain kind of experience and so forth. Charles Taylor, Paul Ricoeur, Alistair MacIntyre and Nel Noddings, amongst others, point to life stories or personal narratives as a way to examine our life's journeys and to respond to these timeless questions.

Narratives (stories) in the human sciences have been defined provisionally as discourses with a clear sequential order that connect events meaningfully for a definite audience and thus offer insights about the world and/or people's experiences of it (Goodson and Gill, 2011; Hinchman and Hinchman, 1997, p. xvi).

Clearly, defining narratives within a temporal, social and cultural framework allows the narrators to recount their life in a certain broad stroke of continuity. This continuity is often claimed to be connected to our identity – a sense of oneself as being the same person and that this life has a certain direction.[3]

Although life's events are never linear and any intention for life to be coherent and progressive in accordance with a 'plan' will constantly be interrupted, still we believe that life does not merely consist of a series of random or accidental events that are completely beyond one's own control and thereby beyond any intentionality. In addition to the temporal continuity found in one's life narrative, we want to bring in another view that the inherent structure of a story or narrative, through the organization of plots and sequencing of events, always points to the value or meaning the storyteller assumes. Indeed, as we mentioned earlier, when human life is being narratively recounted and interpreted, the implicit meaning can thus become explicit in the process of telling.

In context, narrative can come in many forms – some may remind us of the roots of identity or personhood and our sense of belonging, such as the narratives passed on from the elders of many generations before, tales of our ancestors or heroes, myths and legends recounted so as to preserve our culture or tradition, literature and artefacts that celebrate enduring moral virtues; some may relate to memories of ourselves, autobiographies, biographies, anecdotal stories of our life's journeys, encounters, traumas, failures, wounds, pursuits and triumphs; other narratives are concerned with both our daily trivialities and significant moments or encounters of life; others still may offer a personal moral tale to reflect key questions that have been the preoccupation of humanity throughout history.

Thus the way a narrator 'emplots' his or her stories is deeply connected to how people perceive their life's themes and pursues

---

[3] This view has been challenged by many post-structuralist and postmodern thinkers who claim that the psychological construct of a core self is impossible and that the self is in constant flux and being reconstructed in our narratives and through discourses. We hope our discussion on the narrative unity of selfhood in the last section of this chapter will be sufficient in addressing the discrepancies between the humanistic conception of selfhood and the postmodern one.

meaning in their activities and actions. As Taylor points out, narrative allows us to examine life through lived experiences, and to question these experiences in light of their places in our life, their significance and meaning to our being and becoming a person. Although life narratives may appear to be immersed in the past, they are reflective of the present and can lead us to the future. Thus the meaning in narratives penetrates the temporality of narratives – narratives organize human experiences into temporally meaningful continuity. So much so, Kierkegaard famously said that, 'Life must be lived forwards but can only be understood backwards'.

Furthermore, the definition above also suggests that narrative stresses the significance of social interaction in examining our life's encounters and journeys, and by doing so, this social process may help transform human experience into meaning (Gill and Goodson, 2010). This is linked to Taylor's point about the web of interlocutors that we discussed earlier. Meanings can be both discernible or evidential, and latent or dormant, and in both cases we feel the need for investigation and interpretation. Sometimes, the presence of another – an attentive ear, an empathetic companion, a non-judgemental friend – can help us overcome the challenge of interpretation, especially when meaning embedded in the experience is ambiguous and elusive. We shall discuss these diverse characteristics of narrative in more detail in Chapter Three.

Because of the temporality, plot structure and social nature of narrative, it has been perceived to be a uniquely human concept (Barthes, 1975). Similarly, Ricoeur (1988) claims that life and, in some senses, even time become human in and through narrative.[4] That is to say that human life has always been deeply embedded in a web of narratives, which yields the space that individuals, communities, cultures and nations can express themselves as who

---

[4] We will return to this point and discuss it more fully in Chapter 3.

they are, with their origin, how they have lived, what they aspire to as a good life and how they may live in order to align their answers to those questions. Narrative is considered central to being human because much of our sense of purpose and meaning, our self-hood, values and aspirations are considered in narrative forms and as such are essential for humans to construct coherence, continuity and integrity.

BRINGING THESE TOGETHER – LEARNING AS NARRATIVE QUEST FOR MEANING AND ACTION

To understand ourselves is to understand ourselves in action. There is reciprocity between our self-knowledge/self-awareness and our action(s) in the world. The bridge between these two is indeed human values, as illustrated earlier through various people's work. Polkinghorne (1988) writes that narrative covers a wide range of discourse, from personal life stories, to social histories, from myths, fairy tales, to fictions and novels, as well as everyday storytelling – all used to explain human actions.

Our preoccupation with narratives has now become more pronounced as we approach the discussion about human *being* in the world. So far we have seen that narratives can allow individuals to adapt, modify and shift their stories, and that their view of lived experiences can thereby be transformed. As we have seen, human life, whilst meaningful, often appears to be chaotic, whereas narratives, through their plots and temporality, allow the chaotic nature of life to assume a certain structure and configuration. This transformative process is not only an inward-looking exercise but also has an outwardly oriented application so as to develop direction and unity of action in life (MacIntyre, 1984).

Narratives can help explain human actions. MacIntyre argues that in the telling of their lives, individuals place actions in the context of intentions 'with reference to their role in the history of the setting or settings in which they belong' (MacIntyre, 1984, p. 208). This is a reflexive process where individuals take the opportunity to evaluate their actions in connection with their intentions and thus 'write a further part' of their histories. In the narrative construct, human actions are united with their intention, values and purposes. When life is narrated, it is also lived, according to its narrative construction. Life becomes 'enacted narratives' (MacIntyre, 1984, p. 208). This consolidates a mutually constitutive relationship between life and narrative – life forms the fundamental basis of narrative and narrative provides order, structure and direction in life, and helps develop meanings in richer and more integrated ways.

Ricoeur, in the conclusion of *Time and Narrative*, suggests that:

> the self of self-knowledge is not the egotistical and narcissistic ego whose hypocrisy and naivety the hermeneutics of suspicion have denounced, along with its aspects of an ideological superstructure and infantile and neurotic archaism. The self of self-knowledge is the fruit of an examined life ... (Ricoeur, 1988, p. 247)

The ethical self or moral identity is further placed by Ricoeur within culture and community. Similarly, echoing Taylor, MacIntyre focuses on the moral questions in one's narrative personhood:

> man is in his actions and practice, as well as in his fictions, essentially a story-telling animal. He is not essentially, but becomes through his history, a teller of stories that aspire to truth. But the key question for men is not about their own authorship; I can only answer the question 'What am I to do?' if I can answer the prior question 'Of what story or stories do I find myself a part?' (MacIntyre, 1984, p. 211)

Myths and other forms of stories are a key part of educating humans into the virtues. MacIntyre's concern is for humans to live ethical and virtuous lives in an Aristotelian sense. The concept of selfhood, accordingly, 'is a concept of a self whose unity resides in the unity of a narrative which links birth to life to death as narrative beginning to middle to end' (MacIntyre, 2007, p. 205). He challenges the disconnected approach to human life and personhood where:

> a separation is made either between the individual and the roles that he or she plays – a separation … between the different role – and quasi-role – enactments of an individual life so that life comes to appear as nothing but a series of unconnected episodes … (MacIntyre, 2007, p. 205)

For MacIntyre, the disjointed self/selves cannot be the 'bearer' of virtues because virtues are qualities that manifest themselves in all situations rather than just when one is playing a role. Fragmentation of selfhood leads to the fragmentation of morality. MacIntyre maintains that the unity of an individual's life consists of:

> the unity of a narrative embodied in a single life. To ask 'What is the good for me?' is to ask 'What is the good for man?' is to ask what all answers to the former question must have in common. But now it is important to emphasize that it is the systematic asking of these two questions and the attempt to answer them in deed as well as in word which provide the moral life with its unity. The unity of a human life is the unity of a narrative quest. (MacIntyre, 2007, p. 218–9)

MacIntyre defines virtues as those dispositions that will not only sustain practices and enable us to reach the good inherent in practice, but also support us in the relevant kind of quest for the good, by enabling us to overcome the harms, dangers, temptations and distractions that we encounter, and which will furnish us with increasing self-knowledge and increasing knowledge of the good. The catalogue of the virtues will therefore include the virtues required to sustain the kinds of household and the kinds of political community in which men and women can seek the good together, and seek the virtues necessary for philosophical enquiry about the character of the good.

MacIntyre concludes:

> The good life for man is the life spent in seeking for the good life for man, and the virtues necessary for the seeking are those which will enable us to understand what more and what else the good life for man is. (MacIntyre, 2007, p. 219)

Hence narrative is also a narrative quest through which we can clarify that what is good for me has to be good for those communities (family, clan, tribe, institution, city, nation, etc.) that I am part of, and good for the different roles and parts that I inhabit and enact in my life. In this way, the self also has a historical continuity, as it is intimately linked to the past of the family (and to one's ancestors), the city, the nation, the collective pain and wounds, expectations and obligations. The self is also a social identity, as the virtues embodied by the self must be socially constructed and temporally appropriated. Thus one's moral identity finds itself in and through one's membership in the communities, which is the starting point for us to examine not only our moral sources but also our moral limitations. Ricoeur suggests that the notion of narrative identity can be applied to both individuals and communities because individuals and communities are 'constituted in their identity by taking up narratives that become for them their actual history' (Ricoeur, 1988, p. 247).

We can go on to suggest that the ethical self and moral identity are not merely embedded in human narratives; they are further developed in the process of narrating. Narrating lived experience and examining human life as a whole can help us forge a vision of our reality and our purpose in the world, which considers how it was constructed in relation to others, within the wider contexts of our communities and of the social and cultural systems that provide meaning to our existence. Here theory and practice are connected and integrated in the development of the individual's voice and in the narrative quest for a better state of things. Personal meanings and understanding are made explicit and placed alongside concepts, theories and descriptions of practice that come from others.

The narratives we tell explain our efforts to determine our places in the world and to direct our lives relative to the good. However, without action informed by our ethical orientations, without enacting our stories, such a vision will remain sterile and fruitless.

CONCLUSION

In this chapter, we have investigated our learning and pedagogical landscape by looking through its moral, social and narrative features and by looking at how these features are joined together in the domain of action-in-the-world.

We can tentatively conclude that the narrative approach offers important opportunities for individuals to examine not only one's experiences as lived but also one's purpose and meaning in one's life. This itself is a learning process and appeals to our capacities as humans. Indeed our orientation towards the good determines two mutually constitutive elements: the value framework(s) that define our moral and ethical horizons and a sense of who we are and how we act in relation to it.

To achieve this, one must work through one's life history, which is at the same time placed within much broader social, political, historical and personal contexts. This narrative understanding of our place in the world integrates our phenomenological experiences with our moral aspirations, assuming that although one is not there yet, one does not cease to strive. Whilst we are examining our phenomenological experiences, the transition from experience itself to reflection and to interpretation permits us to illuminate our scope of action. This then extends out fruitfully into our capacity for both social critique and social transformation. This is what we will turn to in the next chapter.

Finally, understanding learning from the life narrative perspective can enable us to develop pedagogical strategies that facilitate the individuals' journey through life's nuanced implications, ambiguity in meanings of activities, contradictions and dilemmas. Learning thus takes place in this space of inquiry, questions and questioning, which only an unfolding and coherent narrative can serve to respond. In and through such emergent narrative, we develop a sense of who we are, how we have become and where we are heading.

This view of learning is in contrast with the notion of learning as transmission and acquisition in a conventional sense and as practised in schooling across the world. In this book, we have placed narrative learning and pedagogy predominantly within the growth and becoming of persons in adulthood. This is due to the need to examine one's life as a whole, which demands a broader reflection beyond mere infancy and childhood to include one's past and present experiences and encounters as well as future orientations through actions. It is by no means to suggest that children and young people do not have such narrative capacities and need for deeper reflection. On the contrary, we see a great urgency for schooling to shift its conception of learning to embrace the notion of human becoming and to begin to explore the potential of narrative learning and pedagogy. That, however, would require different exploration all together.

CHAPTER 2

Reframing the Critical
Scherto Gill

Conflict is the gadfly of thought. It stirs us to observation and memory. It instigates to invention. It shocks us out of sheep-like passivity, and sets us at noting and contriving … conflict is a sine qua non of reflection and ingenuity.

–John Dewey, *Human Nature and Conduct*, 1930

INTRODUCTION

In the first chapter of this book, through an overview of the different landscape features within the field of critical narrative, we came to see that learning and flourishing are regarded lifelong as an essential human preoccupation. This is conceived as the process of forming and transforming our fundamental dispositions and qualities, enabling us to live well as individuals and make contribution to the wider world as members of a society or a community. There are intellectual, emotional, moral and ethical dimensions to our growth. Integrated into this vision of education and learning is the view of the development of our capabilities and qualities in supporting our own transformation, as well as that of our fellow human beings and indeed the transformation of the world at large.

Whilst we examine the nature of learning and the aims of pedagogy, we further establish that this process cannot be detached from narratives – stories of our past, present and future. This narrative journey is akin to what Dewey referred to as 'reconstruction', including the reconstruction of our stories and the re-identification of paths towards human becoming.

In this chapter, in order to reframe the critical in the light of learning and narrative, we will first review how criticality is conceptualized in the existing literature and practices, and then take a closer look at how it was conceived in the thinking of Freire and Dewey. Furthermore, we will focus on the dialogic aspect of critical pedagogy that both authors have persistently argued for and promoted in their writing as an important element of critical practice. Lastly, we make a tentative proposal about the potential of critical narrative as pedagogy.

CRITICAL THEORY AND CRITICALITY IN EDUCATION

Claimed to find its origin in the Frankfurt School of Sociology, critical theory was highly influenced by the thought of Karl Marx and is likewise concerned with equality, social justice and human emancipation (Horkheimer, 1982). The key argument can be summarized as follows: In the light of an overall emphasis on the economic growth of any given society, many other aspects of human life, such as culture, arts and values, are ignored. The result is that the majority of western societies tend to inculcate a form of consciousness in their working-class people, which serves to remove them from their own interests through the operation of social institutions, education, and other practices and norms. In this way, working-class people 'learned' to accept uncritically a particular kind of power imbalance, allowing the ruling class to maintain its status quo. A theory is critical in the sense that it seeks to uncover these circumstances that have enslaved people, so that humans can be free from domination and oppression. Embedded in this critical theory is the central role of the ideal of democracy and the conceptions of freedom and justice, including the freedom of individuals considered in a holistic way: that is, the individual in a web of relationships with and within the society as a whole and with nature (Horkheimer, 1982, 1993).

As a strong movement in the 1960s, 1970s and 1980s, neo-Marxists were critical of capitalism and all the societal malaises resulting from it. However, with the collapse of communism, some critical theorists are moving away from the criticism of capitalism and are instead confronting many other sociological issues, such as, ethnicity, gender and, more recently, sexuality. We will return to this point later.

Critical theory has long been integrated into educational theories. Often referred to as 'critical pedagogy' (following Freire's work), critical (educational) theory has been adopted and transformed by generations of educational thinkers and practitioners – so much so that it no longer has a straightforward definition. Yet, what constitute critical pedagogy are those educational practices and strategies that aim to confront social realities and their historical contexts, and to raise students' critical consciousness regarding structural oppression and social domination. The ultimate end of critical pedagogy is supposed to be human emancipation through the development of critical consciousness and collective political activism towards achieving a democratic society. Education plays a central and decisive role in this endeavour.

Critical thinking and critical theory

According to Burbules and Berk (1999), two schools of thought are pivotal in the emergence of criticality in pedagogy: critical thinking and critical theory, both of which find their place in education. Their review of the common concerns of these two schools as well as their differences is highly illuminating.

With respect to the common concerns, Burbules and Berk point out that there is a shared conviction that the majority of people in society have a certain deficiency in their ability or disposition to discern the distortions and falsehoods in the dominant discourse or truth-claims. These deficiencies limit the scope of their action and engagement in the world; these people are subject to an unjust social dispensation. Therefore, to become critical is to be able to uncover such power imbalance and the distortion of truth and to restore dignity.

A critical conception of the world recognizes that education contributes to the perpetuation of unequal power and the unjustness of the status quo through the way in which knowledge is defined, constructed and implemented in the socially formed space. As a response, education should help students become aware of, and push back, the delimitations in order to pursue fulfilment of their whole potential. The end of education in this way incorporates opportunities for individuals to examine their role as moral agents and their potential for shaping destiny, both individually and collectively (Goodson and Gill, 2011).

This is where the two schools (critical thinking and critical theory) part from each other as they take different approaches to education and pedagogy. Critical thinking takes the view that to be critical means having more capacity to discern faulty arguments, generalizations and assertions that are not backed up with evidence, or claims based on some unreliable authority, or obscure concepts. The purpose, then, of critical thinking is to contribute to a shift from an irrational, illogical and unexamined living, to a well-'examined life' aligned with its purposes.

Siegel (1988) argues that critical thinking should aim at self-sufficiency, and that 'a self-sufficient person is a liberated person...free from the unwarranted and undesirable control of unjustified beliefs' (Siegel, 1988, p. 58). The critical thinking approach to education is often criticized for its explicit focus on the individual's critical capacities, a somewhat a-politicized approach to emancipation, perhaps.

By contrast, for critical theorists, educational institutions, especially schools, preserve an unjust status quo and shape individuals in such a way that they become participants in the myths regarding the 'right' order of things and thereby accept the imbalance of power. In this case, the priority of education is to uncover inequitable and oppressive institutional culture and social relations. Critical pedagogy thus aims to unmask the world and then change it. The individual's emancipation is contingent with social transformation (Giroux, 1988, 1994). The approaches to critical pedagogy are often regarded as overtly political; thus, encouraging students to think critically is equated to encouraging them to think politically.

Burbules and Berk's (1999) review observes a certain adversarial commentary by some scholars supporting critical thinking and others occupying the critical theory camp. The review concludes:

> In short, each of these traditions regards the other as *insufficiently* critical; each defines, in terms of its own discourse and priorities, key elements that it believes the other neglects to address. Each wants to acknowledge a certain value in the goals the other aspires to, but argues that its means are inadequate to attain them. (Burbules and Berk, 1999, p. 56)

Despite their respective strengths and limitations, both schools of thought are finding a place in the educational theoretical arena. They continue to challenge the framework of the traditional canon, so to raise students' consciousness about oppressive social structures, and to critique social inequality generated by the system itself.

In developing an appropriate response in terms of classroom praxis, both approaches offer the potential for teachers and students to act as agents of change (Kincheloe, 2004; McLaren, 2000; Wink, 2005).

Critical pedagogy and feminist pedagogy

Inevitably, scholars and pedagogues extend these theoretical and definitional tensions into teaching and learning. There are also additional tensions between the rather masculine theorization of critical pedagogy based on Frankfurt School's sociology, Marx and the other so-called founding fathers of theory, on the one hand, and their feminist counterparts stressing and engaging with sociological topics other than class, including gender, ethnicity, sexuality, ability and culture. Feminists argue that a masculine approach can only further marginalize the oppressed. To this extent, feminists term class-obsessed pedagogy a 'boy thing' and thus hooks (2003), Lather (2001) and others want to reclaim the territory underpinning critical theory for a more justice-oriented rationality. Their intention is to enlarge the field and develop a more inclusive understanding of critical pedagogy.

Whilst these debates and tensions are ongoing and the list of social issues to be included in the field of critical theory continues to expand, there is an increasing sense of frustration as the battleground has moved from educational sites where agents (students and teachers) struggle for emancipation, liberation and social transformation through critical education, to the 'symposia' where academics clash with and confront each other about the textual meanings and endless deconstruction of discourses. Indeed, this is where 'language of critique, devoid of language of hope and possibility, threatens to undermine the very notion of radical theory and politics' (Giroux, 1988, p. 205).

At the same time, scholars such as Ellsworth (1989), have cautioned that critical pedagogy should not be confused with feminist pedagogy, as the latter constitutes a separate body of literature with distinct goals and assumptions. She offers a reflexive note in terms of the task for educators:

> Given my own history of white-skin, middle-class, able-bodied, thin privilege and my institutionally granted power, it made more sense to see my task as one of redefining 'critical pedagogy' so that it did not need Utopian moments of 'democracy,' 'equality,' 'justice,' or 'emancipated' teachers – moments that are unattainable (and ultimately undesirable, because they are always predicated on the interests of those who are in the position to define Utopian projects). (Ellsworth, 1989, p. 308)

We want to highlight here that when the critical becomes the aim of education, or one falls into a deconstruction black hole, critical theory can begin to lose its potency – because, indeed, the critical itself is a route to change and transform the false consciousness inherent in the oppression of our human faculty. The critical is not an end and shall never be an end.

The complexity of applying criticality in education

Breuing (2011) notes that critical pedagogues tend to define and understand critical theory in ways that are both overlapping and contradictory – an aspect of the complexity of applying criticality in education (see also Gur-Ze'ev, 1998; Kincheloe, 2004). Take the action research movement as an example. It has now shifted from a critical educational theory that is too preoccupied with uncovering assumptions and analysing political discourses to a focus on praxis (Freire, 1996). Action research as it happens now aims to empower teachers to reflect on their classroom contexts and practices, to theorize and make changes in order to transform curriculum and pedagogy.

Proponents of critical action research point out the important role that teachers play in investigating the social, cultural and political contexts of schooling through critical inquiry. Goodson and colleagues further suggest that, to launch any inquiry into the practices of teaching and learning, insights must be developed into the way teachers perceive their personal and professional life and how it intertwines and evolves over time with societal, political and human history. Thus Goodson and others initiated a mode of educational research that focused the investigation on studying teachers' lives (Goodson, 1992; Goodson and Hargreaves, 1996). Later, the teacher-as-the-researcher movement places educational action within the realm of teachers' conception of education and learning, and allows insights into the ways in which teachers' life histories, career trajectories and personal values affect their practices and growth. This reaffirms the centrality of the teacher in educational research. Goodson proposes that:

> by tracing the teacher's life as it evolved over time – throughout the teacher's career and through several generations the assumption of timelessness might also be remedied. *In understanding something so intensely personal as teaching it is critical that we know about the person the teacher is.* Our paucity of knowledge in this area is a manifest indictment of the range of our sociological imagination. (Goodson, 1981, p. 69)

Indeed, only by broadening our sociological gaze and imagination can teachers be given the opportunity to transform teaching and learning strategies as their response to the findings of such inquiries; in addition, by empowering teachers as critical pedagogues, it is possible to develop a democratic culture both in schools and in society at large (Carr and Kemmis, 1986; Kincheloe, 1991, 1995). The studies of teachers' lives bring together the personal, the moral and the political. Giroux (1988) points out that when conceiving of teachers as inquirers and as transformative innovators,

> teaching can be linked directly with a political and moral discourse that takes as one of the first considerations the issue of how schools contribute to the oppression of youth and how such conditions can be changed. (Giroux, 1988, pp. 212–3)

Once again, in the field of action research, this dichotomy between practical and critical action research is being observed (Cochran-Smith and Lytle, 1999; Manfra, 2009). Our goal here is not to reconcile the differences in the conceptualizations of critical theory and critical pedagogy, nor to create a new definition. Nevertheless, we see an opportunity for dialogue and thus agree with authors such as Burbules and Berk that such creative tensions should be welcome. If these tensions are seen as conditions that can give rise to refreshing and renewed understanding through dialogic encounter, then we believe that any conflicting perspectives and definitions will serve as the basis for new interpretation and meaning. What really interests us here is an examination of the critical, not necessarily from the perspective of a particular theoretical or ideological framework, such as reviewed briefly earlier, but rather from the following standpoint.

We have seen that the critical refers to a way of thinking and perceiving that involves our ability to question things, to challenge assumptions including our own, to recognize historical, sociocultural and political contexts of views and to understand the world holistically and meaningfully. This is essentially a dialogic approach to being and becoming critical, and it has its proponents in Paulo Freire and John Dewey amongst others, who regard the critical as looking for an appreciation of humanity and progressing towards emancipation.

REFRAMING THE CRITICAL – A RADICAL READING OF FREIRE AND DEWEY

The question of 'what constitutes the critical' is less explored, yet it is a key question in education. If we are not clear about what it means to be critical, how can we continue discussing critical pedagogy? We all have an idea of what the critical is roughly about, but it is necessary to go deeper in our inquiry.

Two key thinkers, Paulo Freire and John Dewey, have significantly influenced the work in critical pedagogy. We will now consider their writings in more depth.

Freire's *Pedagogy of the Oppressed*

In *Pedagogy of the Oppressed*,[1] Freire (1996) noted that the core of radical pedagogy lies in its potential to enable critical discovery amongst the oppressed that their being oppressed and their oppressors' oppressing them are equal manifestations of dehumanization. An act is defined as oppressive when it prevents people from being and becoming fully human. Therefore, the ultimate goal of liberation is the humanization of all people, both the oppressed and the oppressors included.

Freire sharply pointed out that education can be part of the dehumanizing scheme, in that it reinforces knowledge dependency, a hierarchical understanding of authority and a distorted view of history, and therefore undermines the kind of social consciousness needed for individual and societal transformation. For Paulo Freire, education is ultimately humanization, which 'consists in permitting the emergence of the awareness of our full humanity, as a condition and as an obligation, as a situation and as a project' (Freire, 1996, pp. 74–5). Freire considers freedom and emancipation as routes to become fully human, which, as we described in Chapter 1, is man's historical and ontological vocation.

According to Freire, a critical approach starts with problematizing in order to develop an awareness of the reality in concrete situations, understanding one's place in the world and relating this to one's aspirations, and finally taking action. Such action must be connected to people's situated preoccupation, doubts, hopes and fears – and not just discourse. Freire saw people as beings 'in a situation', who:

> find themselves rooted in temporal-spatial conditions which mark them and which they also mark. They will tend to reflect on their own 'situationality' to the extent that they are

---

[1] In this book, most references to Freire's seminal book *Pedagogy of the Oppressed* are taken from the revised edition published by Penguin in 1996. The original work was published in 1970 by Continuum.

challenged by it to act upon it. Human beings *are* because they are in a situation. And they *will be more* the more they not only critically reflect upon their existence but critically act upon it. (Freire, 1996, p. 90)

Understanding the world and our situations within it, changing our individual and collective aspirations and taking a different course of action together[2] in order to become fully human are the essences of Freire's critical existential thinking. Critical consciousness is critical reflection on one's own 'existential experience and human–world relationship and on the relationship between people implicit in the former' (Freire, 1996, p. 78). Thus, 'critical analysis of a significant existential dimension makes possible a new, critical attitude towards the limit-situations' (Freire, 1996, p. 85). *Conscientizacao* is critical investigation, which in turn helps men and women develop a critical form of thinking about their world, through dialogue. The dialogic approach to education is not to impose or convey any existing views, but rather to explore shared understanding about the world. Part of the dialogue is to enable the oppressed to identify that the oppressor has been 'housed' in the oppressed; consequently, the oppressed is a dual being, as he/she continues to carry the oppressor within himself/herself.

Freire further explains that the object of dialogic investigation is not persons as such, but rather 'the thought-language with which men and women refer to the reality, the levels at which they perceive that reality, and their view of the world, in which their generative themes are found' (Freire, 1996, pp. 77–8). In other words, the purpose of dialogue is to name the world with a view to changing it with ourselves in it. Indeed, Giroux (1988, p. 203),

---

[2] Freire himself stressed that action must be reciprocal: that is, in an educational setting, both students and teachers will engage in the actions thus identified.

by quoting Bloch's writing on the *Principle of Hope*, suggests that 'only thinking directed towards changing the world and informing the desire to change it does not confront the future … as embarrassment and the past as spell'. This characterizes the *raison d'être* of the critical – collective actions for a societal future, a common future for all humanities.

Freire proposes a three-pronged integral process to critical dialogue – critical reflection, dialogue and action – and 'only then, will it be a praxis' (Freire, 1996, p. 47). Through dialogue and action, education is constantly being remade, and as Freire saw it, in order for education 'to *be*, it must *become*'. In this way, the critical is not only to shift our thinking and our understanding of the world within which our thinking arises and evolves through education, but also to shift the way we educate ourselves (teachers and students) and the way we approach educating.

Critical dialogue is mutual humanization that determines solidarity between the teacher and her students. To be in solidarity with each other in the process of critical reflection and actions is another central aspect of being critical. In other words, the critical must be reciprocal, which in itself is humanity affirming. Freire further describes that humans are 'beings for another' (Freire, 1996, p. 49). This gives rise to the implication that care or caring is the human thing to do even in a process of being critical.

Thus at the heart of Freire's thesis lies the primacy of ethics – a vision of the good and our quest for the unfolding of human potential. Thus the highest good is to be human, which is equivalent to being ethical and moral. The Freirean ethics of humanization comprise humans' aspiration to transform the world through reflective, critical, dialogical action. The ethical vocation of all human beings is to realize this capacity. Freire later terms this a universal human ethic that underpins 'human living and human social intercourse' and which 'calls us out of and beyond ourselves' (Freire, 2001, p. 25).

Dewey's inquiry-based epistemology

John Dewey's inquiry-based epistemology has resonance with respect to the critical, and the aim of education. He regarded this as the way to develop a freer and more humane experience in which people can share and to which all can contribute (Dewey, 1939). Agreeing with Freire's notion of 'man-in-a-situation', Dewey saw it crucial to understand our experience within the social, historical, cultural and political contexts that have shaped it. Dewey recognized that our lived experience is shaped by habitual modes of behaviour (habits), attitudes and assumptions. Our experiences and attitudes can be self-perpetuating and difficult to modify because they form habits to which we develop a certain attachment. When these habits are interrupted, people tend to react with anxiety and discomfort. Often, prevailing ideologies can be seen as such 'habits' and assumptions, and represent righteousness. Thus these habitual attitudes and assumptions can obstruct social change.

However, when people who embody different 'habits' interact, tensions can arise as a result of the differences, at which point, people feel the need to pause, reflect and examine their experience. Dewey argued that reflection and examination require the rational and the intellect for problem solving. This is a process of critical inquiry that involves a reciprocal relationship between experience and reflection:

> That the subject-matter of primary experience sets the problems and furnishes the first data of the reflection which constructs the secondary objects (reflective inquiry) is evident; it is also obvious that test and verification of the latter is secured only by return to things of crude or macroscopic experience. (Dewey, 1925, p. 4)

This inquiry becomes a thought experiment designed to arrive at a practical judgement as well as an action by which it is anticipated to resolve one's predicament (Anderson, 2010). Thus the inquiry will return to the experience and action that invoked it in the first place. Here the intellect enables articulation and analysis of the situation as well as the development of a renewed course of action and strategies for implementing it. In turn, the more one engages in such intelligent conduct, the more such dispositions become habitual and further enhance the change. Thus, for Dewey, education ought to instil the habits of independent and intelligent thought, critical inquiry, careful observation, active experimentation and imagination, including sympathy with others (Dewey, 1916). It is clear that the critical, for Dewey, is the human's ability to experience, to problematize, to inquire and reflect, and to resolve in order to renew our experience and our action. Embedded in the critical is the relationship between experience and inquiry, or means and ends, which is reciprocally determined (Anderson, 2010). To be critical is to embark on a process whereby, through inquiries and critical thought, humans cultivate and develop sets of dispositions through which we grow, transcend and transform, ceaselessly moving towards a more humane civilization of democratic society (Anderson, 2010).

Dewey's view of the good and his approach to moral ethics are also situated within the method of critical and reflective inquiry. Rejecting fixed and objective notions of the good, Dewey saw the good as the object of desires, which are the fruits of informed reflection, including a critical appraisal of our own characters and dispositions as a crucial determinant for what we ought to desire (Anderson, 2010). In turn, education, learning, inquiry and reflection are constituted in human goods. Furthermore, Dewey's (social) ethics are concerned with the institutional culture and arrangements that influence the capacity of people to conduct moral inquiry intelligently, such as in schools and wider civil society. This means, in the case of schools and other educational institutions, teachers and students ought to be offered the opportunity for developing and investigating ideas and information in active pursuit of their own critical appraisal of social situations. This would resemble the problem-posing and problem-solving approach that Freire has proposed.

Dewey regarded the critical as key to action, especially when individuals regard the moral norms as hypothetical and launch their own investigation by reflecting on their experience in the world, and appraising value and wider consequences. In this way, the critical bridges Dewey's moral ethics and political thoughts. In Dewey's conception, democracy is more than a form of government; more importantly, it is a way of being and living together in and through dialogic and communicated experience. Once again this comes close to Freire's idea of people being in relationship with one another in the dialogic process of mutual humanization. Critical investigation through dialogic encounter helps articulate our moral ideals and directions for action as well as the virtues and non-moral qualities necessary to bring us towards our direction.

Freire and Dewey – common views on the critical

In summary, the critical for both Freire and Dewey lies in the development and cultivation of our critical consciousness. These two thinkers share a conception of the critical, which can be articulated in the following way.[3]

Both authors agree that the end of the critical is encompassed in the end of education, which must have humanization as its core aim. Where Freire explicitly articulates that the aim of education should be to enable men and women to become more fully human, Dewey would agree that education must help individuals develop their full potentialities as good citizens. There are two

---

[3] For a helpful discussion of the differences between Freire and Dewey's educational thinking, refer to Deans (1999). For our own purpose, we only highlight the premises upon which both authors can agree, in relation to the notion of the critical.

connected points here: one is the recognition of the need for never-ending human becoming. As Freire later writes:

> my own unity and identity, in regard to others and to the world, constitutes my essential and irrepeatable way of experiencing myself as a cultural, historical and unfinished being in the world, simultaneously conscious of my unfinishedness. (Freire, 2001, p. 51)

The other is our commitment to overcoming our own limitedness to achieve a betterment of things. Human becoming thus consists of becoming more ethical. Indeed, embedded in both Freirean and Deweyan thoughts is the primary concern for the good, which provides us with a moral compass in our pursuit of meaning and valued ends. In the case of humanizing ends, both authors have pointed out the importance of perceiving one's own good as intimately connected to the goods of others. In other words, as we have seen, a good life must be a life in relationship with others, and our moral obligation is therefore to make our own life and that of others more worthwhile and more humane – a noble aspiration which in turn creates a bond between people, making societies humanized societies. Freire writes: 'Insofar as I am a conscious presence in the world, I cannot hope to escape my ethical responsibility for my action in the world' (Freire, 2001, p. 26).

The critical is perceived by both authors as part of human consciousness. When education is increasingly being used as an instrument to perpetuate a way of thinking and to privilege a certain notion of knowledge, it is crucial to develop a critical consciousness (not just critical thinking, but also human curiosity) that will help people uncover the economic structure, social order and political regime that render an inhuman society and undignified existence for all. Both Freire and Dewey agree that the process of critical inquiry and the process of developing critical consciousness are not separate but integral and reciprocal. In other words, the only way to become critical is to engage in the critical.[4] In the next chapter, we will survey the contexts and the kinds of encounter that would enable us to become critical.

Identifying the prevailing 'myth' of society and liberating us so as to reach new levels of awareness and consciousness involve a dialogic process. The dialogue is a critical act itself, and through dialogue, a course of action is identified, which further serves as the basis for an ongoing dialogue. The key to a dialogic approach to the critical is to be able to question and pose problems. In Freire's words, the foundation of such processes is 'human curiosity', which makes us 'question, know, act, ask again, recognize' (Freire, 2001, p. 19). For both Freire and Dewey this dialogic process is an ideal approach to humanizing ourselves and others, and to breaking down social barriers of class and race, and other boundaries. Thus dialogue, inquiry, reflection, action, praxis and social change are linkages of one transformative chain, as Freire (1996) concludes:

> For apart from inquiry, apart from praxis, men cannot be truly human. Knowledge emerges only through invention and re-invention, through the restless, impatient, continuing, hopeful inquiry men pursue in the world, with the world, and with each other. (Freire, 1996, p. 58)

DIALOGIC APPROACH TO THE CRITICAL – A CLOSE READING OF FREIRE AND GADAMER

Dialogue is at the heart of the Gadamerian philosophical hermeneutics as well as Freirean critical and transformative thoughts. Both Freire and Gadamer saw dialogue as a human phenomenon, involving critical inquiry, relying on the presence

---

[4] This is after Dewey's own saying that 'the only way to prepare for social life is to engage in social life' (Dewey, 1964, p. 116).

of the Other, and focusing on growth and action, as we will consider in this section.

Freire on dialogue

Since we have already covered Freire's thinking extensively in this chapter, we will only sketch his views on dialogue here, focusing on a few elements that Freire sees as important to dialogue.

The first step that Freire took in discussing dialogue was to consider 'the essence of dialogue itself: *the word*' (Freire, 1996, p. 68), which, for him, is not merely a tool or instrument that humans can use to communicate and to have dialogue with. His view of language is totally in line with Gadamer's conception, as we shall see later. However, Freire sees that within the word there are 'two dimensions: reflection and action' (Freire, 1996, p. 68). He regards these two dimensions as in radical interaction with each other, together forming the basis of a praxis, as we have seen. Freire writes that 'to speak a true word is to transform the world' (Freire, 1996, p. 68). Therefore, the word in dialogue is what contains the critical element.

Certainly, for the word to have critical quality and thereby to be transformative, it must be authentic, reflective, problematizing and committed to naming the world in order to change the world. Thus the word is linked to action, change and transformation. Freire passionately claims: 'Human beings are not built in silence, but in word, in work, in action-reflection' (Freire, 1996, p. 69). In this claim, Freire equates word with action and affirms humans' existential characteristics to be in dialogue with one another in order to pursue their destiny.

Freire has famously said: 'Dialogue is the encounter between men, mediated by the world, in order to name the world' (Freire, 1996, p. 69). So clearly, for Freire, denying people's rights and opportunity to the word (to name the world) and to change the world is dehumanizing because dialogue is of 'existential necessity' for human beings. Part of our being is to transform the condition within which we exist and thrive.

As Freire sees it, the aim of transforming the world for the liberation of humankind suggests a 'profound love for the world and for people' (Freire, 1996, p. 70) and 'an intense faith in humankind' (Freire, 1996, p. 71). We would certainly join Freire in recognizing that the act of love is an expression of our ethical commitment and moral responsibility to the goodness of humanity and of the world. Freire writes: 'If I do not love the world – if I do not love life – if I do not love people – I cannot enter into dialogue' (Freire, 1996, p. 71). Having love for the world is the basis for taking the courage to act in order to create and recreate a new world, which, at the same time, transforms ourselves within and with it. In the next chapter, we will return to this topic of self-transformation when we discuss the narrative pedagogy and how naming the world also includes naming ourselves, and how creating and recreating the world include retelling and recreating our own narratives.

Freire further points out that dialogue entails humility, which means that the interlocutors or partners/discussants must perceive each other as having something valuable to contribute to the dialogue topic (i.e. naming the world), and that, by dialogue, we each will learn more about the world through engaging in meaningful conversations about our experiences in the world. Such humility determines that dialogue is a reciprocal exchange and mutual trust as well as a give-and-take relation (as we shall see later, this is a view put forward more explicitly by Gadamer).

Freire's consistent message about humanization is once more being reinforced, in that dialogue is a humanizing act where persons are in solidarity with each other. This fellowship is not static but is formed in active pursuit of betterment and hope. Hope has been an important element in Freire's struggle for human emancipation, to the extent that he writes: 'If the dialoguers expect nothing to come of their efforts, their encounter will be sterile, bureaucratic and tedious' (Freire, 1996, p. 73).

The last but most important ingredient of dialogue, for Freire, is the critical. As we have seen in the previous pages, the critical must be perceived in a radical light in the Freirean dialogue. He writes that the critical:

> discerns an indivisible solidarity between the world and the people and admits of no dichotomy between them – thinking which perceives reality as process, as transformation, rather than a static entity – thinking which does not separate itself from action, but constantly immerses itself in temporality without fear of the risks involved. (Freire, 1996, p. 73)

What is crucial here is that dialogue requires the critical and, at the same time, engenders the critical. This idea is reinforced in Gadamer's thinking.

Gadamer on dialogue

What we touch upon here is mostly drawn from Gadamer's major works: *Truth and Method* and *Philosophical Hermeneutics*. Gadamer's view of dialogue is situated within philosophical hermeneutics. Hermeneutics is applied in situations in which we encounter meanings that are not immediately accessible to us and which require interpretive effort. The earliest situation in which hermeneutical principles were adopted was when interpreters were trying to understand significant texts, such as Holy Scripture, whose meanings were often obscure, resulting in an alienation from the meaning. Hermeneutics apply to all situations of understanding where the same alienation may occur. These situations include when we engage in dialogue or conversation, when we read texts, experience works of art or try to understand historical events and actions.

Gadamer does not regard hermeneutics as a method or methodology, and the emphasis on hermeneutics does not mean a rejection of the importance of methodological concerns. Instead it represents an insistence from Gadamer on the limited role of method and his intention to prioritize understanding as a dialogic, practical and situated activity.

According to Gadamer, interpretation has a temporal character and cannot be carried out by an anonymous 'knowing subject'. To understand is also to understand a web of meanings and contexts within which understanding takes place, including that of the interpreters. Gadamer claims that hermeneutical interpretation can bridge the gap between the familiar world we inhabit and the unfamiliar meaning that resists assimilation into our horizons. This is where he introduces the reflexive dimension of hermeneutical understanding. He argues that any knower or interpreter's present situation (which carries his or her own historicity and traditions) is already constituted in the process of understanding. The interpreters always try to understand within a certain boundedness of their own horizon and this, combined with their temporal distance from their objects (resulting from their own historicity and tradition), offers a rich and productive ground for understanding. Thus Gadamer posits that understanding includes an element of historical consciousness which is 'unavoidable ... when immediate insight into what is said in the tradition is no longer possible' for us to access (Gadamer, 1977, p. 46).

Gadamer employs the notion of prejudice in a radical way. Prejudice, as defined by Gadamer, does not refer to what is unjustified and erroneous and thereby distorts the truth. Prejudice simply means 'a judgement that is rendered before all the elements that determine a situation have been finally examined' (Gadamer, 1975, p. 273). It is where we can start to engage with otherness. Gadamer points out that being situated within traditions and prejudice does not necessarily limit our freedom. He asks: 'Is not, rather, all human existence, even the freest, limited and qualified in various ways?' (Gadamer, 1975, p. 277). Prejudice is closely connected to Freire's notion of man-in-a-situation. According to Gadamer, prejudice opens up possibilities for understanding and defines the premises that the interpreter occupies, from which he or she attempts to understand. Freire would concur with this. In fact, both Freire and Gadamer support the idea that the critical self-consciousness of the interpreter or interlocutor must include an awareness of the continuing power of history and tradition in the finitude of human understanding.

Understanding as a hermeneutical task is not aimed at reconstructing the intention of the author/person who writes/speaks. Understanding is mediation or translation of past meaning into the present, and is thus concerned with the continuity of history, which encompasses every subjective act and object comprehended. Gadamer summarizes:

> Understanding is not, in fact, understanding better, either in the sense of superior knowledge of the subject because of clearer ideas or in the sense of fundamental superiority of conscious over unconscious production. It is enough to say that we understand *in a different way, if we understand at all*. (Gadamer, 1975, p. 296)

The first condition of hermeneutical understanding is an encounter with something unfamiliar, or in Gadamer's words, encountering 'the alien'. This is to say, when a person is trying to understand, he or she is prepared for it to tell them something – something new, something different from what they already know. This sensitivity to 'the alien' is 'neither neutrality with respect to content nor the extinction of one's self' (Gadamer, 1975, p. 271). Later, in Gadamer's discussion about education, he also talks about the importance of the continuous presence of others or the other in our being-in-the-world. This reciprocal character of education is also reflected in Freire's discussion of teacher–student and student–teacher reciprocity. We will touch on this later in this chapter and discuss it in more depth in Chapter 3.

Gadamer proposes that 'we remain open to the meaning of the other', but this openness 'always includes our situating the other meaning in relation to the whole of our own meanings or ourselves in relation to it' (Gadamer, 1975, p. 271). According to Gadamer, in order to attend to the meaning implicit in the otherness, and achieve understanding (rather than misunderstanding), the criterion of questioning is very important. In this way, the hermeneutical task '*becomes of itself a questioning of things* and is always in part so defined' (Gadamer, 1975, p. 271, italics in original).

Gadamer claims: 'The close relation between questioning and understanding is what gives the hermeneutic experience its true dimension' (Gadamer, 1975, p. 271), and the 'real power of hermeneutical consciousness is our ability to see what is questionable' (Gadamer, 1977, p. 13). This questioning of things and Freire's problem-posing approach are both encompassed in the critical that we conceived in the previous section of this chapter. Thus we believe that both authors address the critical in a fundamentally similar way – through inquiry, problematizing, questioning and quest for meaning.

For Gadamer, the critical refers to sensitivity and an awareness of one's own prejudice, without which any otherness cannot present itself and hence loses its potential to prompt our understanding. With the finite determinacy of human thought in mind, Gadamer suggests that the way one's own range of vision can be expanded is through understanding. He describes this vision by using the concept of horizon, which is 'the range of vision that includes everything that can be seen from a particular vantage point' (Gadamer, 1975, p. 301). He introduces the famous expression 'fusion of horizons' to describe the process of dialogue when one continues to encounter the other's horizon, and they fuse into 'something of living value' (Gadamer, 1975, p. 301). As summarized by Linge:

> It is precisely in confronting the otherness ... that ... (our) own prejudices ... are thrown into relief and thus come to critical self-consciousness ... Collision with the other's horizons makes us aware of assumptions so deep-seated that they would otherwise remain unnoticed. (Linge, 1977, p. xxi)

Gadamer sees that the dialogue between the interlocutors involves active reciprocity and equality. It presupposes that both dialogue partners/interlocutors are concerned with a common topic or a common question. In this way, dialogue is never a question of a relation between persons – the dialogue partners – but rather a question of participating in exchange or communication about a topic. It is not a matter of looking *at* the other person, but of looking *with* the other *at* the thing which is the subject of the dialogue.

For Gadamer, the key to the dialogue is questioning of things. This questioning allows the interlocutors to transcend each other's horizons (including the historical horizons embedded in our cultures and ways of thinking), to fuse them and then to transform them respectively towards higher universality, 'which overcomes not only one's own particularity but also that of the other person' (Gadamer, 1975, p. 288). This active reciprocity in a hermeneutical dialogue suggests that genuine understanding is not only intersubjective, but also dialectical – a new meaning born out of the interplay that goes on continuously between the past and present, between different horizons. 'Through every dialogue something different comes to be' (Gadamer, 1975, p. 58). This is Gadamer's principal contribution to the hermeneutics. This view of dialogue and the development of critical consciousness through questioning are fundamentally akin to that proposed by Freire. Implicit in the 'something different' is our understanding of the topic, our understanding of where we came from and how our life has shaped the way we think and act and how we might understand the world, ourselves and our actions differently.

Furthermore, Gadamer agrees with Freire that language is the key to dialogue and argues that understanding as fusion of horizons is an essentially linguistic process, and language and understanding are one and the same process. In this way, language constitutes our prejudices (which constitute our being), and language and understanding are inseparable structural aspects of humans' being-in-the-world.

He defines language as follows:

> Language is by no means simply an instrument or a tool ... Rather, in all our knowledge of ourselves and in all knowledge of the world, we are always already encompassed by the language which is our own. (Gadamer, 1977, p. 62)

Understanding is language-bound, claims Gadamer, and:

> language is the real medium of human being, if we only see it in the realm that it alone fills out, the realm of human being-together, the realm of common understanding, of ever-replenished common agreement – a realm as indispensable to human life as the air we breathe. As Aristotle said, man is truly the being who has language. (Gadamer, 1977, p. 68)

Freire and Gadamer – common views on dialogue

In summary, Freire and Gadamer agree that dialogue is of ontological significance and that, through dialogue, we understand and we become. Both authors recognize the importance of the presence of the other, how such encounter prompts us to recognize that our existing understanding or perspectives are conditioned and that dialogue simultaneously helps us go beyond such conditioning in order to take responsibility to reconstruct and transform. Freire's problematizing and Gadamer's questioning-of-things are key to developing critical consciousness, which in

turn allows us to transcend and transform. Apart from the reciprocal relationship between the interlocutors and their give-and-take
exchange, both authors suggest language be a basis for dialogue
and a medium through which dialogue takes place.

Gadamer's vision of dialogue is, at first glance, apolitical, which
would appear to be in contrast to Freire's view of dialogue. For
Gadamer, the primary focus of dialogue is understanding and
meaning, which shifts as the partners continue engaging in the
exchange. The dialogue never aims to arrive at a final conclusion,
but our understanding through the hermeneutical endeavour will
remain temporal, situated and yet impregnated with endless possibilities, as long as the dialogic process stays open and progressive.
This progressiveness of dialogue reflects Freire's notion of human
unfinishedness introduced earlier. Freire points out that 'because
in my unfinishedness I know that I am conditioned. Yet conscious
of such conditioning, I know that I can go beyond it' (Freire, 1998,
p. 54). In this regard, the Gadamerian hermeneutical dialogue
also 'exercises a self-criticism of thinking consciousness, a criticism that translates all its own abstractions and also the knowledge of the sciences back into the whole of human experience of
the world' (Gadamer, 1977, p. 94).

Thus hermeneutics engenders a critical dimension by enabling
the interlocutors to become aware of social, cultural, historical,
political and ideological influence on our interpretive positions as
dialogue partners, and on the boundedness of language, horizons
and what it is to be known and to be understood. Gadamerian dialogue is critical hermeneutics and is similar to Freirean inquiry,
which in turn invites dialogue.

Although the Gadamerian take on dialogue appears to be less
political, without a focus on ideological critique or unveiling hidden agendas and assumptions, its openness to differences and
reflexivity ultimately helps unfold the underlying cultural, social
and political beliefs and structures explicit in our language and

discourse, which have shaped our own subjectivity and horizons (Sammel, 2003, p.160).

CONCLUSION

In this chapter, through an in-depth review of the relevant literature, we set out to explore a way to reframe the critical within the context of critical narrative as pedagogy. As we have seen, critical approaches have long been integrated in education as part of the transformative pedagogy, and in our review, the critical is reassumed with new meaning in light of narrative, encounter and dialogue.

First, the critical is constituted in the end of education – to become fully human includes developing the disposition of being critically reflective. The reflexivity is connected to a vision of goodness, as we saw in Chapter 1. This critical capacity is connected to our ability 'to intervene, to compare, to judge, to decide, to choose, to desist...' (Freire, 2001, p. 53).

Second, the critical is pivotal to demystifying the politicalized societal narrative intended to sustain a power imbalance. To do this, it is necessary to take a dialogic approach to learning, especially incorporating questioning and problem posing. Indeed, to participate in critical dialogue itself is to embody and enact human relations. Through encounter between persons and different perspectives, the individuals launch investigations and formulate interpretations of questions arising from their lived experiences.

Third, the critical thus allows the deconstruction of certain assumptions inherent in the individual's everyday discourse as the result of education and rooted in their narratives (consciously and unconsciously), and dialogue and 'fusion of horizons' further provide an opportunity to reconstruct their own vision of good life.

Fourth, the critical dialogue can support the individual to develop a sense of themselves in time and locale. In doing so, they may begin to recognize their unfinishedness, but also place it in the social, cultural, political and personal context in which it is located. In the next chapter, we will see that, within the critical dialogical approach, it is narrative that can build bridges linking a person and a community's past, present and future.

Lastly, the critical can make it possible for individuals to de-associate themselves from a discourse or vision of life that is being imposed on them, and by unveiling such views, they then reinte-grate a set of values in their day-to-day being and action.

CHAPTER 3

Critical Narrative as Pedagogy

Scherto Gill

In our making and remaking of ourselves in the process of making history – as subjects and objects, persons, becoming beings of insertion in the world and not of pure adaptation to the world – we should end by having the dream, too, a mover of history. There is no change without dream, as there is no dream without hope.

–Paulo Freire, *Pedagogy of Hope*, 1994/2004

INTRODUCTION

So far, we have described the field of critical narrative through four interconnected landscapes – the moral, the social, the pedagogical and these in light of agency. We chose the metaphor of 'landscape' for a number of reasons: it allows us to locate different approaches to understanding criticality and critical pedagogy within the scope of human learning and development; it gives us a clear idea in terms of the terrains within which such understanding takes place; and finally it can help us develop a more holistic view of the new horizon into which we can move and how different landscapes are located within it and their relationship with each other. By using metaphoric landscapes, we can thus identify our own paths by navigating through the field towards clarity in our conception and practice of critical narrative as pedagogy.

In the second chapter of this book, our exploration of these different landscapes highlighted some of the existing theories of critical and dialogical pedagogy put forward by thinkers such as those from the Frankfurt School of Sociology, post-structural theorists and researchers, philosophers including Freire, Dewey and Gadamer, and others. It offered an opportunity to place more conventional sociologically oriented and politically focused debates on critical thinking next to a more humanistic conception of criticality.

Having reclaimed the potential of criticality in pedagogy in ways that embrace moral goods in education and the transformative agenda, in this chapter, we refocus on criticality in narrative as pedagogy. We start with an understanding of narrative in social research and human interaction. Then we examine narrative's potential in learning and finally begin to develop a framework of critical narrative as pedagogy.

UNDERSTANDING NARRATIVE

As a human phenomenon, narrative is rich and diverse in form and content. In this frequently quoted passage, Roland Barthes (1977) points out that:

> The narratives of the world are numberless. Narrative is first and foremost a prodigious variety of genres, themselves distributed amongst different substances – as though any material were fit to receive man's stories. Able to be carried by articulated language, spoken or written, fixed or moving images, gestures, and the ordered mixture of all these substances; narrative is present in myth, legend, fable, tale, novella, epic, history, tragedy, drama, comedy, mime, painting ... stained glass windows, cinema, comics, news items, conversation. Moreover, under this almost infinite diversity of forms, narrative is present in every age, in every place, in every society; it begins with the very

history of mankind and there nowhere is nor has been a people without narrative. All classes, all human groups, have their narratives … Caring nothing for the division between good and bad literature, narrative is international, transhistorical, trans-cultural: it is simply there, like life itself. (Barthes, 1977, p. 79)

As a social phenomenon, narrative is both 'complex and revealing' (Merrill, 2007), is one of the most 'problematic terms' in postmodern cultural debate (Winders, 1993), but at the same time has penetrated every discipline and profession (Riessman and Quinney, 2005). In our previous work analysing the different definitions of narrative, instead of making an attempt to generalize a definition, we identified a number of characteristics of narrative which social researchers tend to draw upon in their investigations and studies (Goodson and Gill, 2011). Such effort was also made to acknowledge the impossibility of defining narrative in ways that seek common consensus, especially when everything and anything (talks and texts alike) can now be regarded as narratives – from political rhetoric to ethnographical texts; from an individual's small talk to published (auto)biographies; from online chats to personal journals and blogs; not to mention what is in other media and forms, from television programmes, films, photos and visual arts, to dances, songs and music. When social scientists come to examine narratives as both social phenomena and the product of the research interaction, we must be selective in terms of what narrative to include and what to exclude, and how each kind of narrative functions in the research.

The other problem associated with the all-encompassing conception of narrative is that it obscures all differences in the ways that social researchers and practitioners explore the potential of narratives in their work. For instance, Riessman (1997) and Riessman and Quinney (2005) identified an array of narratives being employed in social research: *an entire life story* as solicited by anthropologists and social historians, such as Barbara Myerhoff's studies on the lives of elderly Jews (1992) where narratives are woven together in order to present life as and in a continuum; *a discrete unit of discourse* which is an answer to a single question being posed and analysed by sociolinguists (e.g. Labov, 1982); and *an account or accounts of lived experiences in contexts* which are framed in and through the interaction and as the result of the rapport between the patient and the psychologist/therapist (psychology) and the researcher and the participant (social research). Goodson et al. (2010) offers a good example where the researchers explored the learning and identity development of people from different walks of life. These narratives were developed over time as a result of a series of interview conversations between the researcher and the participants.

The complexity and lack of consensus involved in defining narrative is seen, in Merrill's (2007, p. 5) words, sometimes as 'political and ideological' and at other times as 'analytical'. He thinks that 'failure to reach an agreement on narrative's definition could be the most pressing issue facing narrative scholars' (Merrill, 2007, p. 6). He then resolves this challenge by ignoring the question of definition, and focusing on what narrative does in social sciences – the functions of narrative.

However, we believe that the lack of a common or agreed definition of narrative is a reflection of the diverse understanding of the term/phenomenon/process depending on the fields and professions, and the multiplicity of ways to engage with it. Thus, in a way similar to the effort of Riessman and colleagues, we have been working through the varying definitions of narrative in different disciplines in an attempt to find out if they have anything in common. In other words, we were hoping to identify some unifying features of narrative that are shared across divisions and boundaries. The following characteristics or features of narrative are not exhaustive and there could be many more, but we believe that they serve as a good starting point for understanding narrative's potentials.

Narrative being temporally and spatially located

All narratives encompass a sequence or sequences of events which take place within particular historical, social, cultural, political and individual personal situations. This aspect of narrative also points to human life as temporally and spatially located. In other words, narratives are never context-free and they cannot be constructed (by the teller/narrator), or received (by the listener/reader) as suspended in mid-air. The temporality and spatiality of narratives give rise to an explanation of how events take place and under what circumstances, the settings in which one must act in order to pursue one's goals and objectives and how individuals' lives and experiences are placed within the greater schemes of things.

Postmodern views on narrative bring in temporal multiplicity, especially from the perspective of historical studies. Winders (1993), absorbing some of the conceptions of time from psychoanalysis and modern theoretical physics, writes that in addition to the narrative temporality we described above – that is, the sequence of events that is being recounted, which historians call 'conscious, lived time' – there is also a time, totally at odds with lived time, of 'dreaming, involuntary memory, and repressed drives' (Winders, 1993, p. 28). He goes on to stress that

> At any given moment in our lives, we operate at the intersection of these multiple temporal modes. Any one moment in cultural history provides, in terms of memory, influence, and orientation toward both past and future, multiple experiences of time and therefore complex modes of representing and recounting experience. Multiple narratives, from oral culture to archival record, are therefore generated. (Winders, 1993, p. 28)

Winders' claim that there should be multiple narratives and myriad temporalities at work in human history, and that history should not be studied or viewed as linear progression, is not limited to a postmodern perspective. Equally, narratives of events and human actions are open to interpretation and, as we have seen throughout human history, events are interpreted in multiple ways over time and remain open to interpretation from the perspectives of those who were involved directly, those who came to understand and assess them later and those who want to explore what they might mean today and in the future. This is precisely the temporal and spatial nature of narrative.

Hermeneutical philosophers such as Ricoeur and Gadamer further suggest that there be integration between narrative's temporal and spatial location and our interpretation/understanding of events and people's experience *in situ*. Such integration can take the human existence (which is temporally and spatially located) to the universals. The latter can transcend the situatedness of individual narratives and experiences, so that we can go beyond ourselves in our future intention and action.

Riessman and Quinney (2005), Hinchman and Hinchman (1997) and others propose a connection between sequence and consequence of a story, although much of the cause–effect and many of the meanings in a narrative are largely open to interpretation by the social researcher. Indeed, seeking a causal explanation of narrative's occurrence makes it possible for us to take a critical stance in reviewing the social, political, cultural and personal contexts within which meaning is located. This can lead to the development of important understanding about the world and persons who inhabit it. As we will discuss further, this places persons as subjects rather than passive objects of history and reassumes persons' role as agents in making a change (Ricoeur, 1992).

In Ricoeur's conception, there are two kinds of time: cosmic time and lived or phenomenological time, which together constitute historical time. Cosmic time is the time that 'unfolds as a sequence of uniform, qualitatively undifferentiated moments in which all change occurs, but in which any present is defined simply in relation to what comes before and after' (Dauenhauer and Pellauer, 2011). Lived or phenomenological time, on the other hand, is the time of our lives. People experience lived/phenomenological time differently according to what meaning(s) they assume in different events and activities, and how they would remember (and narrate) them. According to Ricoeur, on a cosmic scale, human life would seem insignificant, yet in our lived or phenomenological experiences, all meaningful questions arise and are being addressed in the life of humans. Thus, when these two kinds of time are harmonized, cosmic time is humanized, and lived/phenomenological time can have greater significance. This integration is found in narrative, which configures time to make it human and temporally spatially whole.

Narrative and its potential to explore meaningfulness in events and actions within its temporal frameworks give rise to purposefulness and intention in human actions, in both current and future sense. As we have touched upon in Chapter 1, this temporal-spatial aspect of narrative is closely linked to its second feature – narrative being a quest for meaning.

Narrative being a quest for meaning

The notion of narrative meaning making is not a new thesis (see Bruner, 1990; Ricoeur, 1988, 1992; Taylor, 1989; and others). However, as Julian Baggini (2005) writes, the question of meaning (of life) can be about value questions, and perhaps consists of many sub-questions, such as 'Why are we here?', 'What is the purpose of life?', 'Is it enough just to be happy?', 'Is my life serving some greater purpose?', 'Are we here to help others or just ourselves?' and so on.

Apart from what-is-the-meaning-of-life questions, in narrating, meanings that are personally and collectively significant are externalized through the accounts of lived experiences. Human actions can be made understandable through narratives which articulate our intentions, purposes and meaningfulness. People tell stories of their actions to render them meaningful.

Whenever we narrate, we speak of meaning (and the self), through interrogation and interpretation (of our lived experiences). It is a matter of the 'questioning of things' (Gadamer, 1975) as we have discussed in Chapter Two. For a social researcher or an interlocutor who attends to others' life narratives, they must consider, amongst other questions: Why are some stories told and not others? Why at this time, and for what purpose? What do these stories mean? How are meanings extrapolated in the development of plots, characters, incidents and actions? What would be the different versions of these stories? What would affect the differences? What part has the listening and attending played in generating these stories? Who interprets whose stories?

Thus meaning articulated and interpreted in the process of our narrating is shaped by a multitude of influences rooted, for instance, in a person's upbringing and belonging, a community's collective narratives and memories, one's education, profession and life journey, and other factors, including gender, ethnicity, political views, religions and faiths and so forth. Hannah Arendt (1998) asserts that humans are always conditioned beings, which is not the same as their possessing human nature. She writes:

> Whatever touches or enters into a sustained relationship with human life immediately assumes the character of a condition of human existence ... Whatever enters the human world of its own accord or is drawn into it by human effort becomes part of the human condition. The impact of the world's reality upon human existence is felt and received as a conditioning force. (Arendt, 1998, p. 9)

In social research, this is further informed by additional influences that have an effect on the meaning that the researcher derives and perceives from the narrative, such as his or her research interests, the agenda of the research institutions, what he or she can do with the findings of the research, etc. In an everyday narrative exchange, the narrative meaning is also affected by the backgrounds of the interlocutor or the listener, the intention of their listening, the quality of the interaction and the effect of the stories on the listener/interlocutor. We will address this aspect more fully later.

Narrative provides an ideal opportunity for the narrator and the researcher or the interlocutor to explore human lives critically, and to investigate how individuals are subject to a certain social political and power dynamics, and how a person as a bearer of a particular social identity is placed in a wide scheme of things that are beyond their choice and preference. In this way, the narrative quest for meaning becomes a critical inquiry. This is where the notion of pedagogy comes in because critical self-reflection is connected to one's ability to deconstruct certain assumptions and to construct and reconstruct meaning. Facilitating critical conversations during narrative exchange is an important pedagogical act. We will return to this point later in the chapter when we discuss critical narrative as pedagogy and how educators can engage students in such a critical process.

In fact, in social research, education, nursing, psychotherapy, social work, end-of-life care, as well as in everyday situations, professionals and individuals have been using critical narratives to challenge assumptions, to re-interrogate the roots of our own perspectives and to arrive at newer understanding of meaning. What is common amongst these fields of practice is that the interlocutors develop meaning together by telling and listening, interpreting the narrative themes, analysing the situations within which one lives and placing them in a wider scheme of things. In this way, seemingly isolated events and experiences and our individual sense of our identity are placed within a larger and grander narrative – historical narrative, political narrative, cultural narrative, communal narrative, institutional narrative and so forth. Thus political structures, cultural norms, institutional practices and other social factors that impinge on our lives are brought under our scrutinizing and critical narrative gazes.

As we have already discussed, the nature of humans as narrative beings demands that we discern the meaning of any event or experience in temporal and spatial relationship to others. Each narrative process is a critical inquiry and reflection in which we actively make connections between parts and a (notion of) whole. In this respect, by narratively connecting the dots (each representing an event or an episode), the quest also becomes an epistemological exploration.

Bruner (2004, p. 699) writes that 'tellers and listeners must share some "deep structure" about the nature of a "life"'. What is this deep structure about the nature of life? Is it a vision of good life, or an answer to an existential question? As we see it, when people recount their lived experiences in narrative or give an account of their life in narrative, such as we described earlier, their narrative often contains some evaluation in terms of what motivated their actions, or what had made their experiences what they were – joy, bitterness or suffering. Narrative thus entails judgements about what people value as good. The good can be conceptualized from the perspectives of both the ethical and the moral. Ricoeur and others have suggested that the ethical is connected to what constitutes the goodness in human life and is concerned with the overall ends of human existence; morality refers to the norms that are more universal and that can be used to discipline our conduct and action. The ethical and the moral are therefore distinguishable and perhaps inseparable.

This aspect of narrative calls for people to critically examine life as lived in the past, but also to consider the meaning and meaningfulness of life lived in the present and to be lived in the future. Ricoeur (1992) argues that the evaluative nature of narrative gives primacy to the 'other-than-self' over the self. One recounts moments of one's responsiveness to others, aiming at contributing to the betterment of life for others and oneself. In this way, Ricoeur concludes, narrative recounts care and care only.

As we touched upon in the previous chapters, Alasdair MacIntyre takes issue with the (post)modern malaise born out of individualism, which resulted in morally vacuous societies cut off from the narratives that encompass the unity of human life, underpinned by a shared vision of the good. MacIntyre defines the unity of life as 'the unity of a narrative embodied in a single life' (MacIntyre, 1984, p. 218). He continues:

> To ask 'What is the good for me?' is to ask how best I might live out that unity and bring it to completion. To ask 'What is the good for man?' is to ask what all answers to the former question must have in common. But now it is important to emphasize that it is the systematic asking of these two questions and the attempt to answer them in deed as well as in word which provide the moral life with its unity. The unity of a human life is the unity of a narrative quest. (MacIntyre, 1984, pp. 218–9)

MacIntyre considers the narrative quest an education which 'will furnish us with increasing self-knowledge and increasing knowledge of the good' (MacIntyre, 1984, p. 219). He summarizes that:

> the good life for man is the life spent in seeking for the good life for man, and the virtues necessary for the seeking are those which will enable us to understand what more and what else the good life for man is. (MacIntyre, 1984, p. 219)

Through critically scrutinizing our lived experiences in narrative, we could reflect on our interests and pursuits and also challenge the greater political structures and institutional cultures by using this criterion of whether they are supporting the 'good life for man'. Thus human life is first lived phenomenologically, then contemplated and reflected upon critically, elaborating its meaning in a quest, and third, relived by embodying the virtues in our ongoing actions and practices. Thus narrative is both an activity of production and an activity of action. But before we turn to this aspect, let us discuss how the encounter between interlocutors shapes the meaning and construction of further narrative.

Narrative being partly the fruit of the social encounter

Proust once famously said that 'The only real voyage of discovery consists not in seeking new landscapes, but in having new eyes; to behold the universe through the lenses of another' (Proust, 2006, p. 657). As we discussed in the previous chapters, encountering the other is an excellent way to assume a different perspective as well as transform our existing views.

All narratives are told to an audience – in our case, an interlocutor – and the plots, the selection and organization of events and the meaning of lived experiences will inevitably be affected by the rapport and relationship between the teller and the listener, and the intention and the motivation embedded in the very act of listening.

As we have seen, narrative is developed in a dialogic act, even when only one person is offering an account of his or her life. The dialogue is achieved in the exchange, the listening and the questioning. It is an existential dialogue between the interlocutors which depends heavily on the encounter between them (See Chapter Two for more elaboration on dialogic encounter). In social research and equally in an everyday narrative encounter, this is an important acknowledgement that the interlocutors (both the social researcher and the participant; or the teller and the listener) are existentially situated, and meaning arises not only from narratives of these actors' experiences in the social worlds, but also from the narrating/storytelling itself.

As we have already stressed, what is being told, under which circumstances (when and where), how it is being told, by whom and to whom are key concerns as these can determine meaning and significance in the narratives. To this extent, Gadamer (1977) and Ricoeur (1992) both point to the importance of a critical examination of the implicit narrative structures as well as dialectical hermeneutics that regards narrative as a two-step dialogue, initially between interlocutors and then between the author(s) of the (research) text and the reader. Meaning is the result from the encounter and dialogue of existentially and socially situated individuals (Holstein and Gubrium, 2000). Thus, why stories are told, when and how, and in what way they are interpreted are hugely influenced by interlocutors caught in different intentional stances themselves (Bruner, 1991).

However, as Pring (2001) succinctly points out, in the narrative encounter we should be more aware that:

> [our] view of the world is not as straightforward as we think. And that by probing what one means, one inevitably raises questions about the nature of knowledge, what it means to be a person, what constitutes a worthwhile form of life, or how our mental activity links with a world external to ourselves. Our private search for meaning takes place within a public world of exploration and argument. (Pring, 2001, p. 163)

Thus the intention of listening, the quality of the questioning, the sincerity and intensity of the attending, the purpose of the myth making (as opposed to the scripts that society imposes on the individual), the selection of themes and the willingness to bear witness to each other's journeys will ultimately determine one's capacity to act and react, resist the imposed script, deconstruct, reconstruct and develop autonomous space for agency.

Narrative being both a process and its 'product'

Following the thread we are using throughout the book that human beings are tellers of stories, who live in a web of stories of our own and those of other people, there is a tendency for us also to live our lives according to the insights developed through telling these stories. Note that this is a different perspective from the conventional claim that *people live the stories which they tell*. We see that narrative is not just a story. It is, first and foremost, a process. As we have seen, the art of narrative lies in its capacity to extract meanings from what would otherwise appear to be isolated events and random acts, and to place them in a flow of time with coherence and continuity, and intention and purpose. We discussed this in the previous pages and termed it a quest for meaning. This process is imbued with new possibilities and creative potential, especially when it offers the narrator/teller an opportunity to articulate what he or she might pursue, and how, in an ongoing life journey. Thus, narrative also unfolds the intentions of a subject or subjects, who, through a web of human relations, engage in actions.

By the narrative process, we are referring to a number of occasions, including life history research and other in-depth qualitative social research, autobiographical accounts, writing, telling, giving an account of one's life in more vernacular settings (in the sense both of the native language and original dialect and of untrimmed everyday situations) and so on. As we mentioned, this process is pregnated with possibilities and opportunities.

First, narrative is a thematizing process where individuals take a broad overview of their own life and identify certain themes. These themes are less a reflection of a 'life as lived' than of a 'life as interpreted' to varying degrees. People's narrative characters differ hugely, and therefore the themes they come up with have a huge range (Goodson, 2013). Some could be themes of natural transitions in life – childhood, adolescence, youth, midlife and old age; or schooling, professional development, career and work life and retirement; other themes may be of personal significance – first love, divorce, coping with illnesses (in oneself and others), returning to education as an adult, losses and so forth;

yet others are connected to themes of deeper exploration – 'who am I?' search, gender and sexuality, living with or breaking away from canonical and collective narratives and memories, rebellion, social activism, ideological quest, spiritual awakening and other existential and identity exploration.

The thematizing process is *life making/meaning making*, as the narrator (re)orders the events in their life, assigns each event and their experience of such an event a certain (renewed) significance, makes connections between episodes, encounters, events and other happenings, modifies and affirms their intentions for actions and thus transforms experiences into a *life* lived, living now and to be lived onward and forward. This does not mean that life did not exist before the narrative. It would be absurd to suggest that if we did not tell the stories of ourselves, then we have not lived.[1] However, we do think that such an idea remains standing amongst the ongoing debate: narrative as a process of life making refers to the development of an overview of one's life through a narrative account of one's lived experience, including one's gifts and talents and persona, and key incidents and important encounters that have helped shape one's love and hate, inspired one's life courses and causes and motivated one's decisions and actions. This can provide an ethical framework within which one can continue to pursue coherence and meaning in life, as we have discussed and will further elaborate later.

Second, narrative is a reflective and interpretative process where people construct something out of the mundane, the ordinary. By articulating our experiences, a certain canonicity of narrative can be revealed and interrupted, or breached (Bruner, 2004), thus making the familiar strange. In Chapter 2, we highlighted Gadamer's and Freire's idea of *questioning of things*, which

---

[1] There has been much debate on the proposition of 'life as narrative' by Bruner (2004). See the most recent challenges to this notion in Hyvärinen (2008) and Williams (2009).

applies in the reflecting and interpreting of narrative. This is why narrative can enable us to go beyond the mere lived experience and question things on a number of levels: personal, cultural-historical, social-political and existential. As we have seen, these questions will take the narrator on a journey of critical inquiry as well as deep *soul searching.*

Thus this reflective and interpretive process is *meaning making* and such inquiry always encompasses questions and continued questioning. Bruner (1986, p. 127) proposes that 'good questions are ones that pose dilemmas, subvert obvious or canonical "truths", force incongruities upon our attention'. Thus narrative inquiry analyses the social, political and cultural through the lenses of lived human experiences as sites where knowledge and understanding are generated. It allows the individual to bring to light certain unethical and inhumane practices and cultures within social institutions and power imbalances that result in marginalization, alienation and dehumanization.

Lastly, this is a transformative process where people develop creative responses to the challenges they are facing. We see that the construction of a self-narrative is a different endeavour from a literary one, even though one's written autobiography appears to resemble the latter more. In a well-written novel or fiction, the focus is on the plots themselves, and events are only woven together in order to develop the story. This would appear to be neat and purposeful. However, in life narrative about oneself, despite the teller's effort to select, organize and order events and experiences, as well as to incorporate his or her emotional and moral responses to them, there is much resorting, reorganizing and reordering to do during the process of narration. As we have seen, such renegotiation of meaning includes the teller's decisions to take any intended actions. There is, therefore, a potential for transforming the way events and experiences are understood and narrated.

However, scholars differ in their view of people's ability and character in developing narrative. Some suggest that individuals mimic the literature in developing the storyline of their life stories (see Booker, 2004); some point out that people may have narrative character traits – from strictly scripted to highly elaborate – which determine the meaning and significance of their self-narrative in their life (see Goodson, 2013); others propose that individuals narrate their life according to certain mythic archetypes of plots and stories, resulting in self-narrative as a process of myth making (see McAdams, 1993). We believe that in these characteristics of plots there resides the potential for revising our narratives, thereby relieving ourselves of the burden of trauma and hurts as well as resolving our existential and spiritual angst and other struggles. In social psychology and psychotherapy, narrative has been regarded as a process of healing because it can help patients transform stories and their meaning in the direction of optimism and hope (White and Epston, 1990).

At the same time, from a sociological perspective, narrative is an ideal platform for the interlocutors (the teller and the listener) to recognize the influence of dominating discourses on individuals' perspectives and how our ideas, beliefs and actions are (often unknowingly) determined by forces that are not always of our own choosing and that are beyond our control.

We are also members of diverse social groups (gender, class, ethnicity, culture, family, tribal community, profession and so on) and we act in accordance with certain norms and expectations that are inherent in these social groups and institutions. Through telling (and listening), we become aware of certain voices and perspectives being privileged or marginalized within the grander narrative that holds power in society, and of how certain experiences are shaped in a particular way. Telling further unfolds our preferred relationships and ways of being for ourselves and for others, and how one can act in pursuit of what is of true value, as we discussed earlier.

Narrative also highlights our stories' boundedness in language, discourse, social-cultural and communal perspectives, but at the same time embodies and demonstrates a series of metamorphoses. Through narrative, we became aware that certain changes (especially changes for the better) are possible on a personal level or a larger scale. Such changes are based on a vision for the world that we began to develop during the narrative process, as we have illustrated earlier, which includes our vision of the good, the objects of our love, what we value in life, those activities that constitute well-being for ourselves and others and how we want to be in the world.

This is a process of 'world making', to use a Freirean expression. In addition, critical inquiry during the narrative process can help reveal the malaises from which society is suffering and how we can follow a course of action in order to transform the world and ourselves within it. This is essentially re-story, or transforming our narrative in order to build a better world.

Hannah Arendt writes that:

> The chief characteristic of this specifically human life ... is that it is itself always full of events which ultimately can be told as a story, establish a biography; it is of this life, *bios* as distinguished from mere *zōē*, that Aristotle said that it 'somehow is a kind of *praxis*'. (Arendt, 1998, p. 97)

For us, such praxis consists of two elements: an understanding of the context and situatedness of our life and a course of action which is a set of informed practices (see also Freire, 1996). Critical narrative offers the opportunity for us as individuals to deepen our understanding of life as lived, developing what we call 'a theory of context', which is a conceptual construction of our phenomenological world through an interpretation and analysis of the social-political, cultural and economic forces that have shaped our experience. Freire terms this social-historical conditioning (Freire, 2001, p. 7). On the other hand, informed practice is the outcome of the critical narrative process, which unfolds the possibilities that reside within the current reality/context for making positive change.

Ricoeur might have described this more vividly. He argues that narrative is reconstructing a self who would act in pursuit of one's purpose and mission in life, which stands at the intersection of 'the space of experience' and 'the horizon of expectation' (Dauenhauer and Pellauer, 2011). The space of experience thus links a person's past, including events, experiences and meaning embedded in these, to his or her present, which serves as the point of departure for a new decision or action in the future. The horizon of expectation, meanwhile, offers a range of possible actions ('projects' in Ricoeur's words) that a person can now embark on so as to pursue their mission and realize their vision for a good and just world. At this intersection, past experiences feed into new perspectives of the future, which in turn inform the current course of action. Thus 'the space of experience and the horizon of expectation mutually condition each other'. In other words, without our experience in the past (and although it is not necessarily always of our own making), it is impossible to put forward a vision for the future because the critical narrative processes enable us to highlight our values and commitment and purpose in life. Hence, the product is the re-storied or re-narrated *next chapter* of our life, an extension from the present and a set of projects or initiatives that will make history for ourselves and for others. The idea of praxis here points to the fact that human life, narrative and politics are intimately connected. Life is indeed integration between *vita contemplativa*, a life in contemplation and reflection, and *vita activa*, a life devoted to public-political matters (Arendt, 1998).

BACK TO LEARNING AND PEDAGOGY

Our understanding of narrative and its key features as human encounter in both in-depth social research and more mundane and ordinary everyday settings might give rise to a further discussion in terms of the part that narrative processes can play in learning. Learning, as we saw in Chapter 1, is conceptualized as human becoming or being and becoming more fully human. Our investigation into narrative in this chapter has offered an important avenue for us to take into the realm of pedagogy in order to explore the narrative's potential in facilitating critical inquiry and learning.

As our narrative journey continued, we began to reconsider what criticality means in the narrative exchange between people, and how narrative journeys have led to a critical approach to reflection on ourselves, the myriads of relationships in our life, our place in the world and how we ought to be and act in light of all these – the integration of *vita contemplativa* with *vita activa*. We see this process as leading us to radicalize pedagogy (see more on this in Chapter 2). During this journey, a few nagging questions that constantly confronted us were: 'Where is the boundary between life itself and learning?'; 'Is all storytelling a narrative process?'; 'If critical narrative is pedagogy, who is facilitating whose learning?'; 'When do stories cease to be just stories and become narrative?' and many more. We were concerned that we might be making sweeping claims about narrative that make it indistinguishable in any form of discourse. The danger is that, when all interactions are considered narrative, real and authentic narrative encounter will lose its potency. Therefore, it is important for us to articulate clearly what constitutes narrative pedagogy.

This section will sum up the pedagogical insights emerging from our earlier discussion in this chapter. We will draw these insights into five defining characterizations that serve to distinguish critical narrative as pedagogy from other approaches to learning.

Deep encounter

Critical narrative can happen in many different everyday settings, whether it is critical dialogue with oneself through (auto)biographical writing, or dialogue amongst people in narrative sharing within a group, or storywriting and storytelling in a community setting (adult students as a learning community, members of an institution, a creative writing class, singers in a community choir, inmates of a prison and so forth), or recollecting individual and communal memories individually and collectively or many other possibilities. Later in this chapter, we will discuss in detail some of these different settings and how learning takes place. The second and third parts of the book will offer case studies within some of these settings to illustrate the working of critical narrative as pedagogy.

One of the important points made so far is that narrative learning, and any form of learning for that matter, is not and should not be considered as a process that *only* takes place in formal educational settings, especially when we define learning as a holistic endeavour of human flourishing and growth. Widening the scope for narrative learning, we believe, can empower people to pursue learning and support each other's learning in diverse situations. Even social research that seeks life stories and narrative can be a site for engendering (new) narrative, learning and transformation. Thus in both everyday and research settings, rigorous processes of learning can be facilitated by individuals who are engaged in the processes themselves. This, however, is by no means to suggest that there be no place for pedagogy or pedagogues.

We defined elsewhere that pedagogy is an art and practice of teaching which is supported by a theory or philosophy (Goodson and Gill, 2011). It refers to a process of guiding the learners and facilitating their learning through well-examined practices. In this book, we argued in Chapter 2 that learning through critical narrative is the fruit of deep human encounter and compassionate engagement. Much of the dialogic dynamics and promise of transformation lie in the nature of the narrative encounter and the encounter between myriads of differences, such as between different lived experiences, worldviews, memories, qualities of listening, capacities to narrate and critically inquire into life stories and challenge assumptions, willingness and capacities to translate

87

understanding into actions and more. Embedded in the dia-logic processes is the recognition that the interlocutors (in social research, the researcher and the participant) who are engaged in the narrative endeavour are both learners and facilitators.

As a result of these definitions, we now have a completely new situation of learning that is in contrast with the conventional – instead of relying on trained pedagogues or teachers to guide their learning journeys, individuals are empowered to learn and facili-tate each other's learning themselves. How is it possible?

As we have seen in our previous discussions, to try and under-stand our life in dialogic narrative learning, there are essentially two aspects to consider: (1) a narrative vision of what constitutes a good life for oneself; and (2) a narrative account of how one has experienced life evaluated against the above vision. These two aspects are intertwined, in that the vision is developed in the tell-ing and narrating, and the stories or accounts provide the empiri-cal premise based on which one consolidates one's vision and purpose of life; concurrently, whilst the above is being developed, one also organizes life's experiences and events in accordance with a particular view of a good life. This reciprocity is funda-mental to one's growth personally, morally and socio-politically.

Thus we can characterize life as in part a critical inquiry, espe-cially when individuals are open to examining their experience in personal, social and political arenas. We have discussed how, when one offers an account of one's life in dialogue with another, one inevitably interprets one's experiences under circumstances and conditions which can be deemed as good or bad, desirable or undesirable. The quality and motivation of listening, the depth of questions and the impetus for questioning, one's narrative charac-ter and other factors can have a significant impact on the inquiry and its learning and transformative potential.

Narrative pedagogy concludes that individuals are both learn-ers and pedagogues as they embark on a narrative journey of inquiry, questioning, facilitating and learning.

Epistemological learning

Learning as growth and human becoming comprises the development of one's knowledge, including not only self-knowledge and self-understanding, but also a broader understanding of our human society and one's place and agency within it. Knowledge is multi-faceted and knowing can be approached from an array of avenues. Yet, in everyday living, we are too occupied by the business of life itself; there is little space to reflect on meanings – private or public/shared. Therefore, the need for a hermeneutical and dialogical space for meaning making has been increasingly recognized. With the assistance of modern technology, there has never before been a time in human history when we could witness such an explosion of narrative spaces – personal blogs, Facebook profiles, tweets, self-published (auto) biographies and more. The pursuit of meaning and understanding has become woven into the everyday fabrics of being and interacting.

Life as a critical inquiry in and through narrative as described earlier offers an avenue for self-study and for confronting knowledge and ways of knowing that are detached from the knower himself or herself. In the meantime, McAdams (1999) stresses the potential of the narrative approach in developing an epistemological framework that centres on engendering knowledge and understanding through intersubjectivity, as narrative questioning and interpretation are fundamentally aimed at addressing the topics of identity, meaning and transformation. Similarly, what distinguishes narrative learning from what usually happens in formal educational settings is that dialogic and narrative approaches aim to 'create the possibilities for the production or construction of knowledge' (Freire, 2001, p. 30). We join these writers and thinkers in agreeing that meaning and interpretation are intersubjective and that knowledge is not found but rather co-constructed in the process of critical inquiry.

It is true that each narrative and each narrative encounter are unique and can result in novel interpretation of events and experiences in time and space. However, we do not believe that this means that knowledge and understanding engendered in the narrative process are equally unstable and volatile. This is because, despite the fact that people's narrative capacities differ tremendously and, in each encounter, the pedagogical potential can result in myriads of paths for learning, our narrative and our vision of life do have some kind of persistent, coherent and stable characteristics. We are not talking about the accuracy of individuals' narrative accounts. Instead, we are concerned with the consistency and coherence of one's identity (*who* one is, not *what* one is) and whether a person can interpret meaning in ways that allow him or her to remain whole. In our contemporary society, competing 'truths' and narratives (public and private) demand individuals to develop a coherent and stable vision for a good life (for oneself and for others) and articulate it through telling one's stories. This is an intersection of language and action (word and deed), according to Arendt (1998), which allows us to start something new 'on our own initiative' (Arendt, 1998, p. 177).

As we have discussed, narrative has the power of connecting seemingly unrelated and fragmented events and experiences, and integrating them into a person's life as a whole without resulting in identity crisis or schizophrenia. This means that narrative interpretations as the fruit of critical inquiry can unfold knowledge and understanding that is robust and satisfying. What is satisfying is illuminating and can further generate new narratives and new action. 'Action and reflection occur simultaneously' (Freire, 1996, p. 109).

Community building in reciprocal learning

As we have discussed, narrative offers a space for encounter – a deeper form of encounter. People come together to engage with each other in profound ways. Narrative, which is at the intersection of words and deeds or language and action, takes place when people encounter each other in 'sheer human togetherness' (Arendt, 1998, p. 180). It was once asserted that to live is to be amongst men (*inter hominess esse*) (Arendt, 1998). So to be and to act is to be and to act in and through a web of human relationships. It goes without saying that the realm of meaning is also situated within the intersection where one's unique life story and the life stories of others meet, which in turn affects the language and action and life courses of all involved.

In our investigations into the features of narrative, we point out that the quality of the interaction and relationships between the interlocutors can determine the potential for learning and transformation. We highlight that the intention and quality of listening, the willingness to engage the 'prejudices' of oneself and those of others, and the openness to encounter and reach a fusion of horizons with others are essential in this inquiring process (refer to Chapter 2 where we discussed Gadamer). Furthermore, we derive that, through narrative inquiries, the interlocutors can become close to each other as the process enables them to enter into communion with each other (also see the case studies in Part Three of this book). This aspect of narrative learning takes us back to Freire's work on dialogue as love (see Chapter 2). Dialogue requires a deep faith – faith in humanity, in our purpose in the world as being and becoming more fully human, with each other. When dialogue is based on humility, love and faith, it becomes an avenue itself for building mutual trust and solidarity amongst all peoples. Dialogue is a humanizing act which allows us to express our profound need and deepest appreciation for each other in our incessant pursuit for the good in the world (Freire, 1996).

Freire also writes that dialogue is the encounter between people, mediated by the world, in order to understand the other, ourselves and the world better. Dialogue expresses humans' need for each other, which can ultimately enrich our thoughts and meanings of our being. Thus at the heart of the narrative inquiry is community building. Carl Rogers (1969) also discussed the importance of relationship in cultivating learning – the personal relationship between the facilitator and the learners.

There are a number of conditions for learning in human togetherness and the facilitation of learning should be conceived within these conditions. The first, as we have already seen, is a genuine and trusting relationship between people, the key to which lies in creating a safe space for deep encounter. In Part Three of this book, we use case studies to illustrate different approaches to creating and maintaining a safe space in diverse settings – in the higher education seminar room, in the meeting place between two former 'enemies' and in prison as a site for learning. The space is safe when there is a sincere intention from all to narrate, to listen, to engage and to reflect. The intention is often seen as grace: that is, not something that can be imposed or forced, but rather something that comes from a source deep within or beyond oneself.[2] When the space is safe, and there is an attentive audience, the narrative shared is more likely to be reflexive, critical and interpretive.

The second is our acceptance of each other and our self-worth as values in their own right, as well as our trust in people's capacity and potential to grow and transform. Rogers regards this as an empathetic understanding. With such a constructive relationship, individuals would have the conditions for self-discovery and growth with a drive for learning or becoming themselves. Rogers uses the words 'self actualization' to describe learning. Yet, self-actualizing learning cannot be detached from each person's stories and narratives. Thus it is important for teachers and students to 'analyse the relationship between their individual biographies, historical events, and the constraints imposed on their personal choices by broader power relations, such as those of class, race and gender' (Middleton, 1992, p. 19).

---

[2] Some may claim that this intention can come from a divine source for them when they are religious or spiritual.

Third is the mutuality and reciprocity of teaching and learning. 'Whoever teaches learns in the act of teaching, and whoever learns teaches in the act of learning' (Freire, 2001, p. 31). Teaching here has nothing to do with imparting factual knowledge or transmitting skills. Teaching, as conceived here, is the very fabric of learning, and learning makes teaching possible. Thus the person is at the same time the learner and the teacher, and he or she is learning and teaching at the same time. In other words, during narrative journeys, individuals listen and are listened to, offer stories and are offered stories, help others get pulled up from their assumptions and prejudgements and are helped to do so, love and are loved, and more. Freire regards this integral whole as coming from the human's recognition of our own finitude and 'historical unfinishedness', which gives rise to our infinite desire to learn. In reflecting on the process of learning, humans further develop (pedagogical) approaches to making it happen. Thus teaching and learning are one integral and reciprocal process. Freire sees this circle of teaching and learning as one wholeness which is simultaneously 'directive, political, ideological, Gnostic, pedagogical, aesthetic, and ethical' (Freire, 2001, p. 32).

As we shall see in later chapters, people are drawn to each other in the humanizing narrative process. Through such community building, we can bring a wealth of wisdom, ideas and nuanced meaning together into an emerging new understanding and new alliance of humanity. Indeed, as Gadamer optimistically projected, human being in the twenty-first century is human being-with-one-another.

Developing a theory of context

In this book, we consider narrative as a critical inquiry during which we as individuals not only make sense of our lived experience and interpret life as a whole, but also examine our values and worldviews as well as the social and political dynamics that have fed into a certain discourse and assumptions. As we discussed, the temporal and spatial situatedness of human life and thereby our narratives determine that our understanding is also situated. To take narrative as a pathway for understanding is to unfold the situatedness of our life, stories and meaning. The narrative pathways take the interlocutors onto journeys of convergence and divergence where we each find the way back to our own self, values, and our language/word and action.

The critical dimension of narrative thus lies in its potential for clarifying our ethical commitments and moral aspirations through our language and in our action (see Chapters 1 and 2). In this way, our critical capacity refers to our ability to understand diverse experience and reality in a more connected and holistic way: that is, knowing its constituent elements, rather than fragments and isolated patches. To have an appropriate vision of our reality, individuals 'would have to reverse their starting point: they would need to have a total vision of the context in order to subsequently separate and isolate its constituent elements and by means of this analysis achieve a clearer perception of the whole' (Freire, 1996, p. 85). We believe that narrative can offer an opportunity for people to come together, analyse, interpret and develop a 'theory' of context – to articulate more clearly the situatedness of our narrative, life, choices and action, which would aid our understanding of how we can engage in and with the social world in ways that might open up the possibility for greater change in ourselves, others and beyond.

Developing a theory of context can in turn shift our narrative, providing us an opportunity actively to dis-embed our stories from certain underpinning assumptions and beliefs and to deconstruct the 'script' we might have uncritically inherited. Equally without a theory of context, it is impossible for us to have a vision for the future and thereby create a new narrative and action towards hope. As many revolutions and people's uprisings in contemporary history have shown, it is relatively easy for one group of people to fight against another, but more challenging to work together towards a common vision. The fighting-against approach tends to dichotomize and engender greater rifts.

The critical faculty that is expressed in our pedagogy is what we mentioned in the previous chapter in all three prominent thinkers' theories – that which is problem-based, curiosity-driven and is about the questioning of things. Teaching, searching, questing and re-searching is another integral process. Pedagogy is essentially about subjecting ourselves to questioning (Freire, 2001). Questioning of things involves a kind of intervention or intervening. In other words, when we notice things, we became curious and we raise questions, and the questions can often intervene in our interlocutor's flow of thoughts – in our case, his or her narrative flow. Interrupted stories are to be retold, offering a site for learning and generating new narratives. Critical consciousness is human curiosity that is reflected in our tireless questioning to discover things that are hidden, to seek, to clarify, to quest for meaning and direction, to see and restore beauty, harmony and coherence.

Narrative as a learning pathway 'permits us to view the intersection of the life history of men with the history of society thereby enabling us to understand better the choices, contingencies and options open to the individual' (Bogdan, 1974, p. 4).

Developing a theory of context and locating our life and stories of our life within a broader temporal and social space can provide a moral basis as well as relational and spiritual resources for responding to the diverse challenges we face in moving towards a better world.

Social action through moral imagination

Our life consists of decisions, choices and directions. These are made based on certain moral and ethical values we hold. In this way, in our *becoming* we constitute our *being*. That is to say that through

95

striving to become, we are, because 'the condition of becoming is the condition of being' (Freire, 2001, p. 39). Freire concludes: 'to transform the experience of educating into a matter of simple technique is to impoverish what is fundamentally human in this experience: namely, its capacity to form the human person' (Freire, 2001, p. 39). As we have discussed extensively so far in this book, this forming of the human person includes the moral formation.

Conventional education through schooling has failed to provide any space for young people's moral formation. Instead, schooling has become a machine for reproducing individuals who will pass exams by giving the 'right' answers to well-rehearsed questions. There is little space in such education to explore within oneself what is beckoning[3] us and what our vision is for a social future. As adults, we are exposed to diverse opportunities of choice making and decision making, and narratives, as we have already claimed, can indeed offer an important social space for negotiating our moral actions.

Critical narrative as pedagogy intends to foster open and public spaces for interrogating and interpreting meaning. Within such spaces, learning for individuals is not detached from our social reality, but instead it allows us to situate a mundane personal life within the socio-political arena in a creative and transformative dialectic. When 'ordinary folks' are engaged in epistemological search and pedagogical practices, assumptions and knowledge that are oppressive for the majority will be rejected in favour of alternative approaches that are proponents of a just and more human culture. It is such aspiration that will ultimately determine people's social action. Thus narrative also serves as the development of a map – a map of our life in the world which explains our past, our motivations, values and activities, cultural norms and socio-political and economic mechanisms.

---

[3] 'Beckoning' is used by Heidegger in his book *Identify and Difference*, published by Chicago University Press in 2002.

Yet, this is a complex pedagogical space as Arendt explains:

It is because of this already existing web of human relationships, with its innumerable, conflicting wills and intentions, that action almost never achieves its purpose; but it is also because of this medium, in which action alone is real, that it 'produces' stories with or without intention as naturally as fabrication produces tangible things. (Arendt, 1998, p. 184)

As we have already highlighted, narratives are also pathways, and not 'products'. Narrative could engender new narratives creatively and imaginatively; such stories are not actions themselves. Indeed, Arendt suggests that although life stories can tell us about the 'hero', they are not 'products' and therefore

nobody is the author or producer of his own life story. In other words, the stories, the results of action and speech, reveal an agent, but this agent is not an author or producer. Somebody began it and is its subject in the twofold sense of the word, namely, its actor and sufferer, but nobody is its author. (Arendt, 1998, p. 184)

Indeed, narrative is essentially journeys to unfold who we are as individuals and as a people, and where we are in terms of the social, cultural and political landscape. Knowing who we are and where we are is a key to determining how we ought to be and to act in the world. Arendt offers some insights here:

action has the closest connection with the human condition of natality; the new beginning inherent in birth can make itself felt in the world only because the newcomer possesses the capacity of beginning something anew, that is, of acting. In this sense of initiative, an element of action, and therefore of natality, is inherent in all human activities. Moreover, since action is the political activity par excellence, natality, and not mortality, may be the central category of political, as distinguished from metaphysical, thought. (Arendt, 1998, p. 9)

The narrative pathway is a creative and formative journey where we consolidate who we are as individuals and communities, find our voice, our place in the world and the story that we belong to and that we are, and where we continue to engage in social actions in our pursuit of being and becoming more fully human. Lederach (2005) calls this re-storying. He writes:

> Restorying as imaginative narrative looks for the deeper social story and meaning, not just of what happened, but how stories are connected to a far more profound journey of discovering what these events mean for who we are as both local and global communities. (Lederach, 2005, p. 147)

As we will see in Parts II and III of this book, re-storying is a key to social imagination and collective transformative action. Through re-storying, individuals can revise their life courses and anticipate the birth of a new life – a life of healing and reconciliation, a life of direction, a life pregnant with hope.

CONCLUSION

An examination of our personal and social landscapes has led us to unfold a number of key questions that we have been wrestling with, including this crucial one: how does one live in dignity and with integrity in the midst of a utilitarian culture which tends to dry out any inspiration. There is enough social critique about why things are not working. So we are interested in narrative as a pathway that highlights those anecdotal stories that can serve to encourage people to embark on their own journeys and embrace the creative tensions between strengths and vulnerabilities, and promises and obstacles, as a way to celebrate the triumph of human integrity and spirit. What we have learned, and will share in the later chapters of this book, is that it is often in the telling that these tensions become more pronounced and in the telling that we understand our courageous and unyielding commitment to the greater goodness. Narrative provides the avenues for individuals to accompany each other's journey of inquiry and quest, and to listen with our hearts, drawing inspiration from the deepest source of our values – a shared humanity. As Rebecca Walker says, a post-capitalist utopian vision[4]:

> must be built upon a moral and spiritual revolution, a narrative of abundance of human dignity and equality for all. A narrative for the common good that is so seductive and so compelling that human beings want to spend more time working to dissipate their greed and fear then they do producing wages or abs or anything else but love. It is nothing less than the massive awakening of the human potential to be and act better no matter the economic or political system of the day.

We certainly agree with Walker that we do not need to wait for the revolution and instead we must start our narrative journey towards a new story of the future. In Freire's words, we must have *dream*.

---

[4] This is taken from 'After Capitalism', a series on the 'Comment is Free' column of the Guardian Online: http://www.guardian.co.uk/commentisfree/video/2012/aug/21/after-capitalism-rebecca-walker-video.

INDIVIDUAL AUTOBIOGRAPHIES AS CRITICAL NARRATIVE

CHAPTER 4

Ancestral Voices

Ivor Goodson

INTRODUCTION

In western societies, certainly since the advent of modernity, ancestral stories have been treated at best in a muted fashion. The stress on individualism, personal identity and selfhood has tended to understate the continuities that characterize not just family communities specifically but human communities generally. This has meant a persistent undervaluing of ancestral accounts in the way in which people choose to represent their life stories.

In some ways the disavowal of ancestral voices is symptomatic of a contemporary postmodern fashion for understanding multiplicity and hybridity. Whilst these new perspectives are important and generative their prioritization has been at the expense of understanding certain continuities and coherences. This is regrettable for various reasons. First, because our evidence shows people themselves do often prioritize the search for coherence and the pursuit of continuity. Second, to ignore certain social continuities is to forego vital elements in the social patterning of experiences. In this sense certain aspects of some postmodern myopia fit well with a world where social analysis and critique are being systematically disvalued and dismantled.

In other cultures ancestral voices are given considerable attention. In China, for instance, a mode of 'ancestor worship' has been a feature of many communities and in so doing the voices of ancestors have both been heard and venerated. Cultures that stress the continuities of the human condition and that seek to live in more sustainable ways that value the continuity of the 'earth' have similarly valued ancestral voices. For instance, Native American culture has developed belief systems around what they call 'blood memory'. This is the ancestral link to tribal memory, song, spirituality and language. Native Indians believe if you lose your 'blood memory' you sacrifice the centre of your being. Likewise aborigines in Australia relate their experiences to historical 'songlines', which encapsulate the ancestral dream and myths of their tribal ancestors. If we lose blood memory and our 'song lines' they would think we have become 'empty selves'.

This is precisely the condition diagnosed by Philip Cushman as commonly evident in contemporary United States. In his article 'Why the self is empty' he develops the links between psychic emptiness and a society characterized by an enduring commitment to consumption and personal wealth acquisition (Cushman, 1990). A condition based on self-gratification in the moment with little concern for previous or future generations. This obsessively contemporary focus inevitably obscures and indeed demeans ancestral voices.

Christopher Lasch has characterized modern American society as a 'culture of narcissism' (Lasch, 1977). He characterizes this as a culture that is obsessed by the gratification and grandiosity of the individual and contemporary self. A culture of narcissism inevitably ignores historical continuity for the individual believes entirely in their own singular sovereignty. Their perception is that they are self-created, self-invented. This capacity makes such a society highly innovative but also profoundly a-historical. The systematic production of 'empty selves' who consume and contrive to 'fill the vortex' with their consumption works against the grain of pedagogy and also against learning that is concerned with understanding humanity in its full perspective. By the latter view the

104

task is to connect each person with their past and their peers. We therefore see the counterculture of narrative work as one route to such a connection.

Developing a critical pattern of both pedagogy and learning might therefore require a reconnection and reappraisal of ancestral voices. In understanding this act of connectivity the link to humankind over time will be re-evaluated. The long view of the historical context of humanity will develop a different vision of the contemporary world. Wilfred Thesiger spent a century on this earth studying native tribes and cultures. His study of the Marsh Arabs is a model of the compassionate and empathetic study of different cultures. Most interesting though is the way his long life and his long view of the human condition allowed him to scrutinize the contemporary world. Unlike those cultures that link to their past and take a long view of humanity and the earth he judged that the contemporary United States had lost touch with its history and with the earth:

> The long term effect of US culture as it spreads to every nook and cranny, in every desert and every mountain valley will be the end of mankind. Our extraordinary greed for material possessions, the way we go about nurturing that greed, the lack of balance in our lives, and our cultural arrogance will kill us off within a century unless we learn to stop and think. (Thesiger, 2002, p. 23)

Linking our work to ancestral voices and to a longer view of humanity would seem then an essential ingredient of a critical pedagogy and an informed process of learning.

ANCESTRAL VOICES

Ancestral voices date back to the time before we were born. This is the zone when our ancestors reach forward into the lives of their successor generations and where we are called back to the places from which we originated. In an essay on the writer Sean O'Faoláin, Conor Cruise O'Brien wrote about this zone of ancestral memory:

> There is for all of us a twilight zone of time, stretching back for a generation or two before we were born, which never quite belongs to the rest of history. Our elders have talked their memories into our memories until we come to possess some sense of a continuity exceeding and traversing our own individual being … Children of small and vocal communities are likely to possess it to a high degree and, if they are imaginative, have the power of incorporating into their own lives a significant span of time before their individual births. (Quoted in C. Tóibín, 2012, pp. 2–4)

In a previous study I have argued that peoples' 'narrative character' constitutes 'a kind of DNA of personal response' (Goodson, 2013). People work on their life narrative and have a capacity to 'produce' aspects of their narrative but they also 'inherit' narratives. They have then both a genetic legacy and the environmental potential to explore, exploit and transcend this legacy in different ways.

In this chapter I want to explore the 'ancestral voices' which underpin our life stories and autobiographical memories. I see this as part of the 'genealogy of context' in which our life stories are embedded and entangled (Goodson, 1992). Family myths are implicated in our personal myths and stories, providing an important backcloth for their elucidation and elaboration. 'Personal mythology is but the flower on the bush: the family myth is the branch, society's conventions form the stem, and the root is the human condition' (Feinstein and Krippner, 1988, p. xi).

Ancestral voices are given different prominences and authorities in different cultures. In Africa ancestral voices are commonly called upon and acknowledged. In China as we have noted ancestor worship is formally acknowledged and sponsored. But also in western societies, whether formal or informal, supported or sponsored, ancestral voices play a key role in who we are. Any critical pedagogy would, therefore, have to provide insights and interrogations into our ancestral legacy. To ignore ancestral voices is to collude with the grandiose, self-invented notions of selfhood that certain cultures of narcissism tend to promote.

Any process of self-discovery or auto-ethnography (see Hayler, 2011) involves 'naming the world' (Freire, 1972) and part of 'naming the world' involves the 'journey back to your ancestors'. As we noted earlier, naming the world also involves 'naming the self' and 'knowing our narrative':

> Personal myths are laden with the hopes and disappointments of prior generations. Your new mythology is your legacy from the past, as well as a source and guidance and inspiration for the future. The family is the crucible in which genetics and cultural mythology are amalgamated into the unique mythic framework, that shape personal development. (Feinstein and Krippner, 1988, pp. 17–8)

There are a range of strategies for coming to understand our narrative and the role of ancestral voice. One of the key exercises in developing a sense of ancestral voice is to 'imagine' ourselves as our same-sex great, great grandparent. Exploration follows four questions and then a bodily procedure:

- What are your major concerns?
- What are your primary sources of satisfaction?
- How do you understand your position within your society – its limitations, privileges, and responsibilities?
- If you look to a non-human authority to explain human destiny, what is its nature? [60-second pause]

107

Once you have answered the four questions, take a step forward and assume a posture that you imagine to be typical of your great-grandparent when he or she was your current age. Dramatize this posture until it begins to symbolize what you know and imagine about this person's life. (Feinstein and Krippner, 1988, p. 20)

I have certainly undertaken this procedure myself and can vouch for its power in developing our series of 'ancestral voices'. But I have, more importantly, witnessed its power in workshops where the participants have begun to get in touch with their ancestral hinterlands and in later sections come to talk at length with other workshop participants.

STUDYING ANCESTRAL VOICES?

This section provides a number of examples of 'ancestral voices'. I begin with some personal analyses of my own ancestral hinterland to provide an entry point to the discussion of how to study ancestral voices.

In my own case I had done a fairly detailed family history before undertaking the exercise described above. My great, great grandparent Edwin Goodson had 12 children; like generations of my family he was a landless labourer, working on a duck breeder's farm in Buckinghamshire. My posture when I 'imagined' him was humble, anxious, deferential, a sort of worried crouch. Above all I was worried that I could provide enough food for the family; and I was concerned about my wife Annie (our first two children were born out of wedlock) as she was known to have a 'wild streak'. Finally I was worried about my relationship with the head duck farmers – my work led me to resent the men in this class and I was seen as a troublemaker with an aversion to people in authority; this distrust of authority was passed on through the Goodson generations.

Many themes carried on through generations. My grandfather James was a milkman who carried on an affair with my grandma, a domestic servant, in Peckham. She fell pregnant and they had to marry in a hurry. Further children followed: 12 daughters and the last, a son, my Dad, Fred. I knew my grandma quite well, but James died five years before I was born, after a drinking session at one of his daughters' weddings where he had 'sung his heart out'.

I wrote the following section about my ongoing search for ancestral voices when trying to understand the origins of my own personal project and myth:

Searching for roots in the post-modern Diaspora, whilst fashionable, is a deeply elusive process. In some ways, though, it is a natural search for me at this moment: my mother is nearly 100 and for the past two Christmases I have watched as my son peppers his grandma with questions about the family history. At New Year she brought out all the family photo albums and got down to serious business.

As the process got underway, I began to realise what a deeply oral culture I grew up in. My mother is quite simply a great storyteller. Neither she, nor my dad, were very much at ease with writing but she can 'tell' stories brilliantly (this storytelling tradition is central to the roots of pedagogy as I practice and understand it).

One paper cutting which she produced this Christmas was the obituary of my granddad, James. James fathered 13 children but appears on all birth certificates but two as 'unemployed'. He apparently grew vegetables and sold them around the village from his tricycle which had a large basket at the back (like my father and myself and my son he was a slow learner with transport technology like the bicycle! My father and I never passed our driving test and my son only did at the age of 32). Another paper cutting says James was one of the most popular fellows in the village. In the local hostelry he was everybody's favourite storyteller.

Only a few years back on a visit to my old village pub, 'The Bull and Chequers', an elderly man approached me:

> You're James's boy aren't you?
>> No, no he was my granddad,
>> I see, yeah he was a great storyteller.

One of the other documents my mother uncovers is my father's deeds of 'Indenture'. Here, the 13-year-old boy is signed over as an apprentice to the Reading Gas Company. At the bottom, somebody has scribbled my father's name in pencil and in a shaky hand the young boy has gone over the signature in pen (he could not write). Thereby, he signed on for a job that lasted 52 years. James had to countersign the 'handing over' of his son. This he did with a firm 'X'. (He had run away from home at 11 years of age and never mastered any writing or reading skills.)

My grandmother was also a wonderful storyteller. Since she lived to the age of 98, I remember her well. Whilst James sold his vegetables and told his stories in the pub, she took in laundry. She taught herself to read and write and kept the family finances written in a great ledger book. She also founded the family motto 'we're a very persistent family'. When she fell pregnant for the thirteenth time at the age of 50, having delivered 12 daughters, the midwife came to aid the birth in the bedroom of the cottage. The midwife screamed out: 'Mrs Goodson, it's a boy!' She apparently replied calmly: 'Yes, I know ... we're a very persistent family'. Indeed, we are and the family motto inscribed in the family stories reflects this.

On my mother's side, it was a similar story. My grandfather, like James, was a younger son growing up on a farm. With 'primogeniture', he inherited nothing and made his living in a succession of shops – butchers' shops, and finally a working man's café in Reading. He also was a legendary storyteller and a man of stridently independent views.

The combination of oral culture and independent views is something I have recently come to understand. A book on the village I grew up in has described Woodley in the nineteenth century. Originally, the village comprised a number of cottages that were 'small owner-occupier tenements' (Lloyd, 1977, p. 14), but as the eighteenth century progressed, the local 'squire' or landlord, James Wheble, began to enclose the land and buy the cottages. 'As the cottages were acquired by Wheble, they were let out to labourers on his estate' on a rising scale of rent (Lloyd, 1977, p. 14). Wheble purchased Woodley Park and the existing estate to the side of his land, from Henry Addington in 1801 (the year Addington became Prime Minister of the country). But not all of the village labourers accepted that the squire could rule their lives and charge them rent.

> One area of Woodley, the 'old village', stood beyond Wheble's enclosures, outside his estate. In the 1830s, they were mainly freelance agricultural labourers, but the Rev. James Sherman noted: 'almost every labourer in that village was a poacher'. (Lloyd, 1977, p. 39)

The village he alluded to was my grandfather's village – the cottages and tenements (and beer houses) along Crockhamwell Road, on Wheelers Green and in Cobblers City and Woodley Green. Given the control of nearly all the land by Squire Wheble: 'new building had to take place either on the few remaining owner-occupier sites in Cobblers City and Woodley Green, or on the lands of the squires with their approval' (Lloyd, 1977, p. 59). Lloyd provides a summary of the community where my family settled:

> Independent spirits, therefore, gravitated to Woodley Village where my grandparents' cottage was located. Only in Cobblers City was a fiercely independent group of labourers able to stay

111

outside the influence of the Squire and his estate managers:
The most fascinating aspect of the area was the concentra-
tion of so many phases of social and economic development,
reflected in the building, into one tiny corner of the Liberty. A
city of cottages, sheds and workshops, created by the independent labourers of Woodley as they did what their forefathers had
done before them – survived within the social and economic
framework created by other more powerful hands around them.
(Lloyd, 1977, p. 76)

Independent survival in the face of a socio-economic order that
has sought to control and possess land and rights is an enduring
part of Cobblers City. It is also, therefore, a part of my birthright
and my scholarly and pedagogic posture. I do not start from the
assumption that new world orders are well intentioned and benign
nor that they are inevitably malign. I am deeply aware from my
ancestral voices that certain groups face dispossession and dis-
placement when new economic orders emerge. Certainly when
Squire Wheble began to enclose the land around Woodley my
forefathers had to respond rapidly, most labourers in the village
accepted the dispossession involved: that my own family chose to
resist this economic order by locating in Cobblers City speaks of
an enduring independence of spirit. This spirit hopefully informs
my own chosen vocation and my pedagogic moments in the new
era, which David Harvey has characterized as 'accumulation by
dispossession' (Harvey, 2003). Patterns of dispossession and dis-
placement, it seems, endure (Goodson, 2005, pp. 14–5).

My own personal project or vocation of searching for the voice
of the disempowered in myriad ways clearly links to my ancestral
hinterland. In developing a theory of context to understand my
own social purpose and life projects the study of ancestral voices
has therefore been indispensable.

This identification of your personal project with ancestral
voices is a common theme amongst artists and writers. W. B. Yeats

and V. S. Naipaul have both written powerfully of the influence of their fathers' (often thwarted) dreams of their life missions. Likewise Colin Tóibín has written about these ancestral voices:

> The twilight zone of time for me goes back decades before I was born. It is always Enniscorthy; and it belongs also to earlier generations of my family. When she died, my mother left me her books and her CDs. Her A Golden Treasury of Irish Verse, edited by Lennox Robinson, is dated in her handwriting: January 27, 1941. She would have been 19 then. At the back of the book are pasted two poems she wrote, which were published in the local newspaper, the Enniscorthy Echo, and then reprinted in the Dublin newspaper the Irish Press in 1941, with a commentary by one of the editors calling the first of them 'lovely' and the second 'exquisite'. The two poems had been published with her initials only, but it was known in the town that she had written them, and it gave her a sort of fame among her friends.
>
> It is something I was aware of as I grew up. I knew how much the poems mattered, as if I had somehow shared the experience myself of seeing them in print, or being around when they were written.

Tóibín writes of his growing awareness of his mother's poetry and how he began to discover an archive of fragments that allowed him to fill out the ancestral picture. We can see here how the process of cultural and generational transmission takes place and how ancestral voices can be reproduced in the new generation.

> Between the pages of another anthology she owned is a cutting from the local paper with the news that a pageant my mother wrote in the mid-1960s won an all-Ireland competition run by the Irish Countrywomen's Association. I remember the pageant being performed; my mother could not go because my father

was too sick. But I went. I think I was the only one of the family who ever saw it performed. It was in rhyming couplets and was recited by actresses representing the women who took part in the 1798 rebellion in Wexford. I can even remember one of the couplets: 'This is about myself, Anne Flood/And how I spilled a Hessian's blood'.

Later, when the Irish Times ran a weekly competition for light verse, my mother entered every week and won sometimes. I remember one of her end lines as it appeared in the paper: 'When the Greeks bring gifts, who fears to get?'

He slowly developed a sense of how this ancestral project provided a context and background for his own developing sense of purpose and identity.

It mattered to her that she could have, or might have, been a writer, and perhaps it mattered to me more than I fully understood. She watched my books appear with considerable interest, and wrote me an oddly formal letter about the style of each one, but she was, I knew, also uneasy about my novels. She found them too slow and sad and oddly personal. She was careful not to say too much about this, except once when she felt that I had described her and things which had happened to her too obviously and too openly. That time she said that she might indeed soon write her own book. She made a book sound like a weapon. Perhaps a book is a weapon; perhaps an unwritten book is an even more powerful weapon than one which has been published. It has a way of filling the air with its menace or its promise, the sweet art of what might have been.

Unwritten books and poems mattered to me when I was growing up; there was a melancholy sense of what was never achieved, and that sense has been vivid for me, and it still is, even more than some things I remember happening, or that I saw coming into being. (Tóibín, 2012)

One of the most common themes in analysing ancestral voices is the manner in which we seek to complete the often-thwarted dreams of our ancestors. This is clearly at work here with Colin Tóibín. But he also points to the ambiguity and ambivalence of the legacy of storytelling.

> I dislike being called a storyteller, and resent the implication that I come from a world where the oral tradition, something primitive and unformed, remained strong or intact. This was not true; the oral tradition was not strong in the place where I grew up. I was brought up in a house where there was a great deal of silence. When my father died, his name was hardly ever mentioned again. It was too much that he had died, too hard; his absence was too palpable, too sad. So it entered the realm of what you thought about and did not speak of, a realm I remain very comfortable in to this day.
>
> But sometimes in the years before my father died, he and his brother and sister talked of their other brother, Philip, who had died of tuberculosis in 1940. I know the date because I found his grave one day when I was looking for my father's grave, and I saw that he had died a very short time after his own father. This fact had never been mentioned at home, but they must have lived through those two deaths and then held them close. The deaths were significant enough not to be mentioned. When I imagined them and put them into my novel *The Heather Blazing*, the older members of the family were, I think, all shocked by those scenes I wrote, but they never talked about them, at least never to me. The book became another thing that the family could be silent about. (Tóibín, 2012, pp. 2–4)

Beyond the uncertainty and the ambivalence it is clear that Tóibín's writerly vocation is closely associated with the ambitions and frustrations of his mother. Whatever the complexity, it is clear that ancestral voices are highly implicated in the 'courses of action' which he defines and delineates for his life. In terms of our analysis of human action ancestral voices provide an important prism through which to interrogate and investigate human agency. Given that critical pedagogy is considerably invested in human agency they provide a vital gateway for understanding how people define their 'courses of action'.

Since this book tries to investigate the juxtaposition of ancestral voices and autobiographical memory let me provide two autobiographical vignettes of how I understand the relationship between some of my own ancestral voices and certain specific courses of action I have undertaken.

One of the most familiar settings for the inscription of family memory was the stories that were told each Christmas at family gatherings in my home. My father had a number of favourite stories and at a certain point in the proceedings – normally when a fair bit of alcohol had been consumed – he would be called upon to tell the family stories. One of the most common stories that I heard as a young child was the story of Field Cottage. The family had taken occupation of an old cottage in Cobbler's City to escape from the domain of the squire. But this cottage had become unavailable to them and in and around the year 1890 the family rented an isolated cottage in the fields, which later became the runway of Woodley Airdrome. This isolated cottage suited our family because at that time there were ten children and James scratched something of a living from growing his own vegetables. Field Cottage had a large garden and this allowed him to pursue his vegetable growing. The downside of living at Field Cottage was that my grandmother Alice had to carry the laundry that she took in a good mile from the centre of Cobbler's City. But clearly it was judged a worthwhile move and from 1890 to 1904 (the year after my father was born) they lived at Field Cottage. The landlord was another squire who lived in the nearby village of Sonning. Thus although they had escaped the clutches of the local squire, James Wheble, they still were part of the landed economy of the squirehierachy. In 1904 without any warning the land agent acting for the squire informed my grandparents that they would have to leave the house. It is conceivable that this was related to some of James' poaching activities but this has never been proven. Anyhow without warning, and this is how my father told the story – the family was evicted and with their few possessions found themselves homeless. This experience of eviction and the stigma that went with it stayed as part of the family memory in a very profound way and when my dad told the story at Christmas he raged against the social system that had elevated the squirehierarchy to such power and had brought our family to such disgrace. So these were my experiences of one story of the experiences of my ancestors, and I heard this story in Christmas gatherings year after year from 1948 through to 1960.

Let me now fast forward to the year 2004. This I might note is the one hundredth anniversary of the eviction of my family. I have by now returned from working as a well-paid professor in North America with my wife and son and we are looking for a place to live in Sussex where I have been offered a new university position. As I walk down Lewes High Street, I catch a view of a thatched cottage (not unlike Field Cottage it must be said) for sale in the village of Rodmell. Something in my heart tells me that I have to have this cottage and that I have to go and live there. At the time I am less than clear as to what the impulse is (the trouble with this retrospective account is that it implies I knew at the time – the truth is I did not) but I immediately made an appointment to see the cottage and was most frustrated to hear it had already been sold. However, on the last day when my wife had returned to Norwich a fortuitous phone call came to say that the original buyers had backed out and that the cottage was for sale again. I visited the cottage, made an offer, made an appointment for my wife to see the cottage and put in train the process of purchasing it.

As I approached the cottage door on 4 May 2004 I had this incredibly odd sensation. Amazingly as I walked through the door

I said to myself, and this must have come from the depths of my subconscious, 'there you are James, there you are Alice we have got it back'.

Only then, and this is absolutely true, only then was I clearly aware of what my subconscious perception of ancestral voices had spoken to me about and how it had quite seriously and systematically framed my course of action with regard to the purchase of the house.

There is a second example that speaks not only to the delineation of courses of action but to my overall political orientation. A second story that my father told was the story of my Auntie Hilda. Of all the twelve Goodson girls that were born to Alice and James, Hilda was by far the most fragrant. She found herself at work in the squire's house in Sonning (yes the same squire that had evicted the family). According to the Christmas story the squire's son took a fancy to Hilda. In due course she fell pregnant. Four months into her pregnancy her body was recovered from Sonning Lock. She had been drowned. The inquest found that it had been death by misadventure and that nobody was involved in her demise. But according to folklore in Cobbler's City and according to the deeply held convictions of my own family she had been pushed into the lock by two of the squire's hired hands. I have subsequently confirmed the veracity of the story and there is a report in the local newspaper about the inquest into Hilda's death. As he told the story each Christmas, my father raged at the political order represented by the Tory squires and made it clear that we should be working for a different social order and one that had moral purposes and moral underpinnings very different from that which he associated with the local squirehierarchy.

Fast forward to 1976 I have moved into a small cottage with my new wife in a village in Sussex. The cottage is not unlike Field Cottage and it was previously a semi-detached cottage for farm labourers. On the green in the village a nouveau riche version of the local squire is ensconced. Over time I become the parish clerk to the very small parish in which the village is situated. One of the tasks of the parish clerk is to scrutinize new buildings in the parish or changes in land use. It becomes clear that the inhabitant of the squire's house has enclosed the lake which was part of the common land of the village and has without planning permission refurbished the barns in his estate. At the same time, it comes to my notice that covert plans are being made to build a whole estate of houses on one of the common land fields in the village. Reaching back no doubt into my ancestral memory it seems clear where my duty lies. I visit the said squire and confront him on the way that he has appropriated the land and refurbished the barn without proper planning permission. I urge him to reconsider his plans for building a new estate in the village. As you can imagine he was furious at the intervention of this young upstart clerk. However, after much thought he withdraws the plans for the new estate.

Both of these autobiographical vignettes (which provide me with a somewhat heroic subtext I have to admit) show how courses of action can emerge from the juxtaposition with ancestral voices and family memories. Undoubtedly, there are several examples of how ancestral voices lead to less-heroic actions and possibly and indeed quite probably undesirable actions. But for the moment I will keep silent about these!

ANCESTRAL VOICES AND PEDAGOGY

Ancestral voices and autobiographical memory are closely inter-linked and allied. In the next chapter, we review the place of auto-biographical memory as a site for the examination, elucidation, exploration, elaboration and enlightenment of historical context. In our memory work, we can see the way that narratives weave in historical context and in this way seek to establish coherence and continuity in our stories of selfhood. This search for overarch-ing themes within the narrative is often a crucial dimension in the construction of courses of action we undertake in our lives. Narratives are not just stories that search for meaning and coherences but compasses as we plot out our action in the world. Life themes can point to the priorities and patterns of our agency and provide key moments for learning and critical pedagogy.

Paulo Freire has talked of 'generative themes' as a central axis in any critical pedagogy. He also points to the unique capacity of human beings to link their past with their present and future activities. He says:

> In contrast to the animals – people can tri-dimentialise time into the past, the present and the future, their history, in function of their own location, develops as a constant process of transformation within which epochal units materialise. (Freire, 1972, p. 82)

In any personal project concerned with developing a critical awareness of human possibility and transformation, the role of ancestral voices seems to constitute an important but yet neglected conceptual space. In some of the most interesting school classrooms I have visited this conceptual space can provide a launching pad for pedagogy. For instance, in Counterthorpe school teachers would begin with their new class in the following manner as a way of introducing themselves. In the centre of the room was a huge box full of the teacher's archives – pictures of family, parents, cousins, etc., old letters, photos of home and villages, family videos and recordings. The idea was that the pupils could ferret around in the material and chat to members of staff about their family history and ancestral hinterland. It provided a wonderful, intimate exchange and preceded a project where the pupils explored their ancestral background. As a basis for critical pedagogy in other schools, it was one of the most successful curricula experiments I have ever witnessed.

Getting in touch with our ancestral hinterland and voices is a major stepping stone in self-understanding and collective understanding. In the last chapters of the book, we explore other collective settings where educational understandings and pedagogic exchanges can be pursued.

Our understandings of our own historical trajectory provide generative insights for the development of more collective memories and aspirations. We would want to say that they provide valuable prerequisites and prompts for the development of collective projects of recovery, redemption and reconciliation. In this sense reconciliation and recovery of our own personal past is itself a pathway to collective understandings and reconfiguration. The chapters in Part Two provide in this sense a bridgehead to the investigation of collective settings in Part Three in this book.

CHAPTER 5

Defining the Self through Autobiographical Memory

Ivor Goodson

It has been acknowledged since antiquity that the relationship between autobiographical memory and identity was intimate and inextricable. The site of 'memory work' was known as a place where life stories were recounted and described but social scientists were historically unsure about the status and significance of these accounts. As McAdams has noted:

> Once upon a time, psychologists viewed life stories as little different from fairy tales, charming, even enchanting on occasions, but fundamentally children's play of little scientific value for understanding human behaviour. (McAdams, 2006, p. 100)

Part of the problem was the belief at that time, and still in many quarters, that autobiographical memory and life stories were simply patchy and selective descriptions of factual events that had happened. Accounts were seen as descriptive, recapitulative and retrospective.

Matters began to change with some force in the 1980s. New perspectives emerged in studying the place of autobiographical memory and life stories in developing our understanding of life experience (Barclay, 1996; McAdams and Ochberg, 1988; Nasby and Read, 1997; Singer and Salovey, 1993). The major shift was a belief that far from being passively descriptive and recapitulative, autobiographical memory was a site of reconstruction and reflexivity and a place for the reworking of personal meaning.

Martin Conway's introduction to autobiographical memory (Conway, 1996) focuses on these points and argued that the 'defining feature of autobiographical memory was that they inherently represent personal meaning for a specific individual' (Conway, 1996, p. 186). He says, therefore, that autobiographical memory represents 'a challenge for the cognitive psychologist and the challenge is how to understand personal meanings' (Conway, 1996, p. 186). Conway concedes that in 1990 'autobiographical memory is a comparatively new area of research for cognitive psychologists' (Conway, 1996, p. xvii) and implies the reason for this is that:

> Autobiographical memory constitutes one of the areas where cognitive psychologists have no choice but to confront aspects of human cognition which are often set aside in mainstream cognitive research. These are aspects such as: emotions, the self and the role and nature of personal meanings in cognition. (Conway, 1996, p. xvii)

This new area has burgeoned in past decades and a new range of work has emerged which focuses on autobiographical memory (Brewer, 1986, 1996; Conway, 1996; Fitzgerald, 1996; Markus and Nurius, 1986; Markus and Ruvolo, 1989; McAdams et al., 1997; Moffitt and Singer, 1994; Neisser and Winograd, 1988; Pillemer, 1998; Reiser, 1983; Reiser et al., 1986; Robinson, 1992; Robinson and Taylor, 1998; Rubin, 1986, 1996, 1998; Schank, 1982; Singer, 1990; Singer and Salovey, 1993; Strauman, 1990, 1996; Thorne, 1995, 2000; Woike, 1995).

This work stresses how autobiographical memory helps define and locate our narratives of selfhood within a continuing and coherent life story. There the memory works in a more improvisational, constructional and creative manner (e.g. Barclay,

1996). In these accounts the life story provides the compass for the delineation of our courses of action throughout life and hence in this version autobiographical memory is a crucial lynch pin for human action and human agency. The implications of where autobiographical memory locates itself on this spectrum of possibility are considerable for their role in identity construction and maintenance as well as in the associated activities of learning and pedagogy.

Other work points to the enormous cultural variability of autobiographical memory. There is a Eurocentric and American perspective which focuses on highly individualized patterns of induction into autobiographical memory. Studies of socialization show how developing our autobiographical memory is partly 'learned behaviour' (Han et al., 1998; Leichtman, 2001; Mullen, 1994; Wang et al., 2000). This learned autobiographical memory work is linked to modalities of 'reconstruction' that we have referred to earlier.

John Dewey, who has much influenced new work by Michael Armstrong on reconstruction (Armstrong, 2012), says that 'education is a constant reorganising or reconstructing of experience'. He says:

> It has all the time ... an immediate end, and so far as activity is educative, it reaches that end – the direct transformation of the quality of experience. Infancy, youth, adult life – all stand on the same educative level in the sense that what is really learned at any and every stage of experience constitutes the value of that experience, and in the sense that it is the chief business of life at every point to make living thus contribute to an enrichment of its own perceptible meaning. (Dewey in Boydston, 1980, p. 54)

The realization that 'memory work' is part of an ongoing process of reconstruction and learning has substantial implications for those involved in all pedagogic endeavours. In part this is all related to a vital shift in our understanding of human inquiry. Postmodern theorists have begun to shift us from the view of rationality and human inquiry fashioned by the Enlightenment: 'The philosophers of the Enlightenment put their faith in reason. Reason was supposed to work like a searchlight, illuminating a reality that lay there, passively awaiting discovery' (Soros, quoted in Rowson, 2011, p. 22). The active and reconstructive aspects of reason were left out in this account of human inquiry: 'The active role, that reason can play in shaping reality was largely left out of the account. In other words the Enlightenment failed to recognise reflexivity' (Soros, quoted in Rowson, 2011, p. 22).

More recently work in social science has focused on the learning and pedagogic potential of social reflexivity. Anthony Giddens has developed a range of work looking at reflexivity and exploring its links with life narratives and autobiography. He, like Dewey, focuses on how these accounts reconstruct our knowledge base. He says:

> Developing a coherent sense of one's life history is a prime means of escaping the thrall of the past and opening oneself to the future. The author of the autobiography is enjoined both to go back as far as possible into early childhood and to set up lines of potential development to compass the future.
>
> The autobiography is a corrective intervention into the past, not merely a chronicle of elapsed events. (Giddens, 1991, p. 72)

The autobiography then is a prime space for the practice of reflexivity and learning. In Giddens' sense, reflexivity refers to the use of information about the conditions of activity as a means of regularly recording and redefining what that activity is. The autobiographical memory is then a site for corrective intervention, in other words for the reconstruction of knowledge.

In Giddens' terms then the self is seen as a reflexive project 'for which the individual is responsible' (Giddens, 1991, p. 75). Hence, 'A person's identity is not to be found in behaviour nor – important though this is – in the reaction of others, but in the capacity to keep a particular narrative going' (Giddens, 1991, p. 54).

The autobiography becomes, by this view, a major site for identity negotiation and production: 'Self-identity is not a destructive trait, or even a collection of traits, possessed by the individual. It is the self as reflexively understood by the person in terms of her or his biography' (Giddens, 1991, p. 53).

The ongoing production of autobiographical 'memories' is then an ongoing process of knowledge production and learning. Central in this knowledge is the capacity that autobiographical memory work has to allow us to dis-embed our understanding of the world. In doing so, we move beyond the birthright scripts we inherit ancestrally into the production of new scripts and visions.

Robert Kegan has written at length about the process of dis-embedding as it begins in childhood. He talks of children looking at other people: 'He cannot separate himself from them; he cannot take them as an object of attention. He is not individuated from them; he is embedded in them. They define the very structure of his attention' (Kegan, 1982, p. 29).

The strategy for dis-embedding our understanding of the world is reflexivity, which Kegan describes as: 'Detaching or distancing ourselves from both the socialising process of the surround and from our own internal productions, albeit in such a way that does not prevent us from connection and joining in community and personal relationships' (Kegan, 1982, p. 22).

Autobiographical memory work becomes a key arena for 'detaching and distancing' as the work of reconstruction and repositioning takes place. As Giddens says, this memory work can act as a 'live intervention' whereby we can transcend the 'thrall of the past' and open up to new paths of development for the future.

In the process of detaching, distancing and development we construct new cognitive maps and contextual understandings. This new knowledge allows us to reframe and reposition our autobiographical memories.

Work on the reconstructive potential of autobiographical memory is, we think, especially important for those exploring the learning and pedagogic capacities of memory work. We can begin to scrutinize the process whereby people dis-embed and reposition their primeval and ancestral memories in the ongoing construction of autobiographical memory. These acts of reconstruction amount to a repositioning of the self and hence may show us how transgression and transformation interweave in the process of personal change. By developing some cognitive distance on our inherited and inscribed memories, we can begin to critically interrogate them, and in doing so the process of personal change is supported and promoted.

Our view here is that the constant reconstruction of memory and narrative is actually a dis-embedding and repositioning of the self. They therefore sit at the heart of learning and pedagogy. To devise educational strategies which ignore this process is to ignore the potential for personal growth in favour of some vision of disciplinary socialization or utilitarian functionalism. By this view critical pedagogy has to realize the considerable potential of this realm of memory and narrative work.

Autobiographical memory is worked on and processed throughout the life course – this means that our experiences and a view of self is in a constant process of reconstruction. These acts of reconstruction of knowledge provide an important point for 'pedagogic leverage' and learning potential. Hence autobiographical memory is a place, a space, where any learning or pedagogy that aims to dis-embed and reposition our ongoing identity project might start.

Whilst I was a professor at the University of Rochester, a group of colleagues developed collaborative research on memory, identity and agency. The group included Dale Dannefer, Paul Stein and Philip Wexler. One of my close colleagues Craig Barclay defined important work on autobiographical memory as a way of undertaking what he described as 'composing the self'. Writing in 1996 Barclay argued:

Autobiographical remembering is an improvisational activity that forms emergent selves which give us a sense of needed comfort and a culturally valued sense of personal coherence over time. One conclusion following from this line of argument is that losing or lacking the generative abilities to improvise selves through the functional reconstruction of autobiographical memories results in the subjective experience of alienation from others in society. In addition we come to a sense of self fragmentation. Under such circumstances it becomes increasingly difficult to ground one's self in the past, to make sense of out of present experiences or imagined possible adaptive futures. (Barclay, 1996, p. 107)

Barclay then expounds the importance of autobiographical memory at the reconstructive end of the spectrum. Intriguingly Barclay argues that we establish what he calls 'proto-selves' through two processes:

The first is instantiation, defined as making public and explicit reconstructed past events (e.g. through rituals) that are objectified with some context... the notion of context presented here includes both private and public contexts. Society and culture are two important contexts within which autobiographical remembering occurs. Societies and cultures are changed by the activities associated with reconstructed remembering activities, especially if those activities occur among collectives working together for some common purpose. (Barclay, 1996, p. 112)

The overarching cultural importance of these assertions is considerable in its scope and impact on our social landscape and memory. Moreover, if Barclay is correct, and we think he is, the cultural significance of memory work is considerable and the role of critical pedagogy within this frame is correspondingly highly significant.

At a broader level, Barclay sees the contextual background as related to the reproduction of 'history':

> History viewed here is the story we wish to be known that justifies our being, culture, or way of life. History provides a context within which local, national and world events are interpreted and understood. (Barclay, 1996, p. 112)

The reconstructive potential of autobiographical memory then works at a broad collective and societal level. We consider some of the reconstructive potential of memory and narrative work at the collective level in Part Three of our book. But the relationship to each personal trajectory is profound and lasts throughout each individual life course.

McAdams has developed a life story model of identity which works in interesting ways with some of this more recent work on autobiographical memory. He says:

> Identity itself takes the form of a story, complete with setting, scenes, character, plot, and theme. In late adolescence and young adulthood, people living in modern societies begin to reconstruct the personal past, perceive the present, and anticipate the future in terms of an internalized and evolving self-story, an integrative narrative of self that provides modern life with some modicum of psychosocial unity and purpose. (McAdams, 2001, p. 101)

This makes it plain that McAdams favours the reconstructive character of autobiography and life story. His work consistently stresses the role of 'composing a self' in our ongoing identity life-work and he focuses on the way in which individual refraction substantially mediates the cultural frame in which narrative work is located.

Life stories are based on biographical facts, but they go considerably beyond the facts as people selectively appropriate aspects of their experience and imaginatively construe both past and future to construct stories that make sense to them and to their audiences, that vivify and integrate life and make it more or less meaningful. Life stories are psychosocial constructions, co-authored by the person himself or herself and the cultural context within which that person's life is embedded and given meaning. As such, individual life stories reflect cultural values and norms, including assumptions about gender, race, and class. Life stories are intelligible within a particular cultural frame, and yet they also differentiate one person from the next. (McAdams, 2001, p. 101)

The intersection between autobiographical memory and cultural settings needs to be closely interrogated. So also does the manner in which particular selections and omissions work through into our constructions of autobiographical memory.

AN EXAMPLE OF CONSTRUCTING AUTOBIOGRAPHICAL MEMORY

In this section, I will use my conversation with Scherto Gill as an example to illustrate a process of arriving at my own autobiographical memory. The following interview section deals with some of these issues highlighted in the Introduction of this chapter. Scherto is concerned with establishing the selectivism and partialities that underpin my own autobiographical memories and to explore the capacities of the 'integrative self' to which McAdams refers.

SG   *In 'The Ego Trick', Julian Baggini investigated into the question about the nature of the self. To begin his inquiry, he used the metaphor of a pearl in the book to problematize notion of an essentialized self. What do you think? Is there such a thing as a core self that persists through time?*

IG   Well that depends what the pearl is of course. The post-modern critique is that there is no essentialized self, there is no centre, and we are just a shifting set of multiple selves represented differently to each people. I both accept that and don't accept it at all. I would say that most of us have some continuing sense of who we are and what we are about and that continuity element can be set alongside other discontinuities of self. But the continuity element is what I recognize as myself, vis-a-vie continuing preoccupations, personality advantages and disadvantages and defects that are me. And so I think that there is something that I recognize as 'me' which other people may recognize in different ways and there are different 'me's over time, but there is also such continuity to me which I think will probably exist for much of the duration of my life. We can talk about what those continuities are and what the discontinuities are. Certain post-modern notions are too stressing of discontinuity and multiplicity, so I think in a sense both the modernist version and post-modern is partly right and partly wrong.

SG   Where would you start if you were to answer the question of 'who am I'?

IG   Well probably one place to start would be some of the continuities of one's sense of space, place, time, purpose. I think there are certain continuities in my sense of purposefulness and in my search for meaningfulness and as Francesca of 'The Bridges of Madison County' says, it always is a combination of daily detail, the details of life. She talks about the wonderful dreams of life and then going back into the details of her life when she returns from abroad, dreams of love with Robert, the photographer and ultimately she embraces the details of life. I would say there are many details to my life, but what melds the details together is a kind of continuity of aspiration around issues of social justice, egalitarianism – treating people equally on a daily basis as well as on an ideological basis. So there is a sort of continuity of belief, a continuity of aspiration which I don't always, of course, live up to, but that I can recognize early where that started. That belief that people should be treated *equally certainly started in my origins which were in the margins of English society, as you know. If you are the son of a manual worker, you are to some extent on the margins of the establishment in this country and that sense of marginality is a great fortune in many ways. One of the skills, I think, is to turn what might look like social misfortune into enormous fortune because of course what it gives you is a great drive to understand the centre.*

Having begun to establish a social context for the way in which my autobiographical memory is conducted, Scherto goes on to question me on the relevance of 'coming from the margins' of English society. Here one outsider in his own culture, me, is trying to explain to somebody from quite outside the culture how margins 'feel' – how the patterns of exclusion so strongly evident in English class society affect our 'internal affairs' and 'external relations'. What is being developed here, in a small way, is a theory of context which we examine in more depth in later chapters. Part of dis-embedding your inherited social script, we argue, is the development of a theory of context and this is often related to a particular 'life theme' (see Chapter 6) which integrated this search for understanding and purpose.

SG   *Could you give us a flavour of life in the margins? In other words, can you depict the 'details of life' you just talked about by recalling your own?*

IG   *The details of marginality... or... yeah... what the flavour is... is that you grow up in a home where you aren't taught to read. One of the reasons that you don't even think about reading is that there aren't any books in the home. Your father has trouble reading, doesn't really read; your Mum reads a bit, but she doesn't read to you, and she doesn't think teaching you reading is important because she thinks, quite rightly in many ways, that storytelling and the oral culture is what our group are about. So I learned to be a good storyteller, not a reader. So one aspect of marginality is that sense of early disempowerment if you see reading as empowerment, literacy as empowerment. But there are many other aspects of marginality in the home, in the sense that you don't see much of your father because he works six day a week, in my Dad's case sometimes Sunday morning. He is always tired when he gets home and he doesn't therefore talk too much because he is constantly exhausted and the only time you will see him is in the one week's holiday a year. Your mother also works, as a dinner lady or in the munitions factory, so you don't see much of her. In my case I didn't go to school until I was six anyhow, we didn't particularly believe in schools in my tribe, and schools were a place where everybody went and they all failed; where all that happened in the end was that you went into a factory anyhow. There was a deep distrust of schools in the community I grew up in. That's what marginality means. It means that all of the beliefs of the society – that literacy is a good thing, education is a good thing, schools are a good thing and so on, don't work because they don't deliver for people on the margins. They only deliver for people in the centre of the society. That is why so much of the discourse about the 'big society' makes no sense at all to me because I always view it (yes, I still do) from what it means on the margins.*

Beyond this overall sense of social marginality, Scherto is concerned with understanding the 'details of life'. She is concerned with establishing my daily 'habitus', my way of living. This leads to an interesting exchange about daily life as inscribed by my memories:

SG *That's an interesting broad stroke type of picture of living on the margins. Now, can we go a bit closer to that life? What is it like to enter the house of your home? What was it like living in it?*

IG *That's a good question…*

SG *Can you recall a moment in your early life at your family home? Once you pinpoint that moment, can you describe your house at the time? At this moment, what was your Mum doing? Your Dad? And what were you doing?*

IG   *Well probably quite a solitudinal moment in some ways.
I mean, not a conventional working class home in many ways
which is a place where everybody mixes together. Umm, I was the
only child, my father was the only son and had twelve sisters and
my mother was one of eight...*

*Our house was a reasonably sized house. Dad was a very
thoughtful and conscientious worker. He looked after his mother
and had his own house. So, in some ways, it is a respectable working class family and quite solitudinal, as I said. I mean my prominent sense of the home would be Dad asleep in the armchair after
a day's work; Mum probably at work or chatting to neighbours,
or generally in a convivial space and myself probably out most of
the time. I was a great lover of the street; I spent a lot of time in
what was called the REC which was the recreation ground. From
about seven onwards every evening I would be in the REC, playing football, playing cards, messing around, doing vaguely delinquent stuff. I was in trouble with the police a few times for messing
around – sawing the Scoutmaster's bike in halves for example and
watching delightedly as he got on it and one half of it broke ... The
police came round about that ... So there were all sorts of small
delinquent acts. I was a fairly street oriented kid, a pretty rough
street kid really and all my friends were exactly the same.*

*The big rupture in my life if you could fast forward is that I
did learn to read when I was eight. Because the teacher comes
to the home and tells my Mum and Dad that they must try to
teach me to read and they must buy me some books and in due
course I do read and I quickly love reading and I become different from my friends in the sense that that happened ... And then
of course the 11+ comes up that you took at the time. Every one
of the friends that I talked about on the street all went to the
local school which was a secondary modern at that time and I
passed the 11+ ... much to my own amazement and everybody
else's ... because I think only one other person in our village had*

every passed the 11+ ... that's how totally marginal the village was and it was quite a big village.

SG   *It is indeed hard to imagine that growing up in such a working class family as you described, you could end up passing the 11+. Your story is very unusual. Tell us more about your village and what happened to the other person who also passed (11+).*

IG   *The place is called Egeley near Reading which had a huge overspill council estate where many people had relocated from London and other places. So it was very kind of working class commuter town/village or progressively suburban village where I grew up. It became more suburban and you got more and more kids there and the pattern of there only being one or two kids at grammar school probably changed. But when I grew up I can remember the only other boy who passed (11+), was a boy called David Cripps. There were only two of us and he never finished at grammar school anyway. He left to become a builder. So I was the only one in a way from that whole village who left the village to go to the grammar school which was 4 miles away and I took a lot of pressure for that because it divided me from my mates.*

SG   *So from being a streetwise boy who was hardly at home, playing happily with other boys, having practical jokes and so on, to becoming the only boy to finish the grammar school, it must have been a huge transformation. Let's first return to an earlier moment when you realized that you could read. This was something your parents were never able to do. How did you feel?*

Asking this question, Scherto evokes incredibly strong memories for me. It is Proustian sensation. I would suspect this is because she is taking me back to a place of 'transgression', a place of 'border-crossing'. For the first time in my life I am going outside the confines of my own tribe. Geographically I am beginning to journey – the library is outside our village (which does not have one), the school I am heading towards is miles away from our tribal territory. She is taking me back to a point of 'rupture' which is vividly remembered:

136

IG   *I remember now, as we speak, the smell of the boards in the library, where my mother took me to get the first book. I remember the first book by Leonard Gribble which I took off the shelf and read and I can remember the smell and the excitement of books. I can remember Mum taking me to William Smith, a book shop to buy books because my parents had been told to buy me books. And being allowed to choose two books, I bought Malcolm Saville's 'Lone Pine 5' which I have still got and I remember then sitting and reading… When I talk about the rift, there is a rift between this raffish streetwise kid, and I was a snotty nosed kid basically who loved to be kicking about with footballs and going out with girls, I loved all that and still do, and this other me that was alone, reading and absolutely absorbed in the world of 'Lone Pine 5', just taken to another place by a book.*

So from the beginning, there is a strange double-side to my personality which continues today: one side is this great love of raffish, romantic street life and the other, a profound isolated scholarly kind of solipsism. They are both part of me.

SG   *How did these two aspects of your persona exist simultaneously in you after you stepped outside of your village? You referred to that moment as a kind of rift, or a rupture. Looking back, how would you consider the impact of such transgression on you and your family? Do you see yourself break away from the fundamentally deprived working class life? Had this new journey set you apart from your family and the others in the village?*

IG   *Well… we talk about various sorts of other people, but I suppose the relationship I spent the most time thinking about as an 11 year old child when I began to go to Grammar school was my father who I loved passionately. Of course for him this was a real difficulty because it was like having a cuckoo in the nest really. You've got this little bird that you've brought into the world and then suddenly the bird is doing a range of things which could challenge your sense of competence in the world. A lot of the things about me came from that moment, for example, from the fact that I never wanted to have my Dad's essential competences challenged. So his essential competences include that he is very good with his hands, he drives a car, and various other things like that. And I always thought the best way to handle this is for him to have his own expertises and for me to have a different set of expertises and for us therefore to be equal, for him to be unchallenged by my unusual emerging competences. So the fact that I still don't drive, and I'm useless with my hands and so on comes back from that moment. Of course, most people would have learnt to do those things some time later, but for me, I hold onto these strange moments of rupture in some strange pathological way.*

And as far as my Mum goes, in what I have come to understand, is that she was a profoundly intelligent woman as was my Dad in a way, but would really have loved to have had a creative, academic life. And I was always aware of that, and felt really sorry for the frustration that she felt with her life as she lived to 104 and was still trying to find a way to be creative. So I think in some ways, my life project was partly related to her sense of frustration, partly guided by it as well. So each of the parents, both of whom are very dear to me (obviously when you are an only child you know your parents in that particular way), had influenced the way I responded.

The difficulties posed by border-crossings were considerable within the working-class family. They were echoed and exacerbated when played out in the wider working-class culture. At this time it is important to stress the culture was well established and broad-based. In my case these tensions were part of the 'negotiations' with my own band of mates. The rupture of going from the village to the grammar school posed particular problems for my gang of mates:

IG   *The biggest problem though was of course my mates and probably to understand the continuity in my sense of self you'd have to really think about what it is like to be the one boy in the village who dresses up in a blue venetian coat with a yellow hat with tassels on, to ride through the council estate to go to school. I can still hear them yelling out 'grammar grub' and throwing mud pies at me on my first day of going to school. And of course the second day, I took off the coat, took off the hat and just rode to school. What I was always able somehow to do was to confront that reaction, which is a collective fear of otherness. There, the tribe was expressing that one of the 'buggers' was trying to escape the tribe and that was me, and I was elected to do that. And how did I handle that? I suppose that's the key to understanding me now – I handled it. Within weeks, I was on the same page with them again and they never commented again. Indeed my best friends, when I got to uni, used to take me out drinking and would not let me pay – they would say it's for you to get through university. So I kind of found a way of negotiating my difference and so I probably have an exaggerated sense of valuing people like that – ordinary people who can cope with your difference and in a sense, your trajectory of escape and deal with it with such beauty.*

So I am trying to honour those people, I think, ever since. I valued their response because it was so generous spirited. If somebody is trying to escape you would think it would be mud pies forever, but within weeks it was, 'Hi Iv, how you doin? Good luck at school'. And that negotiation, that capacity to carry people with you, is something I think I've learnt.

SG   *There is a general tendency to celebrate social mobility and presumably, for any educational system, it is to see more kids from working class backgrounds become young Ivor. That might be considered the ultimate success for some. So looking back, did you recall families in the village telling their children: 'Look, Ivor has made it! If you work hard, you will make it too'. In other words, did the people in your village see going to a grammar school as an escape-route and a path to upward mobility for them?*

Looking back, it is hard to re-evoke the feel of working-class culture in the 1950s. There was a strong sense of solidarity of shared purpose. There was also a sense that the group was 'on the march'. That history was on its side. The 1945 election victory and the enormous achievements of the post-war Labour government had left a mark on the sense of esteem and purpose of the working class. My own uncle George had a workers-of-the-world-unite flag over the fireplace and was forever lecturing us on 'Labour's March to Victory'. So notions of solidarity and shared destiny were set against notions of individual meritocratic advancement.

IG   *Well this is where I think it is difficult to re-evoke historical periods. I was born in 1943, so we are talking about England in the early 50s, a very, very poor country with huge solidarities among the working class communities and a sense of their own growing power. You've got to realize that in 1945, the Labour government celebrates ordinary people and tries to build a world for them a new Jerusalem with a welfare system; build schools and hospitals that would be good for everybody. So there is a strong sense of a class of people that were winning, on the march and therefore a class of people you'd have to be mad to escape from. So social mobility in such a context is a rather odd move and I would say in some ways it still is. But you now face a situation where that sense of class solidarity and class success has been dismantled like the factories. So now all you face is a kind of impoverished lower class from which everybody would want to escape. But in those days, no. It was not normal to wish to escape and it was not even thought to be terribly smart.*

SG   *How did you feel at the time, when departing from your 'tribe' and from that sense of optimism and esteem?*

IG   *Well, let's fast forward. I'm 15. Do I want to go to university? Certainly not because all my mates are coming home with big wage packets from the factory while I am riding about on a second-hand cycle. They have all got large motorbikes with girlfriends on the back and they've got the fastest fashions. They have got everything I want – the motorbike, the clothes, the girlfriends. I am just the boy at the grammar school, still cycling through the council estate, doesn't have a penny in his pocket when he goes out with his friends, they have to buy the drinks, they have to pay for the food. No I didn't feel at all smart. So what did I do at 15, I left school to work in a factory. So in fact, I didn't feel privileged as a grammar school boy except for that other me that I talked about – the sheer joy of learning which never left me. But in terms of its social usefulness, in terms of the attraction, I had very little at that time.*

SG *Before you go on recalling your life stories, could we just pause for a brief moment? I want to ask you something here: do I hear a tension in the way you described 'the life on the margins'? The tension, to me, lies between a picture of marginality, in particular, low level literacy, labour-intense employment and a general sense of deprivation, and a depiction of working class pride and dignity, a sense of solidarity and optimism. Do you not see the tension yourself?*

IG *No, not really. It's seen as the margins by the establishment in the country. They don't see solidarity-based working class people as deserving of pride and dignity, but within the class we were still marginalized. I mean this proud class was not actually ever going to get the commanding power that it thought it was, but my point is that it thought it was on the march, it thought it was heading for power and it thought it was building a new Jerusalem. But in effect, none of that happened because the privileged groups which are now currently in power again made sure that didn't happen. They wanted to keep that group marginal and they successfully did it. And not only did they marginalize it, they virtually emasculated it in the 80s and 90s. That's what I've had to watch that the group I've honoured has been smashed by political forces, quite deliberately. That's a source of enormous sadness to me. I can't even describe how sad that still makes me, and to see such forces in power now, and to see the way they are clearly behaving in the same way, it's quite bizarre, as a bunch of corrupt monsters that I always thought they were...*

At this stage in our conversation I have veered into my contemporary sense of the world. I would stress that there are continuities but Scherto rightly takes me back to an earlier place she is trying to get me to re-evaluate the process we call 'location' (fully developed in Chapter 6). Location is the process whereby we come to understand our own individual life in its cultural and historical settings. We develop a cognitive map, or the 'theory of context' as we call it, of the cultural and political possibilities for living our life. If we do this, it is possible to deconstruct and reconstruct the script – the expectation which society has for us based on the space and the place we came from. In my case, that script pointed clearly to the factory where all my mates ended up or on the dole queue! The rupture came with the unexpected passage to the grammar school. But in the new situation, the landscape of the social order became somewhat clearer to me particularly I think because my out-of-school social milieu still remained the local estate and all my friends at the secondary modern and in the factory. So although I had been educationally relocated, my gaze remained firmly a view through the eyes of my group, my tribe, my mates.

SG   *So shall we return to the point when you started the grammar school – now you were wearing jacket, tasselled hat and riding from your council estate to a different world. Can you recall the other children in the grammar school? In your eyes, what were they like at the time?*

IG   *The school is between Wokingham and Egeley, both of which were quite respectable middle class areas. So only a few people, literally, physically came from the margins of working class villages or council estates. So you are probably talking about five per cent of the school being made up of anybody who was recognizable in my tribe. There are a number of clear distinguishing reasons for that – there are two places you could buy the jacket: one you got blue venetian cloth at Jacksons which was a high class outfitter, or you could get a rather shoddy blue jacket from the Co-op. So* the five per cent of us, my shoddy blue jacket, I know, was paid for on HP. So from the beginning, it was clear who the five per cent were and very quickly the shoddy blue jackets lost their blue and became threadbare so that was all very clearly badged from the beginning. In my class there was one other boy who spoke with very clear Berkshire accents where you drop your 'h's and that's how we talked. I used to love phoning my Dad up and we'd talk like that together. I've lost it to some extent, but, as I say, when I'm drunk I go straight back to it. So it's obviously an editing process has taken over my accent. But we were the two boys in school who talked like that, constantly being told to sound our 'h's and not to speak like that. So the result was that he and I were, there were twenty-seven kids in the class, twenty-sixth and twenty-seventh in every exam. We took our 'O' Levels, I took nine and passed one; he took nine and failed them all.

SG   No doubt it was quite a contrast to your early success when you went to your village school where you were able to pass the 11+.

IG   Well I was among my tribe there you see. I didn't need to realize it as it was shoved right up my nose that I was the wrong kind of a kid to be at grammar school.

SG   Are you saying that the kind of environment at the grammar school didn't really motivate you to do well?

IG   No. It motivated me enormously – to resist with every bone in my body everything they were trying to do. So in English I would not speak the way they wanted me to, so I failed English; I would not accept that grammar and I would not lose my dialect. I would not, in other words, betray my tribe. I just wouldn't. I've always been stubborn like that.

It's more complicated than that because two or three of the teachers in the school were not conventional grammar school teachers. They were Socialists. One of them was a Welsh Socialist, Dai Rees who was a really brilliant man. Another one of them was Joe Pettit who was head of the local Campaign for Nuclear Disarmament. So there were two or three deviant teachers inside *the school who desperately wanted to take the working class kids forward. In fact, after I left school at 15 to work in the factory, Dai Rees essentially was the one who came to the factory and asked me to come back to school. He kind of adopted me. I spoke to him maybe twenty years ago to thank him for everything and he said: 'Christ, you were a difficult kid but you were clever. I could see it, I could see you were a noble savage and I was determined that you wouldn't fail, I was determined that they wouldn't force you out'.*

So I mean it wasn't a monolithic class system to purge us, the reproduction of the middle class, but there were some teachers, as there always are, who were prepared to rebel against that, and to try and nurture some of the noble savages from the working class that crept through the door. So there was a coterie of us, but I was the only one who stuck it out. I was the only one who went to sixth form and then I was the only one who went to university.

I loved the sixth form, I absolutely loved it. It was the thing I could not suppress in myself, even though I could read the social implications of everything, I think, not everything but some of it, I couldn't suppress my deep fascination with learning. When I was able to do History and Economics with this guy, Dai Rees, so that the two things were brought together, he wasn't ambivalent about my nasty class background and his fascination with learning. The fascination with books and history just took me into another zone. So in spite of my social resistance, my sense of marginality, my fury at the way the school ran, I, nonetheless, became a good student.

FROM DIS-EMBEDDING TO RELOCATING – THE JOURNEY OF AUTOBIOGRAPHICAL MEMORY

What this interview extract illustrates is an emerging sense of how we begin to place ourselves in a cultural setting. It also shows how the ongoing construction of our autobiographical memory plays out and inscribes our own changing view of the world. The autobiographical memory is an active intervention and interpretation of the social world as well as a site of learning, pedagogy and politics. Slowly as I progressed through school I began to see how I was perceived and located in the social order. The 'badges' of my class position made 'reading the social context' fairly easy. I was a son of manual workers with a marginal position in society and slowly I developed a 'theory of context' relating to this location. Moreover, at the time, I began to develop a 'course of action' which responded to that theory of context. My own take on 'social mobility' involved simultaneously 'holding on' while 'moving out'. This is not a unique response as many working-class stories evidence. The following extract is from an interview with Melvyn Bragg who has become an official commentator on class and culture in Britain. At the age of 72, Lord Bragg says this about his autobiographical memory:

> I think the working-class thing hasn't gone away and it never will go away. I don't try to make it go away. Quite a few of my interactions and responses are still the responses I had when I was eighteen or nineteen. (Cadwalladr, 2012)

Likewise Frank Kermode has written about the strange autobiographical positioning which comes from such social locations. Not only was he a working-class scholarship boy but coming from the Isle of Man, so he had a double sense of being an outsider. Despite being internationally recognized as a literary theorist and holding many of the most prestigious professorships in his field, he retained his sense of marginality. The title of his autobiography epitomizes this continuing sense of himself and his trajectory. It is called *Not Entitled* (Kermode, 1995). Whatever worldly success he achieved he continued to hold onto a sense of himself as marginal, 'outside' and without an enduring sense of entitlement. This narrative settlement was based on a finely honed 'theory of context' which he developed and his narrative ruminations on the meaning of life have enormous sophistication. He saw the narrative quest, in his felicitous phrase, as 'a search for intelligible endings'.

The process of dis-embedding is strangely ambivalent as my own story and that of Melvyn Bragg and Frank Kermode testify. For whilst the urge to dis-embed involves a quest for 'something beyond', an understanding of the social location and situatedness of a life, it also quite plainly involves a 'holding on' to the meaning of that location. For some that is the case; others of course in the more socially sanctioned version of mobility dis-embed and move on out to another social location.

For many though we follow the insight of Clive James on his migration to England when he says: 'I had to go away to know what was there'. I believe narrative journeys have a similar flavour. In some ways they are a pursuit of 'knowing what is there' and then pursuing the narrative and existential consequences of that knowledge. In our terms, to develop 'a theory of context' is to 'come to know' our social history and social location in order to determine how we should be and act in the world. Only if we do that we can make any assessment of the crucial moral question of 'whose side we are on' and begin to draw up a narrative of social purpose or as we call it later 'a life theme'.

In a sense we return to the spectrum with which we started the chapter. For some autobiographical memory is a rendition of what happened and that which happened often, followed fairly closely the 'birth right script' the person was handed. This is a less agentic, more socially passive version of lived experiences. For many though autobiographical memory provides a platform for social investigation and dis-embedding and provides key opportunities for learning. The route is opened for developing a 'theory of context' to understand our social location, being and purpose. Pursuing our understanding of a 'theory of context' provides a route for developing our 'life themes' which harmonize our social imagination and understanding with our ongoing social purposes. We believe this is a route to active learning and engaged citizenship and that a critical pedagogy situated at this intersection has great potential for social transformation and change.

146

CHAPTER 6

Developing Life Themes
Ivor Goodson

In this chapter, we will review the role of autobiographical memory in 'composing a self'. We will also point out the considerable 'reconstructive' element involved in the ongoing construction of our autobiographical memories. Part of the act of reconstruction, we argued, was that people may develop a 'theory of context' about their life narrative. They come to understand how their narrative is positioned and promoted in particular time and space. They begin to explore the link between their narratives of selfhood and wider socially scripted and underwritten narratives.

The cultural and historical context of autobiographical remembering and of narrative construction is a neglected aspect of most social scientific accounts today. In our work on narrative learning and narrative pedagogy, we have over time developed a number of crucial distinctions in developing what we call 'a theory of context'. In using the phrase 'theory of context' here, we refer to the process whereby people come to understand the historical periodization and cultural location of the resources they employ to construct their narrative and the selections of autobiographical remembering which support the narrative. Some of the work on autobiographical remembering has tended towards a mode of individualism which focuses primarily on the internal conversations that people have about their autobiography and self-narrative. In developing a theory of context one of the crucial distinctions in developing that theory is between the issues of what I call 'internal affairs', which is the internal monologue that people develop about their lives and their life stories, and what I call 'external relations', which is the way they present their life's narrative to the external world and link it to the wider societal narratives. There is often a distinction between internal affairs and external relations and this needs to be explored in social science research as it does in any pedagogic encounter, particularly within a critical pedagogic frame.

Part of this narrative work involves exploring the relationship between the 'internal affairs' of self-narratives and the 'external relations' of the social location of those narratives. In this chapter, we explore how linking the internal and external can often lead to the development of 'life themes', which provide an important compass for people developing their narrative landscape.

What our work has shown is that many people develop an overarching 'life theme' which unifies and provides a spine for their ongoing definition of their life story. Often this theme originates in the desire to overcome a particular social barrier or personal trauma. In confronting this personal dilemma the person is stimulated to develop a narrative theme which offers a route to reconciliation, resolution or reflective compromise. Hence there is a considerable personal and psychic investment in the unifying narrative that is constructed. This act of unifying operates at a number of levels.

In the internal reflexive accounts, the internal conversations that we have as we pursue our narrative work, a unifying theme can integrate the life story that is constructed. So in our internal affairs integration and unification take place. But also integration takes place between our internal account to ourselves and our external reporting to other people, our 'external relations'. A life theme provides internal meaning-making and coherence and an account which is readily understandable to external audiences, in our relations with other people. In the later example, Robert Oppenheimer, we show how crucial it is for people to 'figure themselves out'. Not only is this an internal crisis of meaning and identity but it is an external relations disaster because people see the unresolved narrative and their external relations are therefore unsustainable. In Oppenheimer's case they judged, 'you carried on a charade with him. He lived a charade'.

The development of a life theme is one strategy that people employ, quite a common strategy to integrate their life narrative. This integration takes place both in the internalized life story construction and in integrating the internal and external accounts.

We have argued that this integrative activity is often stimulated by confrontation with social barriers or personal traumas or other critical incidents. For this reason the development of a theory of context often assists this integrative enterprise of developing a life theme. By reflecting upon their contextual background people can see how they have been socially conditioned and in developing a theory of context they allow 'distancing' and 'dis-embedding' and are able to deconstruct and then reconstruct their life narratives. This narrative activity provides a platform for the definition of new and integrative life themes.

Part of the importance of developing a context is that it allows a process of 'distancing' and 'dis-embedding' to take place. This means we can come to understand how the initial scripts that we may have inherited or had inscribed have been unconsciously adopted. In this sense developing a theory of context about our life narratives is a kind of empowerment because it allows us to scrutinize the 'choices' that underpin the development of our life stories and life themes.

Denis Potter has talked about the importance of the process of coming to know yourself, what he calls your 'sovereign self'. He relates this to his work in developing the television play *The Singing Detective* which explored important narrative themes:

> What I was trying to do in *The Singing Detective* was to make the whole thing a detective story but a detective story about how

you find out about yourself so that you've got this superfluity of clues which is what we all have and very few solutions. Maybe no solutions, by that, the very act of garnering the clues and the very act of remembering not merely an event but how that event has lodged in you and how that event has affected the way you see things begins to assemble a system of values.

So it's about how we can protect that sovereignty that we have and that is maybe all that we have and is the most precious of all of the human capacities even beyond language ... the past and present are not in strict sequence because they aren't, they are in one sense in the calendar sense they are not in your head in that sequence and they aren't in the way you discover things about yourself where an event twenty years ago can follow yesterday and out of the morass of evidence of clues and searchings and strivings which is the metaphor for the way we live we can start to put up the structure called 'self' out of which we can walk saying at least I know and you know better than before who we are.

How can be express true values in consumer societies. By attempting to assess how sovereign you are as an individual human being if you know it and that means carefully with all the shapes, all the half shapes, all the memories or the aspirations of your life, how they coalesce, how they contradict each other, how they have to be disentangled as a human act by you yourself, this sovereign self, the beyond and behind all those other selves that are being sold remain this unique sovereign individual. (Yentob, 1991)

This 'disentangling as a human act' that Potter talks about is the quintessential moment of learning and pedagogy. It is close to the notion of dis-embedding that was discussed in the previous chapter. It relates to our own conception of developing a 'theory of context' of our lives which allows us to understand the temporal and cultural settings of our life narrative. The narrator here is trying to dis-embed, deconstruct and disentangle the constructed elements of their social conditioning. This is a precursor and is an accompaniment to what Barclay calls 'composing the self'. The learning and pedagogical leverage at work in this act of composition become clear for autobiographical memory work is indeed, as we quoted earlier, 'an improvisational activity that forms emergent selves which give us a sense of needed comfort and a culturally valued sense of personal coherence over time' (see Chapter 5).

This improvisational activity, which is both internal and external, personal and collective, is the essence of critical learning and pedagogy. In this ongoing improvisational activity we see one of the most generative sites for the critical 'disentangling as a human act' which must underpin our learning mission and pedagogic quest of its essence. The disentangling is an act of constant deconstruction and reconstruction. This is the place where dis-embedding takes place and where new scripts can be imagined and worked for.

DEVELOPING A LIFE THEME: AN EXAMPLE

The importance of ancestral voices in the art of composing a self is clearly evident in many of the life story interviews we have undertaken. In some ways these stories revolve around the idea of an imaginary homeland which is related to ancestral dreams and memories and to 'the notion of roots'. These ancestral places often constitute the starting point in the way that people compose a self and construct a life theme.

This ongoing dialogue between ancestral memory and contemporary self-journeys can be seen at work in the following extract. The life story teller is a 67-year-old Female Norwegian (FN) woman who has lived a life rich in narrative and imaginary journeys. She has lived her life with fidelity to her central dream which is that she belongs to a close family that grew up on a rural farm on an island in western Norway. Her dream has always been to honour and nurture her extended family and to return to the island when her professional work in an urban centre was completed and she retired. As the youngest child in a large family, she has worked hard to honour her family traditions and nurture her family links on the island where she now lives with her older brother. In this regard she is an example of the types of narrative traveller that are found to be commonly present in the interviews and pedagogic encounters in which we have been involved.

Ivor: *So what are the sources of satisfaction, the sources of wellbeing now, because I see that in you, what gives you this sense of wellbeing now more than ever?*

FN: *It is, I have a little place in my world. I have been given a very humble little place where my ancestors were poor people and I'm lucky to own that place and to finish my days there. That's such a great thing, I'm so grateful for that every day, that I know every little corner, I know every grey stone, I can touch the old wooden horse and know my great grandmother was here, she was only thirty-three when she went and I'm now sixty-seven, I can go here, I can live for many years still, that is one important thing, to have a place in the world, which I haven't deserved but it has been given to me, and I live in a country which is so beautiful and which I love so much and where we have not had any wars in my time. The old people remember the war and what a difference that was and not many hours away the war is raging and we live in this big, beautiful country, that is part of my satisfaction, and I must also say my family, they are so dear to me and I am such a lucky person, I have some ... really, I have many, many friends and some really good friends and the person I'm talking to now is one of my best friends.*

The paths of life that this Norwegian has followed lead back to the ancestral homeland but the essential ingredients of the professional life have echoed this destination. In her work she has consistently argued for the values and visions of her ancestors. Her professional voice has echoed these ancestral voices. Her concern has always been to give voice to the concerns and stories of the marginalized, rural people she came from. Her work is known throughout Norway for its emphasis on social justice and narrative enquiry. In defining her paths of life and her life themes she has harmonized her personal dreams with her professional visions. In this way the life theme serves to integrate the journey to selfhood with the workplace and professional aspirations that she consistently embraces and works for. She refers to this path of life she has followed as a long journey:

Ivor: *So what was the journey for? What did that represent in your pursuit of your dream and your…?*
FN: *What the journey was for? Well … along the journey which was sometimes a difficult journey, I learnt more and more and what I learnt and which is so special is that I learnt most from the hard times and as you know I have a belief in there is somebody watching me and taking care of me, I believe in God, and I like to say and I feel it that those hard times in my life, for instance, when I got really ill, they were … they were blessings, they turned out to be blessings, because I survived and I came out as a more grateful and stronger person and I can now relate to other people who are in pain and see that pain and understand that. So very difficult things that has happened to me as a child and as a young person and difficulties at work, I can see I have learned something along the journey and on the journey that I could not be at peace at the same time as I am today if my days had only been happiness and no problems, so I think that's part of it, and I have lots of … and the stories, the journey has been, I see it clearer and clearer by telling stories, and some of the stories could be lies rather than real factual stories, but I am not able to and I resist to discriminate between fiction and fact because I think, oh well, life is in a way dreamlike, it is somewhere between dream and reality and we'll always be on that*

border between ... I like to cross borders both in my proper life and in my existential life, and these stories that have been told, years and years, especially one important story in my life, I'm telling it every day. I understand more of it now, I see it more as a story, and I'm not absolutely sure if everything is true. But to me I want it to be true, it's my storyline, and in a way if I left that storyline I think I ... some people would say to me you could have a better a better life if you, that story, it's doing too much harm to you, it's giving you too much, I don't think so. I think people build the stories they need. But there are stories that can be and should be changed and I know they work with that in therapy, they use narrative therapy, and they ask people to say, for instance, there's questions like, which is the most important part of your story now? Why is that so and what is that person saying to you and what do you answer? So I know about these things, so I am talking to myself sometimes about ... perhaps I could rewrite that story and I could have a better life. Some story telling both as a part of education and research and most of all existential. McIntyre he says, man is a storytelling animal. I wouldn't say I was an animal, I love animals, but I'm something else, but I'm a compulsory storyteller. So that's my conclusion after this thing, the journey through stories. The travel self goes through stories. If you remember my little very humble paper I start by quoting a Norwegian American writer, and it's a wonderful sentence: stories are blood running through a body, paths of a life. So the path of my life has done two, three stories and I can still feel the blood running though my body when I listen to stories and I read a story and that's not all, when I tell my own story, my own story.

Ivor: *So is it possible to imagine a sense of wellbeing without this narrative story capacity to you?*

FN: *No. I would say no. I have discovered how important it is.*

Ivor: *So, just to finish, can you imagine a life, wellbeing of a life without the journey being essentially a story?*

FN: *No, I don't think so.*

We see how a central motif of life as a narrative journey is associated with 'the act of composing a self'. The life theme that is chosen for the journey is worked on and modified throughout the life course but provides a spine, what the life story teller calls 'a path of life'. In this chapter, we look at how life themes or paths of life are discerned, delineated and then lived. In this sense the chosen life theme holds together the improvisational act of living and composing a self.

The salience of life themes relates to a question we have raised earlier in the book. This is the question of whether people have multiple, spontaneous notions of selfhood or whether there is an ongoing search for coherence and thematic continuity. The notion of a life theme certainly places itself at the coherence-seeking end of the spectrum of narrative behaviour. The assumption behind life themes is that the storyteller's actions over time play out and reflect a unique theme which is contextualized within a wider historical background of wider theoretical coherence. An instance of a life theme that was common in past decades was that of the 'scholarship boy' or 'scholarship girl'. Each person adopting this life theme was part of a wider period of historical possibility which allowed social mobility and scholarship roots to have prominence in people's lives. In the current period such stories may be much more difficult to mobilize and composing the self in this way may be more difficult. This is the kind of interaction between historical context and composing the self which the life history method seeks to elucidate.

Contemporary psychological study and investigation focuses a good deal on holistic psychologies that aim to elucidate the continuity in a person's life which results from the creative and coherent structuring of goals and objectives during the life course.

The contemporary focus of some psychology and indeed sociology on coherent life themes is not new in these descriptions. The life history work of the Chicago School dates back to the work of Thomas and Znaniecki, who explored life themes holistically (Thomas and Znaniecki, 1918). The period of the 1930s was an important time in the launch of such studies not just for Chicago Sociology but more generally. In 1938, H. A. Murray's book *Explorations in Personality* developed the notion of a unity- thema which Murray found evident in the case his stories prescribed (Murray, 1938). Gordon Allport wrote a pioneering study of 'The Use of Personal Documents in Psychological Science' (Allport, 1955, p. 40).

Erik Erikson developed new thematic concepts in the evolution of identity: showing in psychological terms how life themes evolve during the life course in association with evolving self-development (Erikson, 1975).

The work of Adler develops a unified notion of life themes, what he called *life style* (Adler, 1927). His work sought to illustrate how during the human life course people develop a set of unified goals and objectives. As in the case of the Norwegian woman, she recounted earlier the life goals may reflect a mix of factual and fictional desires, drives and dilemmas.

Csíkszentmihályi and Beattie have moved from Adler's stress on individual autonomous searching to also examine how in developing their life themes people 'live symbolic codes from their socio-cultural environment' (Csíkszentmihályi and Beattie, 1979, p. 47).

They define a life theme:

As the affective and cognitive representation of a problem or a set of problems, perceived or experienced either consciously or unconsciously, which constituted a fundamental source of psychic stress for a person during childhood, for which that person wished resolution above all else, and which thereby triggered adaptive efforts, resulting in an attempted identification of the perceived problem, which in turn formed the basis for a fundamental interpretation of reality and ways of dealing with that reality. (Csíkszentmihályi and Beattie, 1979, p. 48)

The development of an understanding of life themes was originally suggested by a longitudinal study of artists conducted by Getzels and Csíkszentmihályi (1976). This work:

156

Showed how artists used the medium of visual representation to help themselves discover, formulate, and resolve in symbolic form some central existential concerns which were causing intra-psychic stress. Creative artists tended to find inspiration in deeply felt personal experience, while less creative artists used culturally defined problems as sources of inspiration. (Csíkszentmihályi and Beattie, 1979, p. 48)

Csíkszentmihályi and Beattie collected life stories from a sample of 30 adults to explore the notion of life themes. Fifteen respondents were from highly successful, professional occupations: professors and physicians largely connected with the university. The other 15 were blue-collar workers: plumbers, policemen and steel workers. The reason for the division was to see if patterned and systematic differences could emerge in life themes between two groups holding a socio-economic class of origin constant. The two groups were matched as closely as possible in terms of background characteristics so as to cut down on independent variable.

The professional group tended to remember particular kinds of problems as significant in childhood: they mentioned isolation and marginality most often, followed by feelings of concern and anxiety about performance. The blue-collar respondents most often mentioned concrete problems of physical survival like hunger and poverty.

In practically every protocol obtained from the professional group, the same pattern emerges. The child or young man is confronted by deep stress and questions that threaten his psychic survival. At some point he gets an inkling that what disturbs him is part of a more general human problem. Often this recognition occurs with dramatic suddenness. Once the connection between the personal existential problem and the wider issues as established, a method towards its solution suggests itself. (Csíkszentmihályi and Beattie, 1979, p. 57)

The person has a lifetime's work cut out for him, although he is not always aware that his actions are related to the original problem.

> It would be carrying skepticism too far to doubt the memory of a leading ornithologist about his mother's death from cancer, or to doubt a foremost expert in military affairs when he recalls that his parents had to flee Europe because of their anti-war activities. (Csíkszentmihályi and Beattie, 1979, p. 58)

They also find a connecting thread in the life of the blue collar worker.

> In the first place, five of the blue collar workers end up working at jobs their fathers held. The remaining ten take jobs which give them a certain amount of material security and pride. In this sense their lives become meaningful because their work activity is a solution to the issues of survival and personal worth. (Csíkszentmihályi and Beattie, 1979, p. 55)

Csíkszentmihályi and Beattie see this as a major distinction between the blue-collar workers and the professional workers:

> The work of the blue collar respondents is *external* to them, while the work of professionals is *essential* in that it is an integral part of a life theme which the person has discovered and formulated on his own. (Csíkszentmihályi and Beattie, 1979, pp. 55–6)

The integral nature of the life theme then is where the person's internal definitions of meaning and purpose are integrated with their external process, role and presentation. These internal definitions we call 'internal affairs' and the external realization of these in the outside world we refer to as 'external relations'. The link between the internal zone, and the external zone, is vitally important for our understanding of critical pedagogy and learning. Carl Rodgers has ruminated on the way messages from the internal zone work their way into the external world in the particular case of a writer:

> It seems to me that I am still inside – the shy boy who found communication very difficult in interpersonal situations; who wrote love letters which were more eloquent than his direct expressions of love; who expressed himself freely in high school themes, but felt himself too 'odd' to say the same things in class. That boy is still very much part of me. Writing is my way of communicating with a world to which, in a very real sense, I feel I don't quite belong. I wish very much to be understood, but I don't expect to be. Writing is the message I seal in the bottle and cast into the sea. My astonishment is that people on an enormous number of beaches – psychological and geo-graphical- have messages speak to them. So I continue to write. (Kirschenbauum and Henderson, 1985)

The importance of internal narrative activity and associated external relations can be evidenced in many biographies and cultural productions. For instance, the recent biography of Robert Oppenheimer speaks of him as failing to integrate his story or develop a coherent identity.

His biographer talks about his identity as a set of 'shards' (Monk, 2012, p. 3) of singular intensity and genius but these 'shards' were never moulded into a coherent pattern. He spent a great deal of time reflecting on these matters and trying to develop an over-arching 'theory of context'. In understanding his Jewishness his friend, Rabi, argued 'if he had studied the Malamud rather than Sanskrit… it would have given him a better sense of himself' (Shapin, 2012). In fact his life reminds us of the fate of Nora in Ibsen's play 'The Dolls' House': 'She shows you a woman who is coming to realize that she does not know who she is and has disintegrated into a jangle of performing selves' (Taylor, 2012).

Certainly Oppenhiemer came to see the importance of the search for unity and coherence. He 'thought this brother had problems because he overestimated the inconstancy and incoherence of personal life'.

He concludes: 'There is, there should be, and in mature people there comes more and more to be a certain unity, which makes it possible to recognise a man in his most diverse operations, a kind of personal stamp' (Shapin, 2012).

Oppenheimer however never successfully found 'a certain unity' – his internal affairs remained unresolved.

These failed episodes in the internal affairs translate then into major problems of external relations. The development of life themes and of associated 'theories of context' provides an avenue for the exploration in integration and harmonization of these internal and external zones.

Oppenheimer's case is a particularly interesting example of a man seeking 'coherence' and a certain 'unity' by working out the problem of his internal affairs through a brilliant career lived in the external zone. The impulse to do important work was very clearly rooted in his internal dilemmas but his work life itself presented so many challenges that the hoped for integration never took place: 'He never figures out himself and therefore his life was one long painful and ultimately unsuccessful experiment in personal identity' (Monk, 2012, p. 3).

In Oppenheimer's case, Isidor Rabi says he was 'a man put together of many bright shining splinters' who 'never got to be an integrated personality'. 'You carried on a charade with him. He lived a charade' (Monk, 2012, p. 3). Here we see how these internal affairs provide, or in this case do not provide, a unifying internal theme and associated external relations which allow an integration and harmonization of life themes.

The crucial point to recognize here is the relationship between internal affairs and external relationships and the way the psychodynamic needs which originate in the personal zone are carried over into a 'life theme' which is in many ways consonant and asymmetric and can help resolve dilemmas faced at both the internal and external levels. This is what is meant by a 'life theme' and it is an important part of the process of narrative construction.

For instance, in recent life history interviews we have conducted, one very common theme has emerged in analysing people's life narratives. In an early phase of life there are traumatic incidents. Most commonly these are connected to the abuse of chronic social disadvantage. This experience, especially when it involves an abusive parent, is inevitably a critical incident in the person's development.

We have found that one very common 'life theme' is the attempt to heal this psychic wound by undertaking public service with disadvantaged people. This may mean a career in social work, a brain injury clinic, general medical practice or working in schools in areas of disadvantage and deprivation. In our interviews the life story tellers often acknowledge the primacy of their own needs in the early phase of their public service: 'I know that it is part of healing my own wounds of dealing with my past'. It can indeed, in spite of the creditable public service undertaken, lead to a sense of guilt, 'I am healing, healing my own wounds at the expense of other people's suffering'.

In later stages the primacy of need can shift as psychic healing takes place in the act of public service and the ongoing process of narrative reconstruction and reflection. In the more elaborated cases this can lead onto a stage where the primacy of need shifts substantially to the needs of the clients. The original intentions behind the life theme therefore moderate and more fully engaged social exchanges and encounters become the norm. The interrogation of the life theme becomes a major undertaking in the person's narrative work. This is the point where learning and pedagogy move into a new threshold of possibility.

We have often found in our research that sometimes maybe, at a later stage in life, the original tight link between internal psycho-dynamic experience and external relations and the external production of a macro narrative becomes more loosely coupled. To put it precisely the life theme becomes autonomous. Since, unlike in the earlier stage many of the dilemmas which initiate the narrative activity have been suspended, resolved or put in abeyance, the relationship now between internal affairs and external relationships is essentially renegotiated. This would take the form of following a life project like social justice, not because of its internal promise but because of its own intrinsic validity. Likewise the ongoing internal monologue has less to do with resolving early psycho-dynamic dilemmas than the ongoing clarification and modification of the life story.

In terms of the pedagogic encounter that sits at the heart of narrative pedagogy, this distinction between stages is enormously important. In the first stage the internal and external are tightly coupled; in the second stage they are much more autonomous and therefore their relationship is renegotiated. Since the pedagogic exchange is itself a site for the reconstruction of knowledge, this is a very important way of understanding these things. Most importantly of all though, it throws into high relief the different relationship to a theory of context in stage one to stage two. In stage one the theory of context is trying to clarify the relationship between the internal narrative and its underpinning psycho-dynamic requirements and the construction of a macro narrative which binds some of these life themes together and delineates certain courses of action (whilst at the same time of course involving a reconstruction knowledge); in stage two the theory of context that is being developed is of another order altogether. This time the theory of context includes an understanding of the stage one struggles but seeks to delineate a far more autonomous relationship. This is contextual understanding of a much higher order and it links with our initial five-stage model in narrative pedagogy as the person moves from initial narration, collaboration and location through to integration and wisdom. The culmination of stage two equates to integration and wisdom, but its postulates go beyond that – they also include, because of the differentiation in the theory of context, a different kind of reconstruction of knowledge and a different order in the delineation of courses of action.

The idea behind the grandiose term 'a theory of context' is essentially to find strategies to figure out 'who we are' and how that fits with the opportunities and constraints of our social location in time and space. In Marxist terms 'we make a history but not in circumstances of our own choosing'. The theory of context looks both at our 'composing of a self', at not just an internal task but as a way of finding a place of understanding and possibility in the world. We seek not just to know who we are but how we may act and contribute in the world as the person we are.

LIFE THEMES AND PEDAGOGY

In *Narrative Pedagogy* we looked at this process of exploration, this 'experiment in identity' which in a life could be helped along by the pedagogic collaboration (Goodson and Gill, 2010). Here we need to be reminded of what Freire says about this pedagogic relationship: 'a careful analysis of the teacher-student relationship at any level inside or outside the school reveals its fundamentally *narrative character*' (Freire, 1972, p. 52).

Critical pedagogy should aim to facilitate the exploration of our social context, the site of our identity project. We believe that once we have 'narrated' our story a collaboration aiming at learning and pedagogy should lead to people 'locating' their narrative.

In collaboration the learners come to locate their own narrative in cultural and social time and space and develop thereby a 'theory of content'. Location provides people with a sense of understanding as to why they as individuals tell their story in this way at this moment. We put it this way, 'location involves a process of coming to know the importance of time and social forces as they impinge on a person's stories'. We therefore help people interrogate not just internal affairs but external relations.

We say:

> in a sense the individual cannot fully know what is 'personal'. What has been refracted until he/she comes to understand their stories' historical and social locations. Location then is a highly pedagogic process with collaboration, provides a variety of pedagogic levers. (Goodson and Gill, 2010, p. 128)

In terms of what was earlier called the experiment in personal identity which is our life, the development of a theory of context helps in exploring the relationship between external relations. We saw how a 'life theme' seeks to harmonize this exploration.

Moreover, we saw how in some cases this leads to an amelioration of early personal dilemmas through external courses of action. This amelioration can lead to a development of more autonomous courses of action.

This phase of the life theme comes close to the notion of 'a certain unity' which Oppenheimer so coveted. In developing a theory of context the person can come to feel a sense of wholeness and unity, a new kind of social imagination and holistic vision; although earlier we talked about stages of life theme, in fact this process is not a stage theory or hierarchical but rather an endless spiral of learning and pedagogy. Our sense is that the process of 'location', theorizing and interrogation are points at which critical pedagogy and learning can operate transformatively. Transformative in that they lead us towards living the 'examined life'. But such integration and wisdom is a point in the journey. In the external world, new conditions and transitions emerge and the spiral of learning and pedagogy begins again.

CRITICAL NARRATIVE IN DIVERSE
LEARNING CONTEXTS

CHAPTER 7

From Demonizing to Humanizing: Transforming Memories of Violence to Stories of Peace

Scherto Gill

When I was first invited to a dialogue meeting, I was told that some Muslims would be there and so I'd prepared a very long list of grievances. When my turn came to speak I took out the list but as I read it everyone just smiled. Later a Muslim explained he had brought an even longer list.

Jean-Michel, ex-combatant in Lebanese War (1975–90)

INTRODUCTION

In this book, we propose that memories and narratives are important avenues for the individual to reconsolidate identity, make sense of life, experience emotional wellness and identify one's mission, purpose and actions in the world. Thus the book also supports the arguments put forward by many scholars working in conflict prevention and peace-building that narrative sharing and exchanges of memories can seek to transform an individual's anger and resentment into the ability to live in dignity, harmony and peace with others.[1]

But how can those who have lived through violence and conflict tell the stories that are almost untellable? How do they recall the memories of violence? Yet memories and stories of traumas are an important part of being a person. The question is therefore: 'How do people piece their lives together again if some of pieces cannot be looked at in the light of day?' These pieces are often memories that are so painful or shameful and infused with so much grief or humiliation that they cannot be recalled. Many survivors of wars and traumas choose to forget part of their identity because that part of their story can destroy them and those they had loved. Equally, those involved in that era of darkness might need to forget who they were in the past in order to avoid being brought down in the present. This is an important dilemma – if one cannot tell the stories of one's own life across time, one is dangling in the present, losing a sense of continuity and wholeness. Without these pieces, one's sense of coherence can be hugely affected, which in turn has an impact on living in the now as well as delineating a course of actions in the future.

In this chapter, we reflect on the narrative and storying process of two ex-combatants (a Christian and a Muslim) who fought in opposition during the Lebanese civil war (1975 to 1990). Their ongoing process of narrative sharing has resulted in their arriving at a place where they decided to forgive and embrace each other as brothers. This can be considered the first step towards breaking cycles of violence.

The focus of the chapter is on exploring what happens when two people come together to listen to each other's narratives, even when such narratives are about conflict with, hatred of and pain caused by the other. As we shall see, some stories were so embedded in a (remote) past that they formed the myths that determine

---

[1] We will also explore this topic in the next chapter.

the identity of a community or a people. Other stories were echoes of memories of previous generations, which were integrated in the community's social and cultural fabric and became the key commanding voices guiding individuals' choices and actions at times of threat and fear. Thus the individuals involved seemed to labour in webs that were spun long before their time, and to act unconsciously on some inherited impulses.

So the question becomes: Who is the teller of our stories?

NARRATIVE AND MEMORIES IN CONFLICT AND IN PEACE-BUILDING

Narrative seems to have two faces – on the one hand, in divided societies in conflict, it is often a pivotal means that people use to demonize the Other and create and maintain rifts between communities and peoples; on the other hand, it can be a major avenue for developing empathy, forgiveness and compassion, which serve as the basis for relationship building and peace.

Currently, theories from the fields of political science, sociology and social psychology suggest that violent conflict between groups and communities should best be understood as 'violent culminations of the "identity conflict"' (Aiken, 2008, p. 10), an expression of collective antagonism, of putting oneself against another within societies with multiple ethnic, religious and cultural groups. Systematic discrimination, oppression and social injustice, often caused by the existence of significant cleavages between two or more groups where trust, communication and reciprocity are declining, create the possibility for inter-group conflict (Aiken, 2008). Aiken further posits that when such a rift happens within a society, groups often resolve to frame the actions and beliefs of the Other as villainous, and may therefore subsequently regard all members of this enemy group as outside the normative boundaries, or the 'moral order' of society. This is a process of demonizing (see also Staub, 1989; Volkan, 2006).

An important approach to enemy construction and demonizing the Other in the context of conflict within a divided society is the use of collective memories and myths. Generally speaking, collective memories can create a socially constructed narrative that may have some basis in the actual events but is essentially biased, selective and distorted in order to meet society's present needs (Bar-Tal, 2000). A myth is often a story that has gained wider acceptance and is deemed sacred for its ability to communicate a fundamental 'truth' about the life of a community or a people (Chaitin, 2003). Collective memories and myths can have profound influences, especially when they are integrated in the collective identity by individuals, groups, social institutions and society at large. This is because they often contain archetypal symbols that portray and determine the origins and destinies of a people. These symbols can further shape the 'truth' about a society and underpin a society's psychosocial and political dynamics, cosmology and even metaphysics. In this sense, myths can capture the most fundamental concerns and values of a people, and help preserve their integrity (see Van Evera, 1994).

Collective memories and myths can give rise to meanings and allow people to bridge events in history and develop roles for themselves as actors, tellers and listeners of tales. However, in conflict situations, myths can be used for self-glorification, self-righteousness, victimization or Other-denigration in order to justify one people's violence against another. In these situations, myths can be dangerous and damaging, especially when they are socialized and institutionalized to shape a society's historical 'truths'. As Aiken concludes:

The use of violence to purge society of the enemy other is legitimized and transmitted to successive generations by means of stories, communal memories, and myths that continue

170

to demonize the enemy group and validate its persecution. Ultimately, societies can become trapped within intractable cycles of violence that perpetuate reciprocal acts of violence among communal groups. (Aiken, 2008, p. 10)

Conversely, as we shall see in Chapter 9, one of the ways in which people understand their world and their experiences within it is through the 'narrative mode' of thought, which is concerned with human wants, needs and goals (Bruner, 1986). The narrative mode deals with the dynamics of human intentions, and when in this mode, we seek to explain events by looking at how human actors (including ourselves) strive to do things over time. As we comprehend these actions, we see what obstacles were encountered and which intentions were realized or frustrated.

Telling one's story, through oral or written means, has been shown to be a key experience for those who have undergone severe social trauma, such as violence during a civil war. Whilst the storytelling of their traumatic past does not always have a healing effect for the survivors, it opens up channels of thoughts, feelings and communication that have often been closed for years. Having the opportunity to recount one's traumatic past to an empathic listener can often lead to the telling of deeply personal stories that may previously have been 'forgotten' or 'denied'. This offers an important opportunity to examine the different types of story and how they impact the way we frame the Other. This is essentially a humanizing process.

Next, we examine the role of myths in determining large-group identity (Volkan, 2006) and its relationship to massive traumas experienced at the hand of the Other. We consider how it raises substantial barriers to, but also creates opportunities for, peaceful coexistence between former enemies. This is approached in the light of a narrative learning process of two ex-fighters.

Narrative as demonizing myths

There is a reciprocal relationship between myths, identity and mass atrocity. As we have seen, when conflicts escalate towards violence, communities and groups select those narratives and memories which are useful in demonizing and dehumanizing the Other and thus preparing the ground for wars and mass atrocity against the Other. Furthermore, conflict can result in a total separation between different groups and this separation is additionally expressed through their respective narratives, rituals and myths. These can effectively compress the present into the past and demobilize the future (Volkan, 2006).

Research into the Palestinian and Israeli conflict has identi-fied that the resultant victimhood (as the dominant identity) was originally based on solid individual and collective experiences gained during violent periods. These experiences became a powerful source of identity. They gradually entered the collec-tive memory and then became part of tribal or community myths which were transmitted from one generation to the next through memoirs, stories of family members and ancestors, school books and national symbolic acts and festivals. These narratives have prevented people from reaching beyond their own ethnocentric thinking. In this way, collective memories and myths can con-tinue to demonize the Other, sustaining an ongoing barrier to peaceful coexistence (Bar-On and Sarsar, 2004).

Visible or invisible 'enemies' who have violated a group and thus caused pain and suffering are then categorized and labelled as 'evil', and any actions by the enemy group are considered as evil intentioned. The enemy categorization also imposes a spe-cial status on all members of the group – they are not human. Subsuming distinct individuals into a broad category allows peo-ple from outside to react to the group, forgetting the individual human beings who comprise it.

Often, these divisions are marked by seemingly intransmutable factors of communal identity, such as ethnicity, religion, language or nationality. In this way, individuals' identities collapse into a singular group-identity, social, linguistic, ethnic, religious, racial or whatever else. In times of social and political imbalance, such singular group-identity also includes labels such as the victim, the oppressed, thus preparing the group for potential violence against other groups who are assigned a singular identity of the oppressor or the aggressor. Some have argued that such identity formation through social categorization is fundamental for conflict between groups, and for justifying killing on a larger scale (Volkan, 1996).

As we have seen, a key and effective way to dehumanize the Other is through the narrative of victimhood, pain and suffering as well as the social stigma of deprivation, oppression and disenfranchizing. The more distant the Other is from oneself and one's own community, the easier it is to dehumanize them, and ultimately the dehumanization of the Other leads to the breakdown and corruption of the moral order of society, whereby violence becomes part of a group's responsibility to defend against evil and crime (Staub, 1989).

The dehumanization of the Other further prevents any meaningful social interaction or relationships between the opposing groups. In this way, the enemies are solidly placed outside the moral bounds governing one's own community. According to Aiken (2008), without social contact, the opposing groups would cease to recognize a shared humanity between them. In most cases, such as those illustrated by Bar-On and Sarsar (2004), there is a mutual process of Othering – enemy construction and victimhood construction where both sides see the other as the enemy and themselves as the victim. Mack (1990) terms this a ceaseless cycle of mutual victimization

in which victim identity drives the cycles of violence passed on from one generation to another, bolstered by stories and myths of atrocities committed by the other people, and by heroic acts committed in defence ... by one's own. (Mack, 1990, p. 25)

However, the narrative process of dehumanization does not end with the ceasefire or overt violence. Unless such narratives are shifted and transformed, the same myths will continue to widen and deepen the social divides amongst communal groups formerly in conflict. The undercurrent that perpetuates the violence can be protracted. The memories and the myths of violence may remain selective, exclusive and egocentric, reinstating the identity of victimhood and enemy. Divided societies can thus be trapped in cycles of violence and individuals caught between vengeance and forgiveness. This state prevents the development of social relationships or trust between the antagonistic groups. Moreover, a lack of political and social resolution exacerbates the social strife and division. Society is constantly under threat of another outbreak of violence (see Colletta and Cullen, 2002).

Over time, these narratives will become part of the group's heritage and even characterize its culture. Some of the narratives are so deeply embedded that people who pass them on are no longer able to recognize their roots, as they live them out unconsciously.

We can indeed become our stories.

Narrative to expose and cut through myths

Thus far, we have taken a narrow look at how narratives and myths can serve as carriers of a group's history and identity, contextualizing the collective moral choices and constructing a desired 'moral order', and thereby using a singular group-identity (i.e. that of the victim) to dehumanize the other. However, Rosland (2009) points out that, since victimhood involves a representation of one's experience that elevates certain values and moral imperatives over others, there inevitably exists a paradox that leads to complexity, especially when considering victimhood in the light of agency.

First of all, the construction of victimhood involves an act of humanization: when the stories of the victims are told, the violence is contextualized and also given a human face. When placed

174

within the experience of a particular group or collective, these narratives can give rise to value and meaning, both for the victims and for the perpetrators (as seen from the victims' point of view). On the other hand, owing to the pain involved, the violence and suffering are often mutual, which makes it almost impossible for members of any group to empathize the suffering of the Other. This can therefore render the notion of victimhood paradoxical.

Second, there is the paradox of remembering (Smyth, 1998). In many divided societies, after the overt conflict, many people could not make a choice between remembering and forgetting. Often, one group of people would condemn another group for their deliberate nostalgia; and the other group would point out that remembering can be too much a burden for the community to move on. In either case, Smyth suggests that choice is often the 'privilege of those who are relatively untouched' by the war.

Third, the narrative of victimhood has a paradoxical moral order – it tends to justify one kind of violation against another. Therefore, despite the possibility of humanizing the victim through narratives of victimhood, it is not always possible to moralize the act of violence unless through an overt bias. Irrespective of how the stories are told, there exists a danger of moral disorder. This is partly due to the fact that the experience of war and mass violence implies a loss of conceptual and epistemological framework, resulting in moral disorder in the narratives (Löfving and Macek, 2000).

In many societies suffering from violence and division, the political regime is often plagued by corruption and lack of social justice. For instance, Bar-Tal (2003) examines the apartheid regime in South Africa and points out that the moral disequilibrium was codified and protected in the political and legal framework at the time, so that:

the social system provides the rationales or justifications for the violence, system's organizations train the individuals to carry

175

out violent acts, and social mechanisms and institutions glorify the violent confrontations. (Bar-Tal, 2003, p. 79)

Thus in the approach of the Truth and Reconciliation Commission (TRC) to truth telling, narratives worked to place individuals' and groups' experience within a broader social and political framework, allowing the victims, bystanders and perpetrators to recognize together the broad system of apartheid as a crime against humanity (Aiken, 2008). Such narratives, when met by empathetic and compassionate listening, not only acknowledge the pain and suffering of the victim, but also allow all parties involved to begin to see the complexity of violence and examine their respective responsibilities in it. Instead of the oversimplified approach of assigning a punishment to the perpetrators, a narrative approach may offer an opportunity for all to reflect on the moral disorder, the causes and deeper roots that underlie the cycles of violence. In this book, we see this as a critical narrative approach which has profound pedagogical implications in the process of human becoming.

Narrative is a key to peace-building from a retributive perspective, recognizing the necessity of addressing and readdressing the destructive social political forces that allowed the violation of humanity in the first place (Rotberg and Thompson, 2000).

From demonizing to humanizing

The TRC in South Africa and other parts of the world is essentially a humanizing process, as it allows those who are labelled 'victims' and 'perpetrators' to get rid of the labels and become persons in their own right. Face-to-face meeting itself is extraordinary, as for most of those involved in violence it is often the first time that they have their 'enemy' so closely. The recognition that the enemy is actually a person is often a powerful start.

When individuals' stories are being exchanged, they put the flesh-and-blood human being over the 'evil' image of the mythical and distant 'demon' (Moses, 1991; Staub, 1989). The pain and suffering being shared by the members of one group are often echoed by the pain and suffering of those in the other group. Those involved are therefore encouraged to learn to contain the stories of the Other, to hear their pain and to legitimize their narratives, whilst not negating their own pain and stories. This is a process of mutual telling, mutual listening and mutual acknowledging – a deeply humanizing process. Stories can allow individuals to grieve for themselves and for the Other, especially those narratives about the suffering of the women – wives and mothers – and the children. Through mutual telling, a shared history can gradually emerge, and therefore shared humanity and responsibilities.

Whilst the individuals initiate a shift in their perceptions of the Other, they also re-examine the Other's 'enemy' identity and begin to recognize that the Other is in fact more human than they assumed (Northrup, 1989). This often leads to the thawing of the frozen boundaries between the different communities, and as the distance between the individuals shifts in the narrative and dialogic exchange. Thus the self and the Other enter a reciprocal relationship, which further allows the growth of empathy and compassion.

Gobodo-Madikizela (2009) suggests that, in the truth-telling encounter, there are three levels of witnessing, each contributing to the humanizing process. The first is witnessing at the language level – the use of words to retell the stories of pain. The second is witnessing the trauma at an internal level, which is critical because 'the problem of trauma re-enactment occurs at a deeply unconscious level' (Gobodo-Madikizela, 2009, p. 161). She was particularly concerned that, without such witnessing, these traumas can be passed on unconsciously to other generations as internally unfinished affairs, and become trans-generational trauma. The third level of witnessing is at the level of listening – listening to and hearing the perpetrators, whose narratives can show remorse and their own internal turmoil, shame and guilt for their own actions. Through the multiple levels of witnessing:

> victims and perpetrators speak to each other and bear witness to the stories they bring from all levels of their experience of the past: the stories which find expression through words, and those which are inexpressible. In this sense then, the 'witnessing dance' on a public stage binds victims and perpetrators together in the act of bearing witness, through speech and through the very subtle elements of intersubjectivity in their encounter. (Gobodo-Madikizela, 2009, p. 162)

In South Africa, it was possible to identify victims and perpetrators and those in between. However, in most societies, it may not be so easy to draw boundaries between the different groups. More often, people can be victims and aggressors at the same time, and in fact, everyone falls victim one way or another, including the coming generations.

TRANSFORMING MEMORIES OF VIOLENCE TO STORIES OF PEACE

So it is possible for those who were involved in war and in violence to get together and tell and listen to each other's experiences and come to some sense of them. In this space I will discuss specific interactions in which we tried to understand the narrative process involved. We were particularly interested in the following questions: What is the role of narrative exchange in relationship building? What insights can be drawn from the notion of humanization in order to understand the critical narrative processes when the interlocutors are victim and perpetrator at the same time? How do they deploy narratives of their respective experiences as a way to construct a vision/story of the future? What can we learn from these encounters in order to design educational activities?

Before we introduce the two interlocutors, let us take a quick look at the context within which these encounters and exchanges took place.

Lebanon went through a recent civil war (1975 to 1990) that led to the 'complete and total collapse of all the fields of life' (Hazzouri, 2011, p. 10). Compounded by recent foreign invasions and regional unrest, the country continues to experience conflicts and turmoil due to multiple causes, political, security-related, social or economic, and religious. The ongoing conflict further inflicts psychological wounds and undermines social relationships, as well as individuals' sense of belonging to the society.

In 1991, Lebanon passed a General Amnesty Law which granted amnesty for all politically motivated war crimes and crimes against humanity committed during the 1970s and the 1980s with a few exceptions. This has allowed all ex-combatants in the militias to take no responsibility for the bloody violence in the country.

In addition, sectarianism deepened by the wars became one of the major obstacles to solidarity and human relationship building within society. Instead, group-identity that once brought the communities to war continues to be prominent, supplemented by education, enculturation and socialization, thus becoming a key ingredient of divisiveness (Baalbacki, 2007). There remains an overhanging threat of future violence combined with an uneasy relationship to the violence of the past. The strong sectarian and social identities that made the wars psychologically possible are still active and transmuting, thereby further reducing trust and heightening fears. As a result, there is no shared aspiration or societal consensus regarding how society can move forward.

Khalaf (2011) observes that many young people have chosen to desensitize themselves to a painful legacy of violence and the hostile 'landscape' in which they are negotiating for political and social engagement, public discourse and participatory democracy. She suggests that hidden in such distancing is a desperate longing to share and to be heard in a country dangling in social, political and economic uncertainty.

Therefore, it is necessary to address and heal the deeper roots of conflict, so that Lebanese society can rebuild itself through a positive human relationship and a political culture of reconciliation.

In such a context, Jean-Michel and Tariq met in 2011 for long conversations that lasted for a few days. Jean-Michel and Tariq both fought for the militias during the Lebanese Civil War. Jean-Michel is a Christian and Tariq a Muslim. They were at the ages of 19 and 20, respectively, when the war broke out and when they became actively involved. Jean-Michel was in charge of intelligence, interrogating captives and deciding their fates after the interrogation. Tariq was a leader in the field of fighting and took part in many battles himself. They both are amongst the very few individuals who have publicly spoken about their remorse and asked forgiveness from those whose lives had been sabotaged by the war and by their involvement. This was not the first time they had spoken to each other about the atrocity of the war, but my focus was to understand how they tell and listen to each other and how this narrative process enables them to understand things differently.

Here we share some of the key moments in their interactions.

Sharing the myths about the Other – 'we were pre-conditioned to go to war'

Recalling the myths about the Other was the starting point for both men to explain their reasons for fighting. They were growing up in their respective communities, having little contact with people from the other community.

In Jean-Michel's school, there were a few Muslims, but 'they were not "real" Muslims, they were Christianised Muslims because they were like us, they did not seem different, they did not act different', he says.

Similarly, Tariq did not know any Christians when growing up in a closed Muslim community in Beirut. Both men were taught that the Other were 'dirty', 'having a strange way to pray', 'intending to control the country', 'having all the privileges' and 'denying our rights to live'.

Some of the myths entered into the children's games. For instance, when Tariq was young, the children would play a game where they got together and broke the cross. Later, Tariq found out that the game was aimed at destroying the Christian symbol, as they were told that Christians did not worship God, but only worshipped the wooden cross.

Other myths were in their forebears' tales and legends. Tariq recalls how he drew his spirit from his ancestral legacies:

> I grew up listening to the heroic stories about my ancestors and how they fought in the Turkish army, and how they fought before the Turkish army with the Arabs when they came, during the Islamic war in the area here. I was told that my family is descended from an ancient Arab family that came with the Prophet Mohammed and we fought the Crusaders during the Crusaders era when hundreds of my family were killed. I was told that we are the chosen people. These stories were the basis of my spirit, our spirit.

Tariq had just turned 19 when the fight between the Christians and Muslims started. His father urged him to take up a gun and not to 'stay at home like a girl'.

> We all hated Christians for their evils and their plans to control. Now my father sent me out with my older brothers and cousins to stand up to our rights to exist. I was still young, I was just a student, I wasn't violent, but I was given this responsibility. So I said to myself – I must defend my family, my street, my community. I must defend our own goodness.

181

Hearing Tariq's explanation of the myths and his motivation to fight, Jean-Michel eagerly offered his version:

> For me, the war didn't start on April 13, 1975. It started when I was five-years-old. How come? This was when I first heard jokes about Abdul Hammed. All the stories about him were that this man is uneducated, only thinks of sex, and is violent as he carries a baton or stick. He is big, vulgar, and all that. My parents were not extremists and they were very quiet people. But when this man appears twice a year on TV during Muslim feasts and gives a speech, my parents would ask us all to spit on the television. There are many more similar stories. In fact, for me, the last symptom of the war is the bullet. And they made me. Just like you, Tariq, we were prepared, pre-conditioned to go to war.

Almost echoing Tariq's story, Jean-Michel was motivated by the need to protect and defend his own people from being eliminated by the other:

> Never thought I would harm any creature, let alone a human being, but [in 1975] I dropped university and joined the militia without hesitation. The enemy was so evil and the threat was so big that I felt this strong sense of responsibility to fight for my people and defend my community. So I will carry a gun, I will fight and I will kill because I believe that the Other is evil. Although I had met a few Muslims in school, I believed 'real' Muslims to be evil. I almost wanted them to be because if they were this way, I could be that way.

Both men realized how little they knew the Other; nevertheless, their hatred towards the Other had transformed them from a young person instantly into a 'fighter'. That was the effect of myths demonizing the Other – the word 'evil' was repeated by both men. There were some points in the conversation when they

182

could have been telling each other's story, such as when Jean-Michel cried out: 'This is what they don't understand, Tariq, you fought because you felt responsible for your people. And so did I'. Here they were acknowledging not only each other's myths but also each other's motivations.

Hearing the suffering of the Other

Whilst their myths and stories reinforced the Other as evil, the threat and the image of the enemy, the men at the same time used narratives to construct an image of their community as the 'victim'. Narratives humanizes themselves. There was a point in this part of the exchange when the two men started using the word 'we' to refer to some common experiences.

Shortly after Tariq joined the militia, he and his colleagues discovered that there was a site where quite a few Muslims had been killed. When they went into the village to inspect, Tariq found, amongst the dead, his best friend who was like a brother to him. Tariq, in shock, stayed with the dead body. The dead man, who was only just more than a boy, had been executed in a terrible way, but his eyes were open, still filled with horror. Tariq looked at them without moving and remained there for a long time. At the end, he swore to revenge his friend, and "pushed by the image of death" and the loss of his friend, other colleagues and their families, he became determined to fight in a most violent way.

Jean-Michel returned with a similar story of pain and horror, recalling the humiliation and fear endured by his mother and sister who were nearly killed at a checkpoint, and the atrocities he witnessed in which Christian villages were wiped out entirely, including women and children, and where in a few cases even animals did not escape the massacre.

This kind of exchange was a key to the men realizing that the suffering caused by the war was mutual, no one could escape and there was no winning, and all had lost something significant.

They both agreed: "We are victims and perpetrators at the same time". This acknowledgement further set the ground for them to develop an affectionate connection with one another.

Recounting the stories of violence

The myths and stories of pain and suffering set the scene for the two ex-combatants to recount their most difficult stories – the stories that they were compelled to tell because these were the stories that they had to live with every day – the stories of violence.

They can only tell these stories to each other, as there was so much violence, hatred and horror in them. And yet, telling, however painful and tormenting, has been a significant means for them to understand the extent of their dehumanization and how they had fought in such inhuman ways.

When they narrated the violence, they would first give an account of the event, followed by an analysis to show the extent of their hatred, their mindlessness, the loss of humanity they had experienced, driven by the conviction that the enemy was the demon, the devil. Whilst the majority of ex-fighters have kept silent about their actions during the war, this narrative exchange was a safe setting for the two combatants to share their respective stories.

Listening to each other's stories of violence gave them an opportunity to recognize the madness and absurdity of war, and the irrationality of violence. They began to see that the feeble moral ground on which they stood was situated within a myth where the Other was demonized as well as within a moral framework where oneself and one's own community were the victim and the Other and their community were the aggressor. Listening further allows them to feel the other person's remorse, the torture of having to live with regret and the shame at having committed such violent acts. In this round of narratives, both Jean-Michel and Tariq could hear the human being in each other, the human being whose heart is bleeding for his past acts. Here is an example; after recalling the killing of a Muslim leader, Jean-Michel says:

Somewhere deep in my heart there is injury that never ceases bleeding. He died once, but I die every time I think of him, think of each one of those whom I have ordered to be killed. And there are many of them…

Tariq had similar experience of shame, regret and remorse. He said that he hardly sleeps these days, and that most nights he would be going through in his mind, blow by blow, shot by shot, the images of the violence he had committed during the war. He had not smiled from his heart for years, he admits. He recognized that, entering the war as a teenager, he had been turned into a monster: "I didn't become a man, I became a fighter. A fighter wasn't a man, wasn't a human being".

Together they recognized that, as Jean-Michel puts it: "The war could never be won. If you did win, you are still lost. It is no one's gain, but our loss".

Questioning and placing the stories in a wider context

Jean-Michel said that questioning of things actually started during the war. A particular moment he recalled was during one of his religious confessions with a priest. The priest asked why he wanted to confess about the killing and told him that what he had been doing was right. This reaction from the priest came as a surprise to Jean-Michel. He found himself deep in a moral dilemma.

Through a joint effort, Tariq and Jean-Michel managed to depict a war that was more complicated and more absurd than they could recognize at the time. They realized that the war was not simply about Christians fighting Muslim enemies, and vice versa; instead it was far more complex and intricate. As they exchanged narratives, they were engaged in a critical conversation about the divisions within the Christians, within the Muslims, between the foreign forces and amongst other political powers.

During such discussions, the old myths started to lose their grip on them. They recalled their own moments of doubt – initially it was when they wanted to affirm that the Other was what they had assumed them to be. Both had sought opportunities to verify their conviction of the Other. Jean-Michel says:

> I discovered that the Muslim is not the way I have inherited him, neither the way I have distorted him ... For long years I made it my job to throw away anything positive about the Muslims, any articles, anything pro them, and only keep what is negative about them. And not only that, I also distributed negative stereotypes. So I was a negative dissimulation agent ... Now, when I dropped it all, I actually discovered a lot of very very beautiful things in the Muslims, and that is very important for me.

Interestingly, the men acknowledged what is so distinct about being a Christian or a Muslim, and their respective ways of being, but also realized that some of the fundamental values were not so different from each other after all. In this way, they need each other to complete the fuller picture about the truth. Jean-Michel tried to articulate this:

> I found out that the truth was also somewhere out there between them and me, because they had a part of the truth and I had a part of the truth and those who were up here also had part of the truth, so this means that somewhere, the truth is somewhere between all of us and I was surprised also to discover that there was not such huge differences between them and us. Of course it was obvious that we will never be the same, we will never be the same, I have a different culture from them, I have a different religion than them, etc. etc. We don't have to go out with a full agreement on everything, but at least we can understand what the other has to say.

186

Tariq went through a long process of what he called 're-education'.

> I wasn't able to meet a Christian and in myself he is the enemy
> and he is a killer and he is the devil. It is impossible to meet that
> person if you have this idea. So you have to rehabilitate your
> ideas. You have to rehabilitate the history which you got from
> your family, your society. I carried this particular history for
> thirty years, so I need some time ... But I had questions and they
> brought me to the Christian areas. I went just to see, to confirm
> those images I had of them: they were richer and wealthier
> because they were devilish. But I saw Christians who were poor,
> and who were just like us. I mean they are just people.

This was the beginning of speaking each other's lines in analysing
their history and the war. Tariq said:

> And if you notice, it is very important that you notice here,
> that we are of the same generation so we were exposed to the
> same [recent] history, the same influences, the same pressure,
> the same trauma of the war, but we are the result of [distant]
> history, from the Ottoman Empire era to the 1975 war. Our
> history created us as the fighters. But you must remember, the
> Jean-Michel you see in front of you is a real person and I have
> learned that he is a very kind person and the reason he was what
> he was is because he was someone else created by the history,
> not the person whom I am very proud of meeting, this second
> Jean-Michel. Same with the Tariq you see here, is a new Tariq.

Peace as the new moral imperative

The reaching out for one another was just a start for their actions.
Narrative provides a space within which one is able to develop and

clarify one's own moral commitment. This was apparent in the two men's exchanges.

Both Jean-Michel and Tariq talked about their remorse, their regret, their sorrows and pains at having to live with the scars of the war. They expressed explicit needs for forgiveness from those whom they had hurt during the war. At the same time, they sought actions not to undo, but to make a difference. They saw this as the sole mission of their continued existence. Tariq said:

> God wants this to happen [to go through the war] so that we have a role in this life. Maybe God put us in this experience and prepared the way for us in order to speak. I was assassinated once and I didn't get killed. Jean-Michel was also assassinated many times, but he didn't get killed either. Why? Maybe God want us to have this experience of being saved again. God gave us a mission, to speak about our experience…

Jean-Michel added:

> And you have to explain that you are doing it for the sake of the coming generations and that you don't want them to do the same things you did and this is the important issue. You said earlier that you took your children to see the demolition of Hilton. Why? You wanted them to know the ugliness of the war. One day after the war, my son came home after school. He told me that a friend of his was gesturing vomit when they passed a mosque. That frightened me because I saw myself as a child in these children. I said to myself: oh no, this will not happen again. I must do something.

Both men had asked forgiveness in public and now saw it as their mission to speak about the atrocity of the war, to make people become aware of those deeper roots of violence and to move forward together towards peace. Tariq said:

188

I am not just asking forgiveness from the Christians, or the villages we wiped out. I am also feeling sorry for Lebanon, our country together... If anyone would rewrite this history, it can only be written when we have one spirit and the story will become one from both sides.

Jean-Michel also talked about the need to be aware of our human identity, which is all and beyond all divides:

So this is the thing, not to fear that you are part of a community or a group. But at the same time, you should fear to be over and above all the communities and all the groups. I don't mean that I am better, but I have a consciousness that allows me to be all and beyond all at the same time.

From former enemies to an affectionate friendship, from a shared mission to a we-consciousness, through the narrative process, the two men start to develop a sense of solidarity, without compromising their individual identity. Only now, their identity is multi-dimensional instead of the identity of the victim and the other's identity is no longer the singular of the demon. What is also emerging here is a moral career where both men have shown care for the next generation and for their country together. This solidarity will guarantee a trusting relationship between people and hopefully between communities and groups. This relationship is the bridge to peace.

Peace starts with our becoming the tellers of our own stories.

In this book, narrative is considered as a human act, pertaining to all cultures. As the literature and the story of the two men's encounter illustrate, the narrative process can be a key to building constructive relationships between people and groups. The narrative process, as we have seen, is humanizing due to both the narrative content and the narrative space involved, which engages the self and the Other. When attended to with empathetic listening, narratives can be cognitively, emotionally and morally compelling. Both men realized that Other-denigrating myths and self-aggrandizing myths are sources of violence, whereas the honest recounting of one's lived experience can open the door to trust and human relationships.

Looking back, it would be fair to say that both men did not enter this narrative process straight after the war. There had been some preparation time so that they were ready for this kind of encounter, telling and listening. Nevertheless, we hope that the analysis of their narrative journey will be helpful in understanding the key ingredients in this complex process.

CONCLUSION

It is the humanity within us that compels us to listen empathetically, to show compassion, to forgive and to reach out to the Other in order to move towards a new moral imperative. The humanity embedded in the narrative of suffering and pain and our responsibility for the inhumanity of violence can serve as the basis for constructing we-consciousness, from where solidarity and affectionate connections can be established between people.

During this narrative journey, the interlocutors work together in order to construct new personal meanings from old pains and traumas, and turn division and violence into reconciliation and solidarity. The main principles underpinning narrative approach captured in this chapter are the following.

First, as humans, we generally hold certain narratives which can be in the form of myths and collective memories about who we are as a people. Unconsciously, these narratives can frame the Other in a dehumanizing and demonizing way, especially in times of perceived injustice and when we have a sense of victimhood. These narratives are also imbued with negative meanings of the emotions associated with pain and suffering from mass atrocity.

Second, in a safe narrative space, a person can transform these stories so that they no longer have potency to demonize; instead a new set of narratives can be shared and attended to by empathetic listeners. There begins the re-storying process which is rooted in the ideas of goodness and responsibility to oneself and others.

Third, such a critical narrative process can further facilitate the construction of a collective or shared ethical framework of care that can bring forward a political culture of reconciliation to a formerly divided society. The narrative space thus forges a path from personal reconstruction towards social reconciliation. In this book, we highlight the educative potential that critical narrative has to contribute to learning through humanization and trans-formation. It is therefore necessary to continue exploring ways to integrate such narrative pedagogy in education for peace-building.

However, as this chapter illustrates, narratively humanizing the Other is a mere starting point for a much more demanding pro-cess for building peace. It must be compounded with a political gesture and resolution of justice in order to create the conditions for building positive social relationships between different groups and communities. Ultimately, the forces that perpetuate cycles of violence always involve unjust political systems, discriminative social institutions, a corrupted moral order and cultures of disre-spect. The structural causes of violence must be placed alongside the communal and individual violent reactions to them (Staub and Bar-Tal, 2003).

CHAPTER 8

The Healing Power of Narrative – Learning from Listening and Telling our Stories

Scherto Gill with Marina Cantacuzino, Adam Grant
and Peter Miles[1]

When you listen to a victim's story, you start seeing and you are able to see how things you have done, things you are doing, have affected and hurt others. Then it puts it up front for you to say: 'It's not right.'

–Adam

My change today, where I am at, where my mind is, is totally a lot bigger than it was when I first got arrested. My change when I first got arrested was a change for me. It wasn't a change for other people. It was a change for me ... Now, I know this (The Forgiveness Project) works as it has worked with me. I want to help others to change.

–Peter

---

[1] Marina Cantacuzino is the Founder/Director of the award-winning UK charity The Forgiveness Project, www.theforgivenessproject.com. She and her team have designed and developed the RESTORE programme, launched in selected English prisons in 2009. Adam Grant and Peter Miles were both participants of the RESTORE programme and they continue to be involved in the programme as mentors and, in Peter's case, also as a speaker and a facilitator.

INTRODUCTION

Narrative/storytelling as part of restorative justice (RJ) practice has recently been introduced into the criminal justice process in the UK. It is a relatively new approach within the system, aimed at restoring the relationship between victims and offenders and at transforming conflict between individuals and communities. RJ is carried out both within the criminal justice process and independently, and it has been claimed to have had a large effect in reducing violent crime by as much as 40 per cent (Sherman, 2003).

In this chapter of this book, we will examine how narratives and storytelling serve to promote human values such as empathy, compassion, forgiveness, respect, dignity and responsibility within the context of RJ programmes in English prisons. The case study focuses on RESTORE, an intervention programme designed and facilitated by The Forgiveness Project. It also aims to illustrate that listening and storytelling can allow the victim and the offender to enter a safe space where it is possible for them to deconstruct notions such as 'injury', 'pain', 'grief' and 'suffering' as well as 'anger', 'aggression', 'violence' and 'crime'. By re-storying, the programme further provides participants with an opportunity to reconstruct a sense of self and reclaim respect for oneself and for the other – a starting point for healing and transformation.

In order to rebuild the relationship between people separated by an act of violence, it is necessary to draw on the humanizing effect of narrative as we saw in the previous chapters, and to explore the idea that 'when you forgive, you become human again', another fundamental concept in the restorative process. In this case study, forgiveness and other values promoted by RJ are critically examined in the current prison context in order to re-imagine a justice system that can truly restore human dignity and broken relationships at many levels.

STORYTELLING, FORGIVENESS AND RESTORATIVE JUSTICE

Restorative justice (RJ) has been defined as a set of practices that 'seek noncustodial settlements', 'allow both the offender and the victim much more initiative', orient towards 'peacemaking [rather] than punishment' and aim to 'mobilize the capacities of families, friends, and local communities' in supporting offenders to take responsibility for their actions (Cayley, 1998, p. 10).

The starting point of RJ work is often acknowledging injury and harm (social, psychological and relational) that an offence/crime can cause to people and their communities. It requires that all parties involved in an offence/crime participate in a process of meeting and encounter aimed at responding to the crime and its impact, and empowering offender accountability, reparation and (re)integration into the community.[2]

Zehr (2008) summarizes the principles of RJ as follows:

- focus on the harms and the consequent needs of the victims, the communities and the offenders;
- address the obligations (of the offender, the community and the society) that result from those harms;
- use inclusive, collaborative processes to the extent possible;
- involve those with a legitimate stake in the situation, including victims, offenders, community members and society;
- seek to put right the wrong.

Existing RJ practices include victim–offender face-to-face meetings carried out by trained facilitators; RJ conferences where all the stakeholders in an injustice or an offence come together to discuss the consequences of the wrongdoing and what might be

---

[2] Restorative Justice Briefing Paper, Centre for Justice and Reconciliation, Washington, DC, 2008.

done to repair the harm and restore justice; participatory healing circles[3] and storytelling workshops that focus on listening and developing victim empathy; and so forth. It is person-centred and focused on relationship building, restoring self-worth and dignity (Hicks, 2011) and encouraging self-responsibility and reducing re-offence (Karp and Thom, 2004).

Storytelling (personal and communal narrative) has been introduced as an important and transformative practice within the RJ approach. As we have seen in this book, storying has profound healing power, as through the narrative architecture (Braithwaite, 2006), individuals strive to make sense of their experience of crime/offence as well as the experience of being the victim of a crime. Stories also heal through understanding, compassion and relationship building (Pollack, 2000; Watson, 2010). Re-storying, in particular, plays a critical role in trauma recovery and RJ (Zehr, 2008). As we shall see in the case study presented in this chapter, in victim–offender/perpetrator relations, the power of stories tends to be manifested in a two-way process: allowing the victim to share their often unspoken pain and grievances and to make sense of its impact on their life – the beginning of healing; and offering the offender the opportunity to understand the profound suffering and harm resulting from his/her wrongdoing – a starting point of becoming empathetic and more willing to take responsibility for one's own acts.

As we argued in the first part of the book, personal narrative has an important place in our life because it enables us to locate our being in the world in continuity, coherence and meaning. Violence and aggression can inadvertently interrupt our unfolding narrative in relation to our identity (Gergen, 2009), leading to fractures in our sense of self, our sense of meaning and our relationships with others and with the world at large. Thus, Narvaez (2010) argues that

---

[3] See Colin Tipping's book *Radical Forgiveness*. Boulder, CO: Sounds True (2009).

the aim of any healing process must be to pass from the narration of an offence as hurt feelings into a narration of the offence as an experience of significance. This is important as it highlights a shift from the expected responses of being the victim of violence (i.e. pain, rage, hate and desire for revenge) to the kind of response that liberates one from being imprisoned in such negative, aggressive and debilitating thoughts and emotions. Although not an aim, this liberating response might be described as forgiveness, and often occurs during RJ processes (Armour and Umbreit, 2006).

Enright (2001) suggests that stories of forgiveness are in the interests of both parties – the offended and the offender – and that to forgive requires an emotional transformation in which the person shifts from resentment and desire for revenge to an under-standing of the hurt, respect for the offender and search for empathy. Eide (2010) sees this as a process of rebirth – for the offended, as they shed the burden and grief of the pain; and for the offender, as the forgiveness gives them the opportunity to be reborn and reclaim their dignity as a person.

Eide recounts a ritual in a fictional film, *The Interpreter* (Directed by Sydney Pollack in 2005), practised by the Ku people in southern Africa, who believe that the only way to end grief following the loss of a loved one is to save a life. If someone is murdered, the year of mourning will end with a ritual: after an all-night party beside a river, at dawn, the killer is bound, put in a boat and taken onto the water, where he is dropped in to be drowned. The family of the dead has to make a choice – to let him drown or to swim out and save him. The former decision resolves their need for justice but they will continue mourning till the end of their life; the latter allows them to accept the loss and relinquish the vengeance, as the act of saving life will take away their sorrow. Eide concludes:

This Drowning Man Trial models two modes of justice: retrib-utive (in which a life is sacrificed to avenge a crime) and restorative (in which saving a life allays sorrow). In the restorative form the act of saving a guilty man enacts forgiveness in advance of an inner or emotional transformation with the resulting alleviation of grief, which in turn has the potential to imbue feelings of forgiving. Forgiveness in this fiction takes place in a public ritual in which there is collective participation (an all night party), and predictable rites (the drowning occurs at dawn). (Eide, 2010, p. 4)

As the above story shows, forgiving happens inside us and represents a letting go of the sense of grievance, and perhaps most importantly a letting go of our identity as the 'victim' (Davis, 2002), providing an opportunity for an inner transformation of both the offended and the offender. Thus this transformation is for the good of both parties, allowing neither to forget the aggression or offence, but focusing on whom one has become (Davis, 2002). This is the empowerment we discussed earlier.

Furthermore, as the offended forgives an aggressive act, he or she becomes more open to moving from his or her own perspective of hurt and internal suffering to that of the offender, and thus to embracing the context of and reason for the wrongdoing as well as the offender's present situation (Enright and North, 1998). This helps start another process of fostering compassion, generosity and understanding towards the offended (Enright and North, 1998). This is a humanizing process: as Nelson (2000) claims, when we forgive, we become human again. Yet, forgiveness is not an end in itself; it is a pathway to be free, to be human and to effect positive change.

People have multiple aspects within themselves – those who at times appear to be greedy can be most generous at other times; those who crave power can be inwardly vulnerable; those who have killed can also possess a gentle side. So the key to effective listening and (re)storying is to bring the compassionate self to the fore, at all times. Thus Braithwaite (2006) writes:

even in the worst cases, or especially in the worst cases, the restorative circle is one of our more promising tools for coaxing the offender's compassionate self to the fore and preventing future victimization. (Braithwaite, 2006, p. 434)

Indeed, in narrating lived experience, the multiple voices of oneself can become audible – the voice of the vulnerable and abused child, the voice of the angry and vengeful adolescent, the voice of the fearful person, the voice of the compassionate and loving parent, the voice of a caring and gentle person, and so forth. The storying and listening strategies are situated within the possibility that when the victims and the offenders are brought together in a conversation about life, the 'good' and 'normal' self is interpreted as the 'core' self. It is from here that one aspires for change, and it is here where change is seen as possible.

This humanizing pathway is what we have explored as learning in this book (see Part I). The ultimate aim of RJ is restoring human dignity, relationships and moral action through forgiveness, healing and the fostering of compassion. One pivotal element to creating such noble pathways is to create safe spaces for listening and storying. Neimeyer and Tschudi (2003) suggest that the narrative process (listening and telling) can:

(1) assist persons in finding an authorial voice,
(2) invite meaningful co-authorship of life narratives by ensuring the participation of both protagonists and supporting characters, and
(3) recruit a relevant audience for the performance of a new narrative that transforms the conflict. (Neimeyer and Tschudi, 2003, pp. 171–2)

With a safe space which fosters openness (non-judgement), empathy and acceptance (non-labelling of good or bad, victim or offender), this co-narration or collaborative re-storying can engender greater humility and aspiration for co-construction and change.

199

In summary, RJ practice is value-inspired and value-inspiring. It aims to create spaces for stories, listening and dialogue where it is possible for core values such as empathy, compassion, forgiveness, respect and responsibility to flourish. There has been emerging evidence that RJ can remedy the imbalance between meeting the victim's needs, which normally does not go beyond the sentencing stage, and focusing on the offender's needs for rehabilitation and desistance from reoffending (Braithwaite, 2006).

RESTORE

In England and Wales, Ministry of Justice figures show that 47 per cent of adults are reconvicted within one year of being released. For those serving sentences of less than 12 months this increases to 57 per cent. However, through the introduction of RJ practices, 27 per cent of offenders leaving prison are less likely to reoffend[4]; 55 per cent of those who have had non-custodial punishments are less likely to reoffend.[5]

Many RJ programmes are offered by the voluntary sector, as in the case of The Forgiveness Project (TFP). TFP is a UK charity that uses storytelling to explore how ideas around forgiveness, reconciliation and conflict resolution can be used to impact positively on people's lives, through the personal testimonies of both victims and perpetrators of crime and violence. Since 2009, TFP has been running a programme in a number of adult male prisons and Youth Offending Institutes in England and Wales. The workshop is called RESTORE and comes under the victim/RJ empathy umbrella. In 2012 it was evaluated by Forensic Psychological Services at Middlesex University (Adler and Mir, 2012[6]).

---

[4] http://www.restorativejustice.org.uk/restorative_justice_works/.
[5] http://www.why-me.org/.
[6] http://eprints.mdx.ac.uk/9401/.

RESTORE is a group-based intervention for up to 22 prisoners. The programme encourages the sharing of experiences within a framework influenced by RJ principles and narrative learning potentials, as described earlier. The aim is to open prisoners' minds to an alternative way of viewing themselves and the world, one that makes a crime-free life seem both attractive and attainable. Facilitation adopts a 'leading by example' approach; presenters do it, then participants do likewise. This approach also encourages diverse learning styles.

The methodology and approaches of RESTORE centre on a cycle of storytelling/listening–reflecting–dialogue–(re)storying–integrating. It starts with a half-day induction followed by three (consecutive) days of workshop led by three facilitators, including a victim of crime and an ex-offender. Whilst the victim and offender do not share the same crime, having these two people work together, from either end of the criminal justice spectrum, models a restorative approach.

On the first day of the workshop, the victim of crime shares his or her personal story of trauma with the group. The story is usually extreme, involving loss of life, physical abuse or terrorism. The victim is there simply to share their story and offer insight into how they found the resilience to move forward in their life. They are not here to reprimand, shame or blame, as TFP believes that speaking from a place of anger or attempting to seek answers from the prisoner audience will be counterproductive and only result in defensiveness (from the prisoners) instead of openness.

From the outset there is the recognition that, although convicted of offences, many prisoners themselves have histories of abuse, violence and abandonment. Prisoners are often an angry group of people – angry at society, angry at authority, angry at the people who have hurt them in their childhood and even angry at their victims, whom some perceive as being to blame for putting them in prison in the first place. The RESTORE programme works with this anger by first and foremost asking course participants to listen to the stories of victims. After hearing the story from the victim, prisoners are frequently moved to a point of connection and sharing. The victim's humanity, honesty and vulnerability invite the prisoners to enter the encounter and meet them at the same level.[7]

Having a team consisting of a victim, an ex-offender and an experienced facilitator is the key to creating a trusting and safe space. Throughout the programme, the focus is always on narrative – the victim's story, the ex-offender's story as well as the prisoners' own stories. This further reinforces a space of openness and trust, where dialogue and conversations can then take the stories to another realm, so that the participants are able to reconsider their identities, their vision of life and their place in the world.

In addition, the workshop draws on film and other formats to explore concepts of forgiveness in a framework that aims to foster greater accountability and responsibility. The process enhances participants' victim awareness by looking at the consequences of their actions for others and at what might be done to repair the harm.

During the first day of the workshop, as prisoners witness inspiring personal testimonies, they are invited to consider and discuss the issues raised and later to write in their workbooks reflections on these experiences in the privacy of their cells. This culminates in them sharing with the group some of the painful as well as redeeming events in their own lives, through the medium of drawing their lifelines. This procedure is modelled by the ex-offender facilitator on the morning of the second day and then completed by all participants, who present their stories to the group in the afternoon.

Developing empathy in offenders is at the heart of this work, through dialogue, discussion and the sharing of stories. In some

---

[7] Marina wrote in a note: When I think of this I am reminded of what Jeremy Rifkin wrote about the spontaneous amnesty between so many German and British soldiers in the trenches of Christmas Eve 1914: '*walking across no-man's land, they found themselves in one another*'.

cases, empathy can relate to a specific victim; in other cases, it can relate to a general understanding of human behaviour and why they have made the choices they have. The emphasis is on connection rather than on change, on asking questions rather than on providing answers. Paradoxically it is precisely because of the openness of this approach that there is opportunity and space to shift; participants are remarkably receptive and able to gain insight into themselves.

The workbooks (and the anonymous evaluation forms completed by participants at the end of the course) are surprisingly revealing and moving. Themes which emerge from their writing include: offenders often long for an opportunity to make things right through apology or explanation; many offenders fear that apology would be inadequate and could never repair the harm; offenders seem to grasp the concept that forgiveness is particular and yet universal; that forgiveness brings relief and healing of painful feelings and broken relationships.

On the third day, the workshop uses exercises to explore what empathy means and to enable the participants to further understand the principles and practices of RJ. Although the RESTORE programme is never intended to focus on change, nevertheless after each course, several participants will express interest in meeting their victims and many over time have offered to get involved in the programme in some capacity, including attending the course several more times.

In the space below, Adam and Peter recount their experiences of RESTORE and what happens to them after participating in the workshops.

Adam

Adam grew up in and out of care and suffered the usual negative consequences of early exposure (as a child and an adolescent) to violence and abuse (sexual, physical and emotional). He also witnessed domestic violence. He first ran away from a foster home at the age of six to escape abuse, and later ran away from his own home to escape the ongoing violence. The person whose violence caused Adam the most fear and anxiety in his early life was in fact his own mother. As an adolescent, Adam turned his fear and anxiety into rage and anger, and became involved in a great deal of anti-social behaviour, including substance abuse, thefts, violence and general conduct disorder.[8] He started sleeping rough at the age of 13, and from 17 he was in and out of prisons and other 'corrective facilities'. At 21, he was given a life sentence for killing a man during a fight. Adam described his state of mind at that time as 'distorted':

> so my life was kind of about revenge ... if you hurt me, I'll hurt you ... and ... I'll go to any lengths to do it.

> ...

> I wasn't just angry with this fellow ... I was angry with the world. I was angry with everything ... everyone was to blame.

> ...

> because of the state of my frame of mind at 21 when I killed the person ... you know ... whilst it was an evil act ... it came from a very distorted mind ... that couldn't control it. I couldn't. And I don't offer that as an excuse ... but that's just ... I had no understanding.

In prison, Adam attended many courses recommended to him by prison staff, including an anger management course, and several educational programmes. He also saw a psychologist about his early trauma and in time started to gain some control over his anger. After serving 18 years in prison, he was finally released, but life outside proved difficult to adjust to, and, in his own words, it was just 'not happening' for him:

---

[8] It has been well documented that children exposed to violence and abuses are at risk for various behavioural problems, violence perpetration, drug and alcohol abuse, depression and anxiety in adulthood. (See WHO Europe's publication: *The Cycles of Violence: The relationship between childhood maltreatment and the risk of later becoming a victim or perpetrator of violence.*)

But I was still drinking and that . . . and I didn't last very long. I ended up back in prison. And got out again, recalled again . . . I mean at this point I was, I was really despairing. Because I was getting to the stage where I thought I was thinking, all this work that I've done, all these courses that I've done, and I am not getting nowhere. I am still in prison after 20 years. Because it was getting to a stage where I was prepared to say . . . even with my probation officer . . . I don't want a parole board hearing any more. Just tuck me up somewhere in a cell. You leave me alone and I'll leave you alone and just leave it because it's not happening for me out there.

In February 2009, at a time when Adam was feeling 'low', felt 'despair' and 'was pretty withdrawn', he attended RESTORE's induction session. The charity's founder, Marina Cantacuzino, explained the programme's methodology and Richard McCann, whose mother was the first victim of Peter Sutcliffe, the 'Yorkshire ripper', told his journey of forgiveness and transformation.[9] Adam was very moved by this story:

for me, it was about how this man had dealt with it. You know he was a child when it happened, so he had a really traumatic experience. And it was how he learnt to . . . because I . . . in my head . . . well my life didn't go like that . . . but the traumatic things that happened in my childhood made me a very destructive person. And I didn't deal with my adversity in a positive way. Whereas the message I got from him, although he also became violent . . . was that was what he had done. That was the admiration. That was the kind of inspiring thing that I found really valuable, because I had never really experienced that

---

[9] Richard McCann suffered huge distress during his childhood and early adulthood for the loss of his mother, and at one point in his life, his rage resulted in his being violent and destructive and he served a six-month prison sentence. http://theforgivenessproject.com/stories/richard-mccann-england/.

before. Because everyone I had met in prison, or whatever, had all dealt with their adversity like I did, with revenge and you know being resentful, being angry.

Feeling inspired, Adam and all other prisoners at the Induction decided to sign up to do the three-day RESTORE course. On the first day, although the size of the group (20 prisoners) felt too big for Adam, he was surprised that he did not feel at all uncomfortable. Mary Foley was the first to share her story. Mary's 15-year-old daughter was murdered during a house party in East London,[10] and her story affected Adam on several levels:

> [After hearing the story] I was just stumped for words … And I can remember going back to my group, I was asked to take notes. And I let everyone speak. And one thing that really hit me straight away was that these are people who are in the same boat as me, you know, serving a prison sentence, but they were saying: 'I could not do what that lady has done. If someone took my brother's life, or killed my son, or killed my daughter, I would want revenge'. And it started to make me realise that what I did, you know, the hatred that I can cause, by somebody just hearing a story of it. Remember I am, I am always aware that the parents might resent and hate me, but I didn't think these people who were my, people I lived with, would think that way as well.

Mary's story and her choice to forgive, alongside the inmates' reaction during the group discussions to the act of murder, shook Adam in such a way that he recognized that his crime must have had 'a massive ripple effect' and 'hurt a load of other people'. During the day, Adam talked to Mary and told her about his own offence, and to Adam's astonishment, she just listened, with an

---

[10] More on Mary Foley's story can be found on The Forgiveness Project's website: http://theforgivenessproject.com/mary-foley-england/.

open attitude and 'she really wanted to understand'. This was not only 'one of the most humbling experiences' for Adam, but also invoked a strong sense of guilt and shame in him, so that he could no longer use the usual strategy of anger to defend himself.

During the sleepless night that followed, Adam reflected on the power of forgiveness:

> I was thinking to myself in the night, 'You know what, I want to be forgiven for what I've done'. I don't expect to. But I believe if I was sitting opposite the parents of the person I have killed and they said, and I knew and I could sense that it was real that they forgive me, I think I would break down in tears. Because I do believe that would be a real healing process for me.

Mary's story about the negative effect of holding on to resentment had made Adam aware that he must be prepared to forgive those who had done him wrong:

> And as soon as I could think that way, it just... it made me look at my mum in a totally different way. And I am a great believer in that spiritual side, there is dis-ease which I believe causes disease. What you give off is what you get back. If I walk around angry in a prison I am only going to bump into angry people, but if I am placid and humble, I believe they are the people that I will come across.

Adam also understood that hurt people go on to hurt, and the thought of forgiving allowed him to release some of the anger and rage that had consumed him over the years, as well as to lessen some of the pain he had felt too. From this moment on, Adam decided to embrace the challenge:

> It was just mind boggling really. I never slept all that night and then I went back the next day pretty tired, but still riveted to

want to know what was going to be next. And I latched onto
it really quickly in the sense of, from that first day I knew this
could be something really, really useful. Everyone on the forgiveness project all say it... what you put in is what you get out.
And I just knew I was going to engage in this because I am very
challenging to myself as well to other inmates and I like to be
challenged and I feel that, to provoke that I have to challenge
people because I know that gives them the ammunition to
challenge me back.

On the second morning of the workshop, Adam and his group heard
the story of an ex-offender, Peter Woolf,[11] whose story of meeting
his victim at an RJ conference and consequently changing his life
around was equally inspiring for Adam. Peter Woolf had now been
out of prison for several years, and because Adam doubted his own
ability to lead a life without crime, the story gave him hope and
motivation to change. He decided to 'work at it a lot harder'.

This also led Adam to find the courage to tell his own story to
the group – through the medium of sharing his lifeline.

It took a lot of courage to tell the lads what I'd done. [pause] But
at the same time there was this sense of wanting and needing
to do it. Because I never... and I think this is what I am talking
about, all that stuff trapped in, so damaging, so exhausting, so
energy sapping.

Adam believes that he wouldn't have been receptive enough to
engage in a programme like RESTORE 20 years earlier because
at that time he was entirely 'wrapped up' in his own anger and
rage; 'beating myself up' and 'blaming everyone'. Adam thinks
that the British education system should make children aware of

---

[11] See http://www.why-me.org/about-us/ for more on Peter Woolf's story and his
current work.

domestic abuse and teach young people about forgiveness so that they are not damaged to the extent that he was. The RESTORE programme enabled a certain 'shift' in his life:

> I suppose you can only describe it as like a boil being lanced. Nothing, when I thought about my mum, when I thought about the sexual abuser, there was never that impact that would happen where chemicals would start to go mad in my body. It just, I lost, you know, I lost, like that ability to have that adrenaline pump of rage or stir my mind. And I think that is it. It kind of, it altered my thinking. I think that's quite simply [the shift].

Adam went on to attend many more RESTORE programmes, both to continue his own journey and to provide peer support to other participants. He witnessed prisoners opening up and starting to identify and reveal aspects of their lives they had never shared before. Since leaving prison Adam has learnt to control his anger and aspires to lead a good life. His intention is to continue working with the RESTORE programme in order to help others.

> I really like the fact that I am understanding now, not just for my own needs, because I have needed to understand myself, but that I can be understanding to others. I'm not saying I don't judge people, I think initially something happens and I still can be quick to do it, but then I calm down a little bit or just get things into perspective. I am not judging, I am able to say 'I have not walked in that person's shoes'. [pause] I like the fact that I want to be helpful to others. I do believe I have got something to offer and that, with the right training, I definitely believe I would be good at what this forgiveness project has to offer, because my heart is in it.

Adam has now been out of prison for nearly one year. He is taking a diploma course offered by TFP, so that he can one day become a conflict resolution facilitator. He is also learning to become an anger management counsellor.

Peter

Peter was born to parents who migrated to the UK from the Caribbean in the 1960s. His father was extremely strict with all four children, often using physical violence to discipline them. He was also occasionally violent to Peter's mother. When Peter was ten, his mother left his father and moved to the USA. A year later, she sent for Peter and his twin sister. In order to avoid being bullied and in a desperate need to feel integrated and make friends in a new school and new neighbourhood, Peter did everything he could to 'fit in', which included drinking alcohol and taking drugs. From his late teens, Peter became involved in various drug-related offences and from then on was in and out of prisons in five different states. In his early thirties, he suffered the loss of his twin sister to HIV. He also fathered three children and, in between serving several prison sentences, he worked as a lorry driver and a paramedic. By the time he was in his late thirties, Peter had returned to the UK where he immediately became involved in crime again – mainly driving get-away vehicles in violent robberies. This led to a seven-and-a-half-year prison sentence.

In 2009, while serving this last prison sentence, Peter decided he needed to see some real change in his life, for himself but above all for his children. He was determined now to become a strong role model.

> I said: 'I am tired of this. I am tired of this'. And I also saw the future ... I knew that if I kept doing what I was doing, I would keep getting what I had been getting, and that's jail, that's misery, that's loss of family and loss of self. And I think I have lost myself so many times.

Like Adam, Peter signed up whilst in prison for the RESTORE programme. Listening to stories of crime from both the victim's and the offender's perspectives made him understand 'some of the stuff other people have been through and how they coped'. He also began to consider his own victims for the first time.

> I remember Peter Woolf showed that video 'The Woolf Within' about how he did his crime and how him and the victim just got together and so forth. And I thought that was awesome. It was amazing to see how, because I didn't believe that victims and perpetrators would come together. That was a thing new to me. And I sat there thinking about all my victims. Because in these crimes, in the crimes that I was involved in, there was a lot of victims, because these shops, it wasn't just a shop, or people that were working in the shops, there was customers in there too. So it wasn't like when we did the shops, we didn't just drive by and say 'Oh there's two women working there' because it wasn't like that. It was like, drive in, there's a shop, pull over, let's do it.

Growing awareness of the consequences of his crimes made Peter now want to apologize to the people he had most hurt:

> For me, what was very important was for me to take a look at how I affected all these other people and my family and myself... And I always say I would love to do something like that, to let these people know that I did not mean them no harm, you know. I apologise for affecting their lives and their families, because I don't know what it's like.

The stories of forgiveness brought some new understanding to Peter:

> But the forgiveness thing, what I realized first of all was the most important person I had to forgive was me, because for a

lot of my life I blamed me for a lot of things. I blamed me for a lot of things. I blamed me for my sister's death, I blamed me for me getting on drugs, I blamed me for my dad's hand [being cut by a lawnmower]. I blamed me for a lot of things. And when I first went to prison, I couldn't walk past a mirror. I didn't want to walk past a mirror. I didn't want to see myself. And I was clean. I was clean. I was two months clean, but I didn't want to look at me because I wasn't happy with me you know.

What Peter particularly liked about the RESTORE programme was that the stories from the victim and ex-offender served as an invitation and also permission for the prisoners to then share their own stories:

> The stuff I have heard people mention in their lifeline, and for them to do that they had to feel safe, you know, they had to feel safe that they can say this around us. And that is what makes it so beautiful is that it starts with stories of two people, one from each end, a survivor and a perpetrator. And that allows these guys to realise 'OK they shared with me, I am going to share with them'. That's what it does.

Sharing personal stories also brought participants in the programme closer to each other. Peter noted that this rarely happens in prison because, although two people may share a cell, they will probably not know anything about each other. The RESTORE programme allows for open, honest dialogue in a way that many have never experienced before.

> You see a lot of guys whose stories so much relate with your story, you know, and you would be surprised to see some of the stories that are almost just like yours. And it makes you see the person in a different light. You really do. It makes you see them

in a totally different light ... You know because you have built this bond now and it allows you to open up.

The biggest impact that RESTORE had on Peter was to help build his confidence and to experience feelings of self-worth again. This came from realizing that people do actually care – something he found to be extremely life affirming:

I have talked to numerous guys [in prison], that we just figure nobody cares, you know, and then we don't care. It gets to that point. But listening to the stories, it made me realise that there are some people, like some victims, that want to see people change. They don't want to see you locked up, you know. And that means a lot because my old thinking was they don't care ... That's what the Forgiveness Project made me realise that there are people who care, people that really care. And I met some officers in prison, really good officers that care. It reaffirms that people are good. There are some good people. There are some good people. All the junk I have done, some people don't look at me as junk.

Like many other participants of RESTORE, Peter was moved to want to make a difference, not just for himself, but also for others:

I think the thing is: a lot of people think, it would be good if people changed, if the system changed, or if this changed. But unless I want to step up and try and help it change, it wouldn't happen. Then that's like me sitting on the bed saying: why isn't the TV changing [laughs], you know, instead of me getting up and changing the TV.

It is now a year since Peter was released from prison, and he is working for TFP as an ex-offender facilitator on the RESTORE programme. He finds it especially rewarding to see others go through the programme, begin to consider the impact of their actions on others and become determined to change.

> And it works. It works. And a lot of times at the end of it the guys go round and say how they are so happy that they met this person and 'I'm so glad I was here because I learnt this'. In our group yesterday I have had three or four guys come to me and say 'When I get out, I want to work on this Forgiveness Project'. That's what they say, 'I want to come back to prisons and help other guys like myself'. That's what it's about. That's what it is about because if you keep yourself on that track ... you'll be OK.

Peter believes that it is the use of ex-offenders as facilitators within the RESTORE programme which is key to the programme's success, because it gives prisoners a vision of what they could become in the future and models a way of behaviour that embraces emotion, empathy and change.

> I just knew that this is what I wanted to do. I knew that this is what I wanted to do because this was my way to start planting that seed ... because when they see me and they knew me when I was out there doing drugs, they knew me. So when they see me, they know it is possible, because they knew me when I was one of the lowest of the low. And if I could come up out of there, phhhh, they can. They have got more family and friends than I've got. So sometimes that's all it takes. And that's an awesome feeling. To know that you can go back in and that you have helped one person.

From his own personal experience, as well as from observing others, Peter has plenty of evidence to show that there is no safe space or ongoing support for people leaving prison, and therefore they often end up immediately reoffending. Peter has also taken drug counselling and business administration courses and wants to develop his knowledge and skills in this area, so that he can set up a halfway house to support ex-offenders after release.

In addition, Peter works as a mentor on TFP's mentoring programme. He believes it important to provide continuing support to all offenders, but particularly to young offenders:

> We started this mentoring thing now at young offenders' and it's an awesome thing. We have got eight young offenders and I go in there and see them once a month now and they have made a commitment. This is something that we are doing it while they are in prison and then if they get moved to another prison, we will continue it, when they get out we will continue it because I think that was one of the biggest downfalls that you do all the stuff in prison and when you get out there is nobody out there to continue it.

Today Peter has many plans and sees many opportunities to help others change their lives around. He is confident that he will not reoffend or return to a life of crime.

> Today I can look in the mirror. And I say 'What are you looking at?' and I just smile. [laughs] Because I know who I am, I know what I am about, and I know I am about good. Forget what I've done. I know I am about good. And that's all I need to know.

CONCLUSION

The RESTORE programme is broadly aimed at reducing 'the number of victims of crime through the rehabilitation of offenders'. It creates a safe space for sharing stories as experienced by Adam and Peter – stories of victims, stories of ex-offenders, as well as stories of the participants. Through sharing stories, prisoners are able to change the narrative of their lives and start to engage in positive dialogue. Concepts such as forgiveness, victimhood, revenge, empathy and compassion are further explored during these workshops, so that facilitators and participants are able to take their understanding of these concepts to a new level. For instance, Adam came to an understanding that forgiveness can be 'separated into three areas – being forgiven for what I'd done, forgiving those who had done me wrong and also forgiving myself'. Another example is about understanding the notion of 'victim'. Prisoners not only become aware of the harm they have caused to the victim and their families (through the ripple effects of crime) but also begin to explore the relationship between the victims of their offences and themselves as victims: in other words, they begin to have an idea of how victimization leads to a cycle of violence. The narrative pedagogy that centres on stories and deep human encounter also results in the participants' increased self-worth and self-respect, a revised worldview and moral inspiration.

From ongoing reviews, RESTORE is considered to have consistently demonstrated a shift in offenders' motivation to change, as illustrated in Adam's and Peter's stories. A recent independent programme evaluation concluded that RESTORE has improved the participants' general attitudes to offending and that they are less likely to anticipate reoffending (Adler and Mir, 2012).

There are many ways in which RESTORE can be expanded to reflect the nature of the encounter, the pedagogical intention and the diverse relationships embedded in the programme processes. To conclude from Adam's and Peter's experiences, we would offer one perspective on understanding RESTORE:

- **R**eceiving stories in a safe space – the participants (offenders) were drawn in first by the victim's story as it tells his or her vulnerability, pain, suffering and inner struggle, but also his or her resilience, forgiveness and willingness to reach out and accept any attempt to put the wrong right. This gives the participants an opportunity to be open to narratives as they can recognize that the space is safe, and non-blaming and non-judgemental. They are then ready to receive the ex-offender's story: narrating one's own journeys of entering into the offence, taking responsibility and highlighting the possibility of change, of putting the wrong right.

- Empathetic listening and dialogue – as the participants are open to the storytellers' pain and suffering, as well as their regrets and remorse, they also become more empathetic and more able to engage emotionally with the stories; and a dialogic exchange further offers the participants the opportunity to appreciate the storytellers' humanity and courage to overcome adversity or take a stand in order to make changes.

- Storying and reflecting – the lifeline presentation is the participants' first attempt to story their life and to see their life from a reflexive distance. This allows them also to become more compassionate with their victims, and also with themselves and those who might have done wrong to them in their own lives, and thus to begin to see how and why they are where they are.

- Transgressing – both storying processes enable the participants (offenders) to transgress in their narratives from the bystander (attending to the victim's and ex-offender's stories), to victim (narrating their own stories of abuse and early trauma) and to offender (confronting their own crime/offence). In the transgression, they experience profound humanity and compassion for others but also for themselves. Through their emotional engagement with pain and grief, they reassess suffering in their own life and the damage and loss and suffering they have imposed on other people due to their acts. This is also when forgiveness takes place for some.

- Orientating and ordering – the transgression gives the participants an opportunity to (re)orient themselves towards the good. Some experienced moral outrage whilst attending to the victim's stories, whereas the ex-offender's stories allow them to reorder their timeline so as to see the value of goodness, a life in love and helping others. This orientation towards constructive and positive relationships creates a further step of transgression – to become someone who will change in order to put the wrong right.

- **Reclaiming and re-storying** – narrative process is a humanizing act that allows the participants to reclaim their self-worth and self-respect, and to reflect on their life as a whole. Often the reordering and reorienting helps them to reassemble the broken pieces of life in ways that make it possible to construct a future with purpose and direction. This is also an opportunity to re-examine their individual experience (and the offence) from a life-course perspective and to see that there is still hope for a better prospect through the onward journey.

- Enacting a new story – re-storying expresses the participant's hope and determination for a new journey, which can only be truly embarked on when they enact on this new story. Similar to Adam and Peter, many participants have also expressed they want to get involved in RESTORE as they see themselves playing a new part in the new story.

Crime and punishment cost our society hugely, in the economic sense, the social sense and, above all, the human sense. Therefore, notable effort has been put in to (re)educate the prisoners so that better learning and training opportunities can help prevent them from reoffending, and enable their reintegration in the society (Schuller, 2009). Current emphasis has been on enhancing prisoners' employment prospects and developing skills and capabilities for participating in civic life within a society.

However, in this chapter, the participants' experiences at the RESTORE programme have made a compelling case to suggest that any educational endeavour within prisons must also be focused on helping the offenders (and the victims) reconnect with values and moral ethics, reclaim their humanity and reconstruct their identity as dignified persons. This is indeed one of the core messages of this book – learning is ultimately about enabling us to become more fully human and pursue a meaningful life in ways that contribute positively to our own wellbeing and to the wellbeing of others and the wider society.

At the same time, as we saw in Adam's and Peter's critical narrative analysis, crime is often an expression of wider social malaise, which requires deeper healing and which is best addressed at the root level.

CHAPTER 9

Biographical Learning in Higher Education – Critical Dialogue and Praxis

Scherto Gill

Katrina has returned from the washroom, eyes red but unembarrassed about her emotions. Chitra walks up and gives her a warm hug and the tears well up again in Katrina's eyes. As she returns to her seat, she passes Andrew, who puts a hand on Katrina's arm, giving it a firm squeeze. She nods with acknowledgement.

Behind Katrina, on the wall, there hangs a large sheet of poster paper on which she has drawn 'a river of life' – her life history. Her 'river' meanders from a happy childhood in a working-class family, to an adolescence of disengagement in schools; from the joy of becoming a parent, to the trauma of divorce; from the struggles of being a single mother with two young children, to the optimism of discovering her talent in the arts and training to work in them; and just at the juncture where the river of life is ready to follow an open course, it hits yet another sharp turn – the threat of mortality while battling with cancer.

But Katrina isn't crying because she feels sorry about her own ill-fate; instead she is in tears of gratitude as she is deeply moved by her peers' compassionate listening, their loving tenderness towards her and the overwhelming support she has received from the group.

MA in Education Studies Class Observation

INTRODUCTION

This scene above is not a counselling group or therapy group, although it does resemble it. In fact, Andrew once said: 'This is what AA must be like'. In fact, the scene took place in a seminar room on a master's programme at a UK university. Katrina had just presented her 'learning biography' to a group of peers whom she only met four weeks earlier, but she was already telling them about her intimate personal journeys and stories.

In this final chapter of the book, I will use the case of teachers' biographical learning in postgraduate higher education to illustrate narrative learning as a process of enacting critical pedagogy through whole-person engagement. The case study further demonstrates that, when sharing personal biographies with a group of teachers/educators, the participants become more reflective and reflexive about their own experience of learning. I argue that such deeper forms of reflexivity engender critical distance from one's self and self-understanding, thus leading to profound questioning of key issues and concepts in educational practices and the institutional and socio-political contexts of such practices.

Whole-person learning involves all aspects of what it means to be human. These include emotions, intellect, moral intuitions, connections (self-awareness and sense of identity, connection with others and the world around us) and one's sense of aesthetics, spirituality and actions. These diverse aspects of being human overlap and are not separable from one another. For instance, as we saw in Chapters 1 and 3, our action is not merely a response to some universal principles or moral codes. Instead, we act in such ways because we attend to the realities of others; therefore, moral ethics is not a matter of conformity, it has an inherent affective dimension to it. It is relational and emotive, and it integrates care, compassion, empathy and so forth. At the same time, our action is also motivated by our perception (as we perceive certain ends as valuable and thus decide to pursue them), which is connected to our cognition and our rational thoughts. Our experiences in engaging the diverse aspects of ourselves also constitute an important process of human flourishing.

Thus the purpose of this chapter is to examine the role that critical narratives play in teachers' learning. In particular, the focus is on exploring the effect of narrative learning through biographical writing in a group setting. Using the unique example of master's students (who are themselves teachers) working together to develop their individual learning biographies, we hope to illustrate that the critical dialogic process involved in the group's narrative learning not only engages the participants as whole persons, but also serves as an important starting point for them to begin transforming their educational practice and themselves with it.

BIOGRAPHIES IN TEACHER EDUCATION AND WHOLE-PERSON LEARNING

Biographical learning in higher education is a rarely explored field, and yet it is claimed to be a profound experience involving whole-person learning and transformation (Alheit, 2009; Alheit and Dausien, 2002; Dominicé, 2000; Goodson and Gill, 2011; Karpiak, 2000; Rossiter and Clark, 2007). Some have pointed out that this is an under-researched area due to the challenge of integrating biographical learning within mainstream higher education (Yorks and Kasl, 2006). We will return to this point in the paragraphs below.

As we discussed in Chapter 1, the individual's identity and their sense of self are rooted in many sources, particularly their narratives and life stories. In our previous inquiry (Goodson and Gill, 2011), we drew on Parker Palmer's (1998) work to understand the interplay between our identity and integrity in teacher education. Palmer maintains that our identity resides in 'a moving intersection of the inner and outer forces that makes me who I am, converging in the irreducible mystery of being human' (Palmer, 1998, p. 13) and that through the pathway of integrity, 'I become more whole ... more real by acknowledging the whole of who I am' (ibid.). Thus we conclude that biographical writing allows teachers to examine their lives from 'the mystery of self', which 'is at the centre of education and learning' (Goodson and Gill, 2011, p. 123).

We humans have a deep relationship with our past experiences, as 'each occurrence is charged with echoes and reminiscences of what has gone before, where each event is a reminder of other things' (Dewey, 1920, p. 1). The reason we recall our own life stories is because they can contribute to our present, be it an understanding of ourselves and our place in the world, our relationship with others and with the world around us, or the motivations of our action. Our memories of life are emotional, first and foremost, as well as intellectual and practical. Dewey further maintains that:

> To revive it and revel in it is to enhance the present moment with a new meaning, a meaning different from that which actually belongs either to it or to the past ... [T]he conscious and truly human experience ... comes when it is talked over and re-enacted ... into a whole of meaning ... (Dewey, 1920, pp. 2–3).

Thus we have regarded the narrative as a process that

> consolidates a mutually constitutive relationship between life and narrative – life forms the fundamental basis of narrative and narrative provides order, structure and direction in life, and helps develop meanings in richer and more integrated ways. (Goodson and Gill, 2011, p. 6)

For teachers and educators, the narratives of learning through echoes of the past can often determine their current commitment and approaches to teaching and learning, and their modelling of a relationship with their students. At the same time, as we have seen in this book, narratives and their sociocultural and historical echoes can shape our identity in ways that are totally beyond the individual's conscious examination. Biographical writing with a focus on the concept and processes of learning can allow teachers/educators to break away from destructive and paralysing stories about the past, to analyse them and to examine the ways they have structured their meanings and actions. They can use emerging stories to undo such negative stories and together they can create a new way of understanding and engaging in education and learning. This is the critical element in narrative learning that we discussed in the first part of the book. In this process, we shall argue that two elements are pivotal: a whole-person approach in order to embrace the narrative process fully; and a safe space within a small group so that the participating teachers/educators can support each other's journeys in reflection.

Tedder and Biesta (2009) argue that biographical or narrative learning is a whole-person engagement because it entails not only the cognitive and reflective dimensions but also the emotional, the embodied and other aspects of being human. We discussed in earlier chapters how narrative reflexivity, in addition to helping form and consolidate our identity, can further help us elaborate our moral horizons and our directions for action, individual and collective (see Part One of the book, especially Chapter 3).

So in this section, we will focus our exploration on the emotional aspect of learning in higher education and how teachers' biographical learning as an emotional journey also encompasses other aspects of being human. Later, when we discuss the case study, we will further illustrate the role of the group or community in supporting whole-person narrative journeys.

Emotion, being human and critical learning

Many have argued that, when learners are engaged as whole persons, the experience is first and foremost an emotional one (Blum, 1994; Heron, 1992; Ingleton, 1995, 1999; Noddings, 1992; Yorks and Kasl, 2006). Undoubtedly, the emphasis on the emotional journeys of the students (who are also teachers/educators) within a higher education institution can create tension between the need to work with 'rigorous' scholarly practices and standards, and the perceived risk of merely being self-indulgent with emotions through 'touchy-feely' programmes (Yorks and Kasl, 2006, p. 44). Academics are relatively accepting on a conceptual level of the significance of emotions in students' learning, but are often unwilling or unable to engage with students' intense emotions during seminars or tutorials (Tisdell et al., 2000; Yorks and Kasl, 2006). So it is not surprising that the effect of the emotional life in learning remains largely unexamined and undervalued in the higher education literature (Ingleton, 1999).

For a long time, rationality has stood in opposition to the emotional aspect of human nature, and emotions have been considered an irrational force. However, in the twentieth century, philosophers such as John Macmurray (1961), neurologists such as Antonio Damasio (1994) and psychologists such as John Heron (1992) and Daniel Goleman (1995) have begun to argue that emotions are deeply associated with human reason, and emotions are central to our own perceptions of reality, meaning and personhood.

Macmurray's opening phrase in his book *Reason and Emotion* asserted that: 'Any enquiry must have a motive or it could not be carried on at all, and all motives belong to our emotional life' (1961, p. 3). He argued that in a conventional sense, the disassociation between reason as 'a state of mind which is cold, detached and unemotional' and emotions, which belong to another world 'more colourful, more full of warmth and delight, but also more

226

dangerous' (Macmurray, 1961, p. 3), is a false dichotomy. This is because reason is more than pure intellect. In the long extract below, Macmurray summarized the main thrust of his argument that emotional reasoning is what makes us human. He wrote:

> Reason – the capacity in us which makes us human – is not in any special sense a capacity of the intellect. It is not our power of thinking, though it expresses itself in our thinking as well as in other ways. It must also express itself in our emotional life, if that is to be human ... Reason reveals itself in emotion by its objectivity, by the way it corresponds to and apprehends reality. Reason in the emotional life determines our behaviour in terms of the real values of the world in which we live ... The development of human nature in its concrete livingness is, in fact, the development of emotional reason. (Macmurray, 1961, p. 49)

Macmurray pointed out that pure intellect that rejects the emotions cannot be a source of our critical learning or action because it also rejects creativity, 'a characteristic which belongs to personality in its wholeness, acting as a whole, and not any of its parts acting separately' (Macmurray, 1961, p. 45). Therefore, to educate the person in their wholeness is, above all, to encourage the development of their sensitivities and emotional experiences. As argued by Macmurray, an awareness of the world around us means having a direct 'emotional experience of the real value in the world, and we respond to this by behaving in ways which carry the stamp of reason upon them in their appropriateness and grace of freedom' (Macmurray, 1961, p. 45). Macmurray concluded that, in contrast to conventional belief, the emotional life is not subordinate or subsidiary to the intellectual life; it is 'the core and essence of human life' (Macmurray, 1961, p. 75). The intellect and reason find root in the emotions, and draw nourishment and sustenance from them.

The emotional life is profoundly influential in the education of the whole person because it is in and through emotional experiences that we develop the unity of identity and action (both individually and socially). In other words, emotions are the unifying factor in human life. Therefore, any education programme where only the intellect is challenged will result in the disintegration of the personality and a disjointed existence.

In the late twentieth century, there were further attempts to work in the conceptual space of 'emotions in learning'. Accordingly, understanding emotions and being able to engage with one's feelings and emotions in educational contexts have become interesting topics for investigation. Some authors, such as Daniel Goleman and Howard Gardner, take the lead in placing emotions at the 'centre of aptitudes' for human livelihoods, and suggesting that they underlie our moral stances and rational thinking (Bar-On and Parker, 2000; Goleman, 1995).

As we reviewed in our early chapters, Freire's critical pedagogy has extended the idea of emotion-intense learning into the realm of relation-based learning. Let's revisit some of his views. To be critical, Freire argues, we must engage in dialogue, and a Freirean dialogic pedagogy is nourished by love, humility, hope and faith in humanity. These virtues involve the integration of the emotional, intellectual and spiritual, and they define our 'human duty' to attend to each other, to overcome our own limits and to embrace differences. Through love, humans thrive on by being-in-relation with each other, and in caring and nurturing, we become more human. Similarly, Palmer (1998) supports an approach to pedagogy that enables the convergence of the intellectual, emotional and spiritual. Freire highlighted four essential virtues that are important in education: humility, courage, acceptance and lovingness.

Dewey (1938) also maintains that our method of inquiry should involve all aspects of human experience, including feelings, desires and thoughts, within the environment where we find ourselves, which is simultaneously cultural and physical. Thus when we launch an inquiry, it should be an intellectual, aesthetic, religious, moral and social endeavour at the same time, besides comprising the interrelationships amongst all.

Bell hooks (2003) puts forward an ideal learning environment as one imbued with a combination of care, commitment, knowledge, responsibility, respect and trust (hooks, 2003, p. 131). Indeed, human relationships are the key to learning, around which all else happens and through which learning becomes meaningful.

The absence of whole-person approach in learning theories

Whilst Macmurray's philosophical thinking stresses the importance of educating the emotions and suggests that this can be done through allowing individuals to experience and encounter emotions for their own sake, other authors highlight the interdependence between the emotions and cognition in the learning process (Goleman, 1995; Illeris, 2004; Piaget, 1951, 1953). The general consensus is that emotions provide a foundation for understanding and meaning from which the learner's self-concept begins to take shape.

Critics have pointed out that existing learning theories and well-regarded learning models do not always seem to address this notion of emotions (Ross, 2006). For instance, influential adult learning theories within (social) constructivism, including experiential learning theory (Kolb, 1984) and transformative learning theory (Mezirow, 1994, 2000), have not sufficiently acknowledged emotions in the process of learning.

Feminist author Michelson (1996) points out that emotions are rarely considered in Kolb's work. She contends that, for the majority of constructivists, emotions are considered either as blocks to be overcome in learning, or as positive attitudes to be promoted, or are the result of self-reflection (i.e. anxiety, etc.). Emotions are rarely examined as a 'path to learning'. Michelson argues that this disregard for the affective is a theme of control, a gendering of epistemological values. Referring to Kolb's cyclic model of transformative learning, she concludes that it was the emphasis on the reflective, analytic and objective that led to an unspoken hierarchy that prioritizes rational thinking (masculinity) over learning that is based on raw experience, pre-consciousness, emotions, motives, intentionality and intuition (femininity). Michelson regards a constructivist view of learning as a form of control, which denigrates the affective and its crucial role in learning and knowing.

Similarly, critique on transformative learning theory also rests on the lack of attention paid to the affect in the process of transformation. Some argue that the theory centres on perspective transformation and places too much emphasis on rationality (Edward Taylor, 1997; Kritskaya and Dirkx, 2000).

Over the last two decades, some scholars have begun to explore the role of emotions in transformative learning, heralded by the work of Boyd and Myer (1988), Boyd (1991), Dirkx (1998, 2000), Yorks and Kasl (2002) and Ingleton (1999). Dirkx (2000, p. 4) explains that knowing and learning through engaging the emotions is 'felt to be mediated largely through images rather than directly through concepts or traditional forms of rationalism'. It has a focus on the deeper personal emotional and spiritual dimension of learning, so that feelings, emotions and images are 'given voice, expression, and elaboration' (ibid.). The idea is to develop a sense of wholeness, by 'paradoxically, differentiating, naming, and elaborating all the different' dimensions of ourselves that make up who we are as persons (ibid.).

WRITING LEARNING BIOGRAPHIES – THE CASE OF TEACHERS' EXPERIENCE OF WHOLE-PERSON NARRATIVE LEARNING

The context of the case study is a Master's in Education Studies (MAES) programme at a British university. I am the designer and leader as well as the facilitator of this particular part of the programme. The MAES is a flexible research-based degree. Most of the students

are part-time mature students who are themselves teachers or educators. The MAES allows the participating teachers/educators to
construct their own coherent integrated learning experience through
library-based work and empirical research in the field, and/or inquiry
at the workplace. The core teaching of the programme focuses on
seminars, group meetings and one-to-one supervision with a tutor.

Most of the participants in the MAES share an interest in 'person-centred education', which is underpinned by a set of values
that regard the aims of education as enabling the flourishing of
the whole person, and which highlights the importance of human
relations in the process of teaching and learning (see Fielding,
2000; Gill and Thomson, 2012; Lamb, 2001; Standish, 1995 for
further definition and discussion of this concept). The design of
the programme has attempted to address some of the challenges
identified in the earlier section of this chapter.

Thus the MAES programme features a unique project – a self-
inquiry into some of the key topics in education through the writing of a learning biography. The motivation for including this
project originated from a shared concern for (a lack of) whole-
person learning. The aim is two-fold: (1) to continue developing teachers' understanding of whole-person learning through
reflecting on their own (learning) experiences; and (2) to explore
ways in which teachers/educators as learners could integrate an
understanding of whole-person learning in their everyday experience of teaching and learning within diverse institutions.

The final task for the project is the writing of personal biographies, including selected personal stories of learning, the interpretation of lived experiences and the theorization of learning. The
concept of learning biography used here is based on Dominicé's
(2000) definition of educational biography, which is an interpretation made by an adult about his or her life journey in learning.
Learning here is no doubt a broader term which, as we discussed
in the early chapters of the book, consists in all aspects of our
growth and becoming more human. The approach to the project

was also inspired by Dominicé's educational biography seminar design at the University of Geneva, and Goodson's (2001, 2006) methodological discussion of using life stories and biographies in research inquiry. Goodson argues that personal lived experiences

> concern with time and historical period, and context and histori-cal location. In studying learning, like any social practice, we need to build in an understanding of the context, historical and social, in which that learning takes place. (Goodson, 2006, p. 19)

Thus, as pointed out by Goodson and Gill (2011), the life stories of learning as narrated individually are no longer sufficient to understand the social and historical contexts within which edu-cation and learning takes place. Collaboration between the nar-rators of the stories through dialogue and interaction is one way to achieve greater understanding of one's lived experience. In this way, meaning becomes intersubjective (Charles Gadamer, 1976; Taylor, 1985), and our understanding of the social realities and our experiences within them becomes more critical.

The process of writing learning biography

To enable the participating teachers to inquire into their life's journey in learning, this part of the MAES programme includes:

a) **An introductory seminar.** The purpose of the seminar is to pre-pare the participants for a deep reflection, help them understand the methodology of writing the learning biography and explore some of the key concepts involved in the biographical writing. During the seminar, the group will engage in dialogue about the self-inquiry in adulthood through life history and memories, learning theories, personal identity and other connected con-cepts. Often the participants express their excitement with this project, as they 'have never done anything like this' in their lives, especially within the formal learning context of higher education.

b) **Individual reflection**. As a preparation for the learning biography, the participants are invited to reflect on their life as a whole, particularly the key experiences, people, activities and events. The participants are encouraged to consider questions such as 'Who am I?', 'How have I become the person who I am?', 'What are the key transitions in my life and in what way have they shaped my views of myself, my understanding of learning and the way I see the world?' and 'What are my values and how do I integrate my values in teaching and learning in my day-to-day practice?'. As this is learning biography, the core of the individual reflection is on learning, which is yet to be conceptualized and illustrated through the writing of the learning biography. The participants tend to conceptualize learning from a very broad perspective that involves any experiences of learning: that is, growth in oneself intellectually, emotionally, ethically, relationally, physically and spiritually, and from childhood to present, from formal learning in schools or other educational institutions, to informal, incidental and accidental learning.

This preparation and reflection is mainly carried out individually, where the participant experiences what most of them term as 'an internal dialogue', and one is in constant conversation and debate with oneself in terms of the meaning(s) in the event or memory and how one ought to interpret and understand one's lived experiences. In addition, the participant has to consider how his or her experiences would be interpreted by a reader – in this case, one's peers, supervisor(s) and examiners. Through this to-and-fro of viewing and reading one's life stories from multiple perspectives during this part of the project and transgressing the boundaries between the diverse roles one occupies, the participant engages in a profound dialogue involving multiple 'voices', including the voice of their ancestors (see also Chapter 5 of this book), those of the dominant authority, the voices of class, gender, ethnicity, religion and spiritual traditions, the moral voice and, above all, the human voice which is beyond but also contained in all other voices.

c) **Sharing oral narratives**. This takes place in a small group of six to eight participants, over a study weekend, starting on Friday evening, with a seminar introducing different learning theories and engaging the participants in a dialogue and discussion about the topic. I usually give an oral presentation of my own learning biography, with two to three vignettes, interpretation and reflection as well as theorization of learning in light of my life history. The participants are encouraged to ask questions about the project and how they might shape it based on their own experiences.

On Saturday, the whole day is devoted to sharing and listening to each other's life stories. The size of the group makes it safe enough for individuals to open up to tell their stories; and the very act of storytelling itself also seems to take people into a safe space – stories themselves invite people to listen and to engage. This is often the most creative and engaging session in the entire programme. Participants use diverse media to show their journeys: posters, a slideshow of photos, drawings, music and songs, objects and memorabilia and so on.

Participants initially work in a group of three or four in order that each person has sufficient time to make their presentation and peers can provide feedback and offer further questions to ponder.

d) **Exchanging written biographical vignettes**. The purpose is to explore one's tentative ideas and receive formative feedback from others in the group through the platform of a Virtual Learning Environment (VLE) or emails. All the posts are visible to the participants, the group facilitator/tutor and the supervisor(s) of each student. Feedback is often in the form of questions in order to encourage the author to think further and more deeply about the meaning of their lived experiences. Some participants may suggest books or articles to help the author expand their thinking and deepen their reflection; others might highlight the possible links between one story and the other, and how they are located within a broader cultural, social, political and institutional context.

e) **Presenting the first draft learning biography to the group.** When preparing the draft, participants have to make a selection of the stories that they would like to focus on as the basis of their theorization, highlighting the connections between these narratives and the idea of learning that has been developed. This process often involves dialogue with tutors and peers, and collaborative interpretation and analysis, in order to locate individual stories within wider historical time and political contexts as well as social and cultural practices.

This presentation takes place four weeks after the initial oral sharing of personal narratives. It is done over the course of one day, allowing each student at least 30 minutes to present their project and more time for their peers to provide detailed feedback, including challenging the author to think more deeply, to make connections and to conceptualize learning more holistically.

f) **Further reflection and desktop research.** In order to consolidate one's own understanding (and theorization) of learning, reflection is necessary through ongoing writing, analysis and interpretation, by engaging in critical self-reflection and dialogue with peers, and with the help of guided reading and critical discussion of literature.

g) **Sharing the finalized learning biography.** This takes place over the third study weekend when the participants focus on methodological reflection on the process of self-inquiry, interpretation of the narrative vignettes, theorization of learning and exploration of ways to integrate the new understanding in one's ongoing teaching and learning practices as well as one's ways of being.[1]

Although this process prioritizes group work, participants also work closely with their supervisors/personal tutors on a one-to-one basis. Tutors suggest reading materials and help the participants' theorization move forward. In this way, the final written assignment of the learning biography integrates participants' learning from each of the above stages, capturing the richness of the narratives and constructing meaning from lived experience.

h) **Programme evaluation**. When the participants have received the marking sheet for their project, including comments and formative feedback from the examiners, the group gathers for a debriefing session to evaluate this process and offer feedback to the programme design. During this time, the participants discuss openly the learning experienced and the challenges encountered whilst completing the project. This is often an occasion where each expresses gratitude for the support received throughout this emotional and often difficult process. And there is a celebration of being part of a unique journey which has just begun.

Reflecting on the journey of whole-person learning as critical pedagogy

The scene introduced at the beginning of the chapter took place during the first study weekend described earlier. There are six participants[2] in this particular group:

---

[1] More details on the design of the MAES programme and some of the participants' experiences can be found in Goodson and Gill (2011).

[2] The names given are not the participants' real names.

- Katrina is an art teacher in her late forties. She teaches arts and classics in a small alternative secondary school in the West Country.
- Andrew is a therapist in his early forties. He is a trainer and educator for counsellors and therapists, and has been working within adult lifelong learning for over ten years.
- Chitra just turned 22. She is Asian and has just obtained her first degree in education in her country. She is studying the MAES as a full-time student.
- Dermot is a business manager in his fifties. He runs a small company, but is interested in e-learning and how to build an online learning platform for sole traders in his field.
- Thomas is a science teacher in his early thirties. He became a secondary teacher three years ago and he is interested in starting an innovative programme in his school in order to motivate some of the young people who seem to exhibit apathy in school.
- Tanya is a teacher and educational manager in her thirties. Tanya works in a special unit of a state secondary school. She is a passionate advocate of the idea of a 'common school' and education for all.

With such a diverse group, each participant's experience of the whole-person process of writing the learning biography was different. However, these narrative journeys can be located from three broad pathways: (1) reconstruction of self; (2) finding our own stories; and (3) oneself in action. Here we will give voice to each participant's experience. We want to acknowledge that although the participants' experiences are presented in pairs below, each journey was absolutely unique, and indeed took more than just one pathway.

Katrina and Andrew – reconstruction of self

Being very self-conscious of her lack of conventional educational qualifications and of failing several important educational benchmarks, Katrina was initially reluctant to see her life stories as of any value. The group quickly sensed Katrina's vulnerability and they encouraged her to use her artistic talent and present her life history visually. This did indeed shift Katrina's approach. Overnight, she drew what she called the 'River of Life' on an enormous canvas and when it was her turn to share her life stories, she gradually opened up.

Katrina recalled a particular legacy which is the story about how her grandparents (eastern European immigrants arriving in England during the Second World War) used to sing songs and read poems as a way to deal with the hardship of settling in a new country during the war. The story and the songs and poems reassured Katrina's working-class parents and they continued to reassure herself and her children when she was told that she had 'failed' her education, during her divorce and throughout her cancer treatment. Although Katrina's own journeys, as described at the beginning of this chapter, were full of twists and turns, she wrote with optimism:

> Learning, for me, is the growth that takes place deep inside myself when I relentlessly follow my interests and curiosity, endlessly discover new things about myself, continuously search for the path that will take me closer to my dreams. I may never realise my dreams, but it is the journey that matters because in this journey, the growth within will allow me to blossom without.

When looking back at the process, she said that the writing of learning biography was 'one of the hardest things' she has ever done:

> I did many drawings, each representing a moment or a story in my life and laid them on the table. When I looked closely at them, I felt as if I was meeting myself for the first time. I laughed and cried, I was emotional and philosophical, I sang and I went silent, I danced and I lay still, I emptied myself and I refilled myself with images and stories. So my project is about selecting, creating connections and rebuilding myself from the bits I just unpacked and off-loaded.

Reclaiming her dignity and self-worth had become one of the key tasks for Katrina's project together with her attempt to reframe a sense of herself and her life in light of her aims and hope. In other words, Katrina's learning biography is itself a process of personal growth in examining her inheritances, encounters, artistic experiences and spiritual nourishment. She prioritizes her own inner depth, passion, moral aspiration and integrity. Thus she has identified her research focus for the MA as exploring young people's self-expression in arts.

Andrew embraced the whole-person narrative process straight away. He also encouraged others to remain gentle, especially when it comes to memories that are difficult to recall or painful to examine. Based on his own experience, Andrew saw the writing of learning biography with a group as an excellent opportunity to explore oneself and to launch an investigation into one's own identity. He focused his reflection on questioning how the myths of the self are created, developed and modified in the process of narrating. He wrote:

> The stories I told appeared unbidden, without thought, in consciousness. When I inquired into where significant learning had occurred they were at the front of the queue, larger than life, and waiting to be told. In the telling of my stories I do not pretend to historical accuracy for I do not think that is possible. The stories are current interpretations, interpretations of past events that explain, through an imagined developmental connectedness, my experience of the learning biography itself and the nature of the self that the learning biography has been pointing toward.

In this way, for Andrew, the process of writing the learning biography and his reflection on life is a learning event in itself and one that has radically altered his self-perception. It has highlighted 'the roles and functions of meaning-making, fantasy, imagination, and myth in self-creation'. Andrew, having been a Rogerian practitioner, defines learning as becoming a 'real' person (Jarvis, 2006) and therefore recreating oneself is a form of learning, as personal truth is experienced in a very 'real' way.

> The stories I will tell and my experience with the learning biography point toward integration, expansion, sense-making, and an experiencing of a deeper sense of self. This has not necessarily been through the stories themselves but through their telling and consequent integration in light of current knowledge. It is THIS that is of interest to me from a theoretical perspective. The process of the learning biography is of course dependent on the narratives but it is their integration that is transformative. It seems that a mysterious alchemy takes place when, with the benefit of hindsight, we revisit the past and describe what we find there; past hurts and pains can be put in their proper place; we can imbue them with meaning and what was maybe a continuous cause of suffering can be transformed into an integral part of our own mythology. I will therefore explore aspects of transformative/transformational learning theory with emphasis on not only the cognitive but also the emotional.

Andrew discussed the meaning of whole-person engagement in his learning biography. His project consists of selected episodes and key transitions in his life – the passing of a former partner and the love he offered and received, which transcended the boundaries between life and death; a descent 'down the stairs', at the bottom of which were his daemons; and his quest for spirituality and participating in the life within a Buddhist monastery – a community of 'learners', as he called it. The peers in the group commented that when reading Andrew's learning biography, they were invited onto an emotional and philosophical journey of reflection. They said they were able to understand concepts such as love, forgiveness and healing in much more profound ways than ever before. For his research, Andrew focused on exploring how these 'tools' for self-reflection and transformation might be integrated into his own work with adults especially when his own teaching involves supporting the learners to become self-reflective practitioners themselves.

To some extent, Katrina's and Andrew's learning journeys resemble each other, in that they both centre on recreating oneself in narrative. It was a whole-person engagement where they explored some conflicting aspects of oneself – love/hate, beauty/beast, spiritual/profane, good/bad, morality/decadence. Thus Andrew wrote that it was disintegration for reintegration. Their narrative interpretation of life and articulation of meaning embedded in it created a critical distance between themselves and their experiences. Thus the narrative reflection becomes critical reflexivity. As we saw in our early chapters, their biographical writing is a process of deconstruction in order to reconstruct. Although Katrina and Andrew explicitly focused their reflection and interpretation on the reconstruction of the self, they nevertheless deconstructed the contexts within which the self was constructed, and in doing so, they each reconstructed themselves and re-determined their actions accordingly.

Chitra and Dermot – finding our own stories

Having just completed her undergraduate studies with a focus on alternative education, Chitra was eager to quench her thirst for knowledge about person-centred education. That was one of the reasons why she came to study in the UK. When the learning biography project was introduced, Chitra hesitated, as she did not think her 22 years of life were worthy of self-inquiry. Yet she was surprised as she became aware that the writing of learning biography is 'transformational as I get in touch with myself in a more soulful and enriching way'.

What transpired for Chitra was her realizing of the stories that she lives by – some are inherited from her ancestors and a collective past, some from her religion, some from her culture and community, and others from the media and popular sources. For

Chitra, being able to distinguish the different kinds of stories and how they influenced her as a person was a major learning experience. Her emotional experience during the reflection and spiritual contemplation enabled Chitra to develop a further story of action:

> However, this interesting process brought in a fresh perspective of learning as personal development and my learning biography focused on finding the stories of my action. I felt honoured and reassured that these different stories had enabled me to construct my own stories within an inspirational moral framework.

Through dialogue with peers in the group, Chitra was encouraged to be more critical with some of the stories she experienced and encountered. One such story was within the realm of racial discrimination in an English school. Since her brief stay in England as an adolescent, this was the first time that Chitra had been able to confront a 'humiliating' past of 'bullying and torment'. Listening to another participant's friendship with an Asian child at school which was a stark contrast with Chitra's own experience, Chitra and the group discussed how the educational institution's ethos, culture and practices, and the role of the teacher, can affect a child's relationship with other children.

Chitra also saw that a relationship of care and trust within education can re-engage the energies of the child/learner (Noddings, 2007). She realized that educating moral beings must start from the teacher's own ethical dispositions.

> I will begin with a reflection on my own moral purpose. This is my 'Inner Voice' inspired by other voices, especially my religion, and I want it to guide my research and my future work in education.

From here, Chitra launched a research into the British policy of inclusive education in secondary schools, followed by further inquiry into teacher training and how teachers are educated in order to appreciate human differences and to help the children respect each other In this way, Chitra has found her own narrative.

Although Dermot also examined the stories in his life, his experience was very different from Chitra's. To begin with, Dermot viewed his life 'uniquely through the emerald green glow of my Irish heritage' – 'hardworking, calm, warm and supportive', but 'devoid of feeling and emotion'. Therefore, he called himself a 'traditional man' – a 'hardworking business man' and a 'family man' who embodied his heritage. On top of his Irish 'script' was a religious script of being good and he was 'unquestionably obedient, respectful, observing all religious ceremonies and submitting to clerical authority'.

Dermot's reflection and interpretation focused on questioning why these important scripts in his life only resulted in his turbulent divorce and losing all that mattered to him – house, job, wife, children and even the church, as he was 'berated as the seed of Satan'. Initially, in his presentation, he regarded his '180 degree' change from the 'traditional man' to a 'modern man' who danced in boardrooms, sang in choirs, acted in theatres, exercised in gyms and socialized using new technology and gadgets as a 'triumph', symbolizing his overcoming his own lacking in emotions and feelings as well as 'worldly skills'. Yet, in conversation and dialogue with his group, who encouraged him to question further, Dermot realized that he had simply escaped from one set of scripts and adopted another set of scripts.

> The writing of learning biography has been an illuminating process. I was able to reconsider and re-examine all the scripts I have unconsciously been living, and I felt that I can now venture to write my own script and this project is the starting point…The story of myself will never be divorced from my Irish heritage, my religious background or the appeal of modern script. Instead, they provide a platform or a stage upon which I re-identify myself. The deeper I look, the more I realise that I can only integrate these stories so that they truly become my own.

For Dermot, learning is closely associated with finding one's authentic self and finding one's stories. The research he proposed was aimed at creating holistic and collaborative online learning opportunities for small business owners like himself.

Tanya and Thomas – oneself in action

When looking back at the experience of writing the learning biography, Tanya said that it was one of the most challenging things to do:

> The process was an emotional roller coaster at times, being almost too personal to write down and consider how other people, who you had never met you and didn't know you, might read about you. It made me very clearly aware that on a daily basis I encounter people, places, have thoughts, emotions etc. and these can change us, take us on a different path, influence our decisions, help us or others learn and it is almost impossible to stop learning – you'd have to try quite hard to do so.

Tanya's own learning biography was 'to use prose and poetry to describe five pivotal incidents in my life that have led me to become the person I am today'. These 'dots' of pivotal incidents of her life were chosen from amongst many other possible ones and were put together into a meaningful thread that comprised Tanya's personal journey of growth. What facilitated her learning was often her own curiosity, which led to some new discoveries; her questions, which resulted in a deeper understanding of things; and her making a choice in terms of how to act when facing a moral dilemma. For Tanya, learning is about uncovering certain assumptions about oneself and the world, and being able to challenge the status quo and make some changes, large or small.

Tanya supports students with special educational needs. Reflecting on the power in the world, power in the hands of parents, teachers, authorities, social services and people of the middle class, she expressed her interest as a teacher in empowering the children:

> Many of my students have seen the power of others as a destructive force in their lives. They live with domestic violence, drug and alcohol dependencies and crime. They can often become aggressive or submissive and need appropriate social skills and support to become assertive and powerful in respect to their own safety, choices and opportunities. I would like to provide them with opportunities to learn and grow through positive action, enabling them to have their own direct experiences of joy and capability that many other children take for granted.

The learning biography made Tanya realize that 'we are a product of our upbringing, but our opportunities are not limited or prescribed by our social class beginnings'. Her own pathways point to the power of learning, education and training, and the positive influence a teacher can have on a child through his or her own course of action.

> I have an on-going interest in the role of students in their own learning and how they are able to express their needs, wants and directions they would like to explore in adult life. Working with students who have autism and speech and language difficulties I am aware that the usual routes to student voice are predominantly through literacy – listening, speaking, reading and writing – with which many of my students have significant problems.

Tanya's project focuses on how to help these students to develop their voices.

Thomas regarded the learning biography as 'an excellent way of easing my way back into academic writing'. He started the process by just writing up episodes from his life, ordering and trying to discern strands of influence.

> This was probably the most enjoyable aspect of the process, as it involved a certain degree of creativity while being based in lived experience. In the learning biography I mention that I once went to France to try to write a book, only to find that my prose was 'contrived and uninspired, while the journal I kept was effortlessly readable'. So it was nice to return to writing about my own experiences, which I find comes much more easily.

Through the project, Thomas was able to 'problematise things', but he also noted a fascinating aspect of the human narrative, as the storying process itself seems to allow a tendency to frame one's choices and actions in more noble terms. As we discussed in Chapter 1, the narrative process inevitably makes explicit one's ethical convictions, and therefore, in our telling, we tend to discard those stories of self-interest in favour of the notion that our life has been a long search for meaning.

Although Thomas accepted the possibility of becoming emotional in reflecting on his pathways in life, he had not expected it to be so intense:

> The process of systematically looking at how one's life has been shaped necessitates a much longer, harder look than one might ordinarily be inclined to take, and as such the emotional impact is much greater.

For Thomas, the 'main avenue of emotion' arising from the learning biography was that

> it helped clarify my sense of anger with the current state of education, and my recognition that this gap between vision and

reality can be seen as a source of creative energy ... The overriding sense from my short time as a state school teacher ... is one of frustration: with the inflexibility of the system, with the apathy among the students, and with my own shortcomings as a teacher within that system.

This anger and frustration fed directly into Thomas' ambition to help bring about change in education. Similar to Tanya, Thomas drew on his learning and understanding through the learning biography and the strength of his own moral rage to design an action research project within his school – introducing critical thinking into teaching the course of PSHE (Personal Social and Health Education). Through the critical dialogue during PSHE, he and his students explored the way they think and feel about education. In particular, Thomas 'challenged them to examine their attitudes, values and beliefs, such that they are able to justify them in the face of opposition, and amend them where they feel it necessary to do so'. He believes that critical thinking is a key to students' developing their capacity to examine and challenge assumptions. Thomas also discovered an extra dimension to his work:

> I have since come to realise that education reform is not possible without political reform. I am still interested in leading change in education, and I still place high value on education research ... However ... I am now of the opinion that the responsibility for changing a system lies with each individual in that system, and that wholesale education reform cannot happen until the politics that shapes education is itself reformed.

Thomas was really excited about this opportunity to put into practice the theories and ideas he had embraced throughout the MA course.

CONCLUSION

This sketch of the whole-person journey to understanding oneself and learning has illustrated that, by weaving the personal narratives of teachers and educators into academic discourse, learning biography makes it possible to enable profound personal growth and professional development. In so doing, this approach may also have the potential to help resolve the longstanding tensions between the emotional and the intellectual in higher learning, and in personal and professional learning within a scholarly context. This has been theorized as a process of narrative learning, particularly when it not only involves the teachers as whole persons, drawing on their implicit knowledge of learning which has been kept alive within, but also allows them to use narrative self-inquiry as an avenue for an expression of their inner integrity, personal growth and professional development.

There is little scope for higher education to integrate biographical learning and narrative pedagogy. At the same time, as this case study illustrates, such approach to learning and pedagogy is holistic, encourages reflexivity and engages the learner at many levels: existential, social, political and professional. This story of an MA class might serve to help us reframe our understanding of higher education from the standpoint of personhood.

Bibliography

Adler, A. (1927), *Understanding Human Nature*, Garden City, NY: Garden City Publishers.

Adler, J. and Mir, M. (2012), *Evaluation of the Forgiveness Project within Prisons*, London: Forensic Psychological Services at Middlesex University.

Aiken, N. (2008), 'Post-Conflict Peace-Building and the Politics of Identity: Insights for Restoration and Reconciliation in Transitional Justice', *Peace Research, the Canadian Journal of Peace and Conflict Studies*, Vol. 40, No. 2, pp. 9–38.

Alheit, P. (2009), 'Biographical Learning-Within the New Lifelong Learning Discourse', in K. Illeris (ed.), *Contemporary Theories of Learning: Learning Theorists—In their Own Words*, London: Routledge.

Alheit, P. and Dausien, B. (2002), 'The Double Face of Lifelong Learning: Two Analytical Perspectives on a Silent Revolution', *Studies in the Education of Adults*, Vol. 34, No. 1, pp. 3–22.

Allport, G. (1955), *Becoming: Basic Considerations for a Psychology of Personality*, New Haven: Yale University Press.

Anderson, E. (2010), 'Dewey's Moral Philosophy', *The Stanford Encyclopedia of Philosophy*, Fall 2010 Edition, http://plato.stanford.edu/archives/fall2010/entries/dewey-moral/, accessed 11 March 2013.

Arendt, H. (1998), *The Human Condition* (2nd revised edn.), Chicago: University of Chicago Press.

Armour, M. and Umbreit, M. (2006), 'Victim Forgiveness in Restorative Justice Dialogue', *Victims and Offenders*, Vol. 1, pp. 123–40.

Armstrong, M. (2012), 'Education as Reconstruction: Another Way of Looking at Primary Education', *The Brian Simon Memorial Lecture*, Institute of Education, November 24.

Baalbacki, A. (2007), *Around the Obstacles of Development: Social-Cultural Approach*, Beirut: Dar Al Farabi.

Baggini, J. (2005), *What's it All About? Philosophy and the Meaning of Life*, Oxford: Oxford University Press.

Barclay, B. (1996), 'Autobiographical Remembering: Narrative Constraints on Objectified Selves', in D. C. Rudin (ed.), *Remembering Our Past*, Cambridge: Cambridge University Press.

Bar-On, R. and Parker, J. (eds) (2000), *The Handbook of Emotional Intelligence*, San Francisco: Jossey-Bass.

Bar-On, D. and Sarsar, S. (2004), 'Bridging the Unbridgeable: The Holocaust and al-Nakba', *Palestine-Israel Journal of Politics, Economics and Culture*, Vol. 11, pp. 63–70.

Bar-Tal, D. (2000), *Shared Beliefs in a Society: Social Psychological Analysis*, Thousand Oakes, CA: Sage.

———. (2003), 'Collective Memory of Physical Violence: Its Contribution to the Culture of Violence', in E. Cairns and M. Roe (eds), *The Role of Memory in Ethnic Conflict* (pp. 77–93), Houndmills, England: Palgrave Macmillan.

Barthes, R. (1975), *The Pleasure of Text*, New York: Hill and Wang.

———. (1977), 'Introduction to the Structuralist Analysis of Narratives', in R. Barthes (ed.), *Image—Music—Text*, London: Fontana.

Blum, L. (1994), *Moral Perception and Particularity*, Cambridge: Cambridge University Press.

Bogdan, R. (1974), *Being Different: The Autobiography of Jane Fry*, New York: Wiley.

Booker, C. (2004), *Seven Basic Plots: Why we Tell Stories*, London: Continuum.

Boyd, R. (ed.) (1991), *Personal Transformation in Small Groups: A Jungian Perspective*, London: Routledge.

Boyd, R. and Myers, J. (1988), 'Transformative Education', *International Journal of Lifelong Education*, Vol. 7, No. 4, pp. 261–84.

Boydston, J. A. (ed.) (1916), *John Dewey: The Middle Works, 1899–1924*, Vol. 9, Southern Illinois: Southern Illinois Press.

Braithwaite, J. (2006), 'Narrative and "Compulsory Compassion"', *Law and Social Inquiry*, Vol. 31, No. 2, pp. 425–46.

Breuing, M. (2011), 'Problematizing Critical Pedagogy', *International Journal of Critical Pedagogy*, Vol. 3, No. 3, pp. 2–23.

Brewer, W. F. (1986), 'What is Autobiographical Memory?', in D. Rubin (ed.), *Autobiographical Memory* (pp. 25–49), New York: Cambridge University Press.

———. (1996), 'What is Recollective Memory?', in D. Rubin (ed.), *Remembering Our Past: Studies in Autobiographical Memory* (pp. 19–66), New York: Cambridge University Press.

Bruce, J. D., Read, D. G. Payne, and Toglia, M. P. (eds) (1998), *Autobiographical Memory: Theoretical and Applied Perspectives* (pp. 125–44), Mahwah, NJ: Erlbaum.

Bruner, J. (1986), *Actual Minds, Possible Worlds*, Cambridge, MA: Harvard University Press.

———. (1990), *Acts of Meaning*, Cambridge, MA: Harvard University Press.

———. (1991), 'Narrative construction of reality', *Critical Inquiry*, Vol. 18, pp. 1–21.

———. (2004), 'Life as Narrative', *Social Research*, Vol. 71, No. 3, pp. 691–710.

Burbules, N. and Berk, R. (1999), 'Critical Thinking and Critical Pedagogy: Relations, Differences, and Limits', in T. Popkewitz and L. Fendler (eds), *Critical Theories in Education* (pp. 45–66), New York: Routledge.

Cadwalladr, C. (2012), 'It's not where you come from ...', in The New Review, *The Observer*, February 12.

Carr, W. and Kemmis, S. (1986), *Becoming Critical: Education, Knowledge and Action Research*, London: Falmer Press.

Cayley, D. (1998), *The Expanding Prison: The Crisis in Crime and Punishment and the Search for Alternatives*, Toronto, ON: House of Anansi Press.

Chaitin, J. (2003), 'Stories, Narratives, and Storytelling, Beyond Intractability', in E. Burgess and H. Burgess (eds), *Conflict Research Consortium*, Boulder: University of Colorado, http://www. beyondintractability.org/bi-essay/narratives, accessed October 2012.

Cochran-Smith, M. and Lytle, S. L. (1999), 'The Teacher Research Movement: A Decade Later', *Educational Researcher*, Vol. 8, No. 7, pp. 15–25.

Colletta, N. and Cullen, M. (2002), 'Social Capital and Social Cohesion: Case Studies from Cambodia and Rwanda', in C. Grootaert and T. van Bastelaer (eds), *The Role of Social Capital in Development: An Empirical Assessment* (pp. 279–309), Cambridge: Cambridge University Press.

Conway, M. (1990), *Autobiographical Memory: An Introduction*, Buckingham: Open University Press Buck.

———. (1996), 'Autobiographical Knowledge and Autobiographical Memories', in D. C. Rubin (ed.), *Remembering Our Past: Studies in Autobiographical Memory* (pp. 67–93), New York: Cambridge University Press.

Csíkszentmihályi, M. and Beattie, O.V. (1979), 'Life Themes: A Theoretical and Empirical Exploration of their Origins and Effects', *The Journal of Humanistic Psychology*, Vol. 19, No. 1, pp. 45–63.

Cushman, P. (1990), 'Why the Self is Empty: Towards a Historically Situated Psychology', American Psychologist, Vol. 45, No. 5, pp. 599–611.

Damasio, A. (1994), *Descartes' Error: Emotion, Reason, and the Human Brain*, London: Vintage.

Dauenhauer, B. and Pellauer, D. (2011), 'Paul Ricoeur,' in E. N. Zalta (ed.), *The Stanford Encyclopedia of Philosophy*, Summer 2011 edn, http://plato.stanford.edu/archives/sum2011/entries/ricoeur/, accessed 11 June 2013.

Davis, L. (2002), *I Thought we'd Never Speak Again: The Road from Estrangement to Reconciliation*, New York: HarperCollins

Deans, T. (1999), 'Service-Learning in Two Keys: Paulo Freire's Critical Pedagogy in Relation to John Dewey's Pragmatism', *Michigan Journal of Community Service Learning*, Vol. 6, No. 1, pp. 15–29.

Dewey, J. (1916), *Democracy and Education: An Introduction to the Philosophy of Education* (1966 edn), New York: Free Press.

———. (1920), *Reconstruction in Philosophy*, New York: Henry Holt and Company.

———. (1925), *Experience and Nature*, LaSalle, IL: Open Court.

———. (1930), *Human Nature and Conduct: An Introduction to Social Psychology*, New York: The Modern Library Publishers.

———. (1938), *Experience and Education*, New York: Collier Books.

———. (1939), *Experience and Education*, New York: Macmillan.

———. (1964), 'Ethical Principles Underlying Education', in R. Archambault (ed.), *John Dewey on Education: Selected Writings* (pp. 108–40), New York: Random House.

Dirkx, J. (1998), 'Transformative Learning Theory in the Practice of Adult Education: An Overview', *PAACE Journal of Lifelong Learning*, Vol. 7, pp. 1–14.

———. (2000), 'Transformative Learning and the Journey of Individuation', *ERIC Digest* No. 223.

Dominicé, P. (2000), *Learning from Lives: Using Educational Biographies with Adults*, San Francisco: Jossey-Bass.

Eide, M. (2010), 'Forgiveness: An Introduction', *South Central Review*, Vol. 27, No. 3, pp. 1–11.

Ellsworth, E. (1989), 'Why Doesn't this Feel Empowering? Working Through the Repressive Myths of Critical Pedagogy', *Harvard Educational Review*, Vol. 59, No. 3, pp. 297–324.

Enright, R. (2001), *Forgiveness is a Choice: A Step-By-Step Process for Resolving Anger and Restoring Hope*, Washington, DC: American Psychological Association.

Enright, R. and North, J. (1998), *Exploring Forgiveness*, Madison: University of Wisconsin Press.

Erikson, E. (1968), *Identity, Youth and Crisis*, New York: WW Norton and Co.

———. (1975), *Life History and the Historical Moment*, New York: WW Norton and Co.

Feinstein, D. and Krippner, S. (1988), *Personal Mythology: The Psychology of Your Evolving Self*, Los Angeles: Jeremy P. Tarcher, Inc.

Fielding, M. (2000), 'The Person-Centred School', *Forum*, Vol. 42, No. 2, pp. 51–4.

Fitzgerald, J. M. (1996), 'Intersecting Meanings of Reminiscence in Adult Development and Aging', in D. C. Rubin (ed.), *Remembering Our Past: Studies in Autobiographical Memory* (pp. 360–83), New York: Cambridge University Press.

Freire, P. (1972), *Pedagogy of the Oppressed*, Harmondsworth, Middlesex: Penguin Books.

———. (1994/2004), *Pedagogy of Hope*, London: Continuum.

———. (1996), *Pedagogy of the Oppressed* (2nd edn), New York: Continuum.

———. (1998), *Pedagogy of Freedom: Ethics, Democracy and Civic Courage*, Maryland: Rowman and Littlefield Publishers.

———. (2001), *Pedagogy of Freedom: Ethics, Democracy, and Civic Courage*, Lanham, MD: Rowan and Littlefield.

Gadamer, H.-G. (1975), *Truth and Method*, New York: Seabury.

———. (1976), *Philosophical Hermeneutics* (David E. Linge, ed. and trans.), Berkeley: University of California Press.

———. (1977), *Philosophical Hermeneutics* (David E. Linge, trans.), Berkeley: University of California Press.

Gergen, K. (2009), *Relational Being*, New York: Oxford University Press.

Getzels. J. and Csíkszentmihályi, M. (1976), *The Creative Vision: A Longitudinal Study of Problem Finding in Art*, New York: Wiley.

Giddens, A. (1991), *Modernity and Self-Identity: The Self and Society in the Late Modern Age*, Stamford, CA: Stamford University Press.

Gill, S. and Goodson, I. F. (2010), 'Narrative and Life History Research', in B. Somak and C. Lewin (eds), *Handbook of Social Research*, London: Sage.

Gill, S. and Thomson, G. (2012), *Rethinking Secondary Education: A Human-Centred Approach*, London: Pearson Education.

Giroux, H. (1988), *Schooling and the Struggle for Public Life: Critical Pedagogy in the Modern Age*, Minneapolis: University of Minnesota Press.

———. (1994), *Disturbing Pleasures: Learning Popular Culture*, New York: Routledge.

Gobodo-Madikizela, P. (2009), 'Working Through the Past: Some Thoughts on Forgiveness in Cultural Context', in P. Gobodo-Madikizela and C. van der Merwe (eds), *Memory, Narrative, and Forgiveness: Perspectives on the Unfinished Journeys of the Past* (pp. 148–69), New Castle, UK: Cambridge Scholars Press.

Goleman, D. (1995), *Emotional Intelligence: Why it can Matter More than IQ for Character, Health and Lifelong Achievement*, New York: Bantam Books.

Goodson, I. F. (1981), 'Life History and the Study of Schooling', *Interchange* (Ontario Institute for Studies in Education), Vol. 11, No. 4, pp. 62–76.

———. (ed.) (1992), *Studying Teachers' Lives*, New York: Routledge.

———. (2001), 'Social Histories of Educational Change', *Journal of Educational Change*, Vol. 2, pp. 45–63.

———. (2005), *Learning, Curriculum and Life Politics: The Selected Works of I. F. Goodson*, Abingdon, NY: Routledge.

———. (2006), 'The Rise of the Life Narrative', *Teacher Education Quarterly*, Fall, pp. 7–21.

———. (2013), *Developing Narrative Theory: Life Histories and Personal Representation*, London: Routledge.

Goodson, I. F., Biesta, G., Tedder, M. and Adair, N. (2010), *Narrative Learning*, London: Routledge.

Goodson, I. F. and Gill, S. (2011), *Narrative Pedagogy*, New York: Peter Lang.

Goodson, I. F. and Hargreaves, A. (1996), *Teachers' Professional Lives*, London: Falmer Press.

Gur-Ze'ev, I. (1998), 'Toward a Non-Repressive Critical Pedagogy', *Educational Theory*, Vol. 48, No. 4, pp. 463–86.

Han, J. J., Leichtman, M. D. and Wang, Q. (1998), 'Auto-Biographical Memory in Korean, Chinese, and American Children', *Developmental Psychology*, Vol. 34, pp. 701–13.

Harvey, D. (2003), *The New Imperialism*, Oxford: Oxford University Press.

Hayler, M. (2011), *Autoethnography, Self-Narrative and Teacher Education*, Rotterdam: Sense Publishers.

Hazzouri, P. (2011), *Development and Peace-Building in Lebanon*, Beirut: Peace-building Academy.

Heron, J. (1992), *Feeling and Personhood*, London: Sage.

Hicks, D. (2011), *Dignity: The Essential Role it Plays in Resolving Conflict*, New Haven, CT: Yale University Press.

Hinchman, L. and Hinchman S. (eds) (1997), *Memory, Identity, Community: The Idea of Narrative in the Social Sciences*, New York: State University of New York.

Holstein, J. and Gubrium, J. (2000), 'The Self in a World of Going Concerns', *Symbolic Interaction*, Vol. 23, No. 2, pp. 55–115.

hooks, B. (2003), *Teaching Community: A Pedagogy of Hope*, New York: Routledge.

Horkheimer, M. (1982), *Critical Theory*, New York: Seabury Press.

———. (1993), *Between Philosophy and Social Science*, Cambridge, MA: MIT Press.

Hyvärinen, M. (2008), 'Life as Narrative Revisited', *Journal of Literature and the History of Ideas*, Vol. 6, No. 2, pp. 261–77.

Illeris, K. (2004), 'Transformative Learning in the Perspective of a Comprehensive Learning Theory', *Journal of Transformative Education*, Vol. 2, pp. 79–89.

Ingleton, C. (1995), 'Gender and Learning: Does Emotion Make a Difference?', *Higher Education*, Vol. 30, No. 3, pp. 323–35.

———. (1999), 'Emotion in Learning: A Neglected Dynamic', Paper Presented at HERDSA Annual International Conference, Melbourne, 12–15 July.

Jarvis, P. (2006), *Towards a Comprehensive Theory of Human Learning*, London: Routledge.

Karp, D. and Thom A. (eds) (2004), *Restorative Justice on the College Campus: Promoting Student Growth and Responsibility, and*

Reawakening the Spirit of Campus Community, Springfield, IL: Charles C. Thomas.

Karpiak, I. (2000), 'Writing Our Life: Adult Learning and Teaching Through Autobiography', *Canadian Journal of University Continuing Education*, Vol. 26, No. 1, pp. 31–50.

Kegan, R. (1982), *The Evolving Self*, Cambridge, MA: Harvard University Press.

Kermode, F. (1995), *Not Entitled: A Memoir*, New York: Farrar, Straus and Giroux.

Khalaf, R. (2011), 'Lebanese Youth Narratives: A Shifting Landscape', Paper Presented at the 11th UKFIET International Conference on Education and Development held on 13–15 September 2011 in New College, Oxford.

Kincheloe, J. (1991), *Teachers as Researchers: Qualitative Inquiry as a Path to Empowerment*, London: Falmer Press.

———. (1995), 'Meet me Behind the Curtain: The Struggle for a Critical Post-Modern Action Research', in P. L. McLaren and J. M. Giarelli (eds), *Critical Theory and Educational Research* (pp. 71–90), Albany: State University of New York Press.

———. (2004), *Critical Pedagogy*, New York: Peter Lang.

Kirschenbauum, H. and Henderson, F. V. (1985), *The Carl Rogers Reader*, Boston: Ploughton Mifflin.

Kolb, D. (1984), *Experiential Learning*, Englewood Cliffs, NJ: Prentice Hall.

Kritskaya, O. and Dirkx, J. (2000), 'Mediating Meaning-Making: The Process of Symbolic Action in Transformative Learning', in T. Sork, V. Chapman and R. St. Clair (eds), *Proceedings of the 41st Annual Adult Education Research Conference* (pp. 216–20), Vancouver: University of British Columbia.

Labov, W. (1982), *Sociolinguistic Patterns* (2nd edn), Philadelphia: Pennsylvania State University Press.

Lamb, W. (2001), 'The "Whole Child" in Education', *Journal of Philosophy of Education*, Vol. 35, No. 2, pp. 203–17.

Lasch, C. (1977), *Haven in a Heartless World*, New York: Basic Books.

Lather, P. (2001), 'Ten Years Later: Yet Again', in K. Weiler (ed.), *Feminist Engagements: Reading, Resisting, and Revisioning Male Theorists in Education and Cultural Studies* (pp. 183–96), New York: Routledge.

Lederach, J.-P. (2005), *The Moral Imagination: The Art and Soul of Building Peace*, Oxford: Oxford University Press.

Leichtman, M. D. (2001), 'Pre-Schooler's Memory Environments and Adults: Recollections in India and the US', Paper Presented at the Symposium on Culture and Memory, Third International Memory Conference, Valencia, Spain.

Linge, D. (ed.) (1977), *Hans-Gerog Gadamer: Philosophical Hermeneutics*, Berkeley: University of California Press.

Lloyd, F. (1977), *Woodley in the Nineteenth Century*, Reading Borough Council, UK: Reading Libraries.

Löfving, S. and Macek, I. (2000), *On War Revisited*, Stockholm: Department of Social Anthropology, Stockholm University.

MacIntyre, A. (1984), *After Virtue*, Notre Dame, IN: University of Notre Dame Press.

——. (2007), *After Virtue: A Study in Moral Theory*, Notre Dame, IN: University of Notre Dame Press.

Mack, J. (1990), 'The Psychodynamics of Victimization Among National Groups in Conflict', in V. Volkan, D. Julius and J. Montville (eds) *The Psychodynamics of International Relationships, Vol. I: Concepts and Theories* (pp. 119–29), Toronto: Lexington Books.

Macmurray, J. (1961), *Reasons and Emotion*, London: Faber and Faber.

Manfra, M. (2009), 'Action Research: Exploring the Theoretical Divide Between Practical and Critical Approaches', *Journal of Curriculum and Instruction*, Vol. 3, No. 1, pp. 32–46.

Markus, H. and Nurius, P. (1986), 'Possible Selves', *American Psychologist*, Vol. 41, pp. 954–69.

Markus, H. and Ruvolo, A. (1989), 'Possible Selves: Personalized Representation of Goals', in L. A. Pervin (ed.), *Goal Concepts in Personality and Social Psychology* (pp. 211–42), Hillsdale, NJ: Erlbaum.

McAdams, D. (1993), *The Stories we Live by: Personal Myths and the Making of the Self*, New York: Guilford Press.

——. (1999), 'Personal Narratives and the Life Story', in L. Pervin and O. John (eds), *Handbook of Personality: Theory and Research* (2nd edn) (pp. 278–500), New York: Guildford Press.

——. (2001), 'The Psychology of Life Stories', *Review of General Psychology*, Vol. 5, No. 2, pp. 100–22, http://www.sesp.northwestern.edu/docs/publications/430816076490a3ddfc3fe1.pdf, accessed 13 March 2013.

——. (2006), *The Redemptive Self: Stories Americans Live by*, Oxford: Oxford University Press.

McAdams, D. P., Diamond, A., de St. Aubin, E. and Mansfield, E. (1997), 'Stories of Commitment: The Psychosocial Construction of Generative Lives', *Journal of Personality and Social Psychology*, Vol. 72, pp. 678–94.

McAdams, D. and Ochberg, R. L. (eds) (1988), *Psychobiography and Life Narratives: A Special Issue of the Journal of Personality*, Durham, NC: Dukes University Press.

McLaren, P. (2000), 'Paulo Freire's Pedagogy of Possibility', in S. Steiner, et al. (eds), *Freirean Pedagogy, Praxis and Possibilities: Projects for the New Millennium* (pp. 1–21), New York: Falmer Press.

Merrill, J. (2007), 'Stories of Narrative: On Social Scientific Uses of Narrative in Multiple Disciplines', *Colorado Research in Linguistics*, Vol. 20, pp. 1–26.

Mezirow J. (2000), 'Learning to Think Like an Adult: Core Concepts of Transformation Theory', in J. Mezirow and Associates (eds), *Learning as Transformation: Critical Perspectives on a Theory in Progress* (pp. 3–34), San Francisco: Jossey-Bass.

———. (1994), 'Understanding Transformation Theory', *Adult Education Quarterly*, Vol. 44, No. 4, pp. 222–32.

Michelson, E. (1996), 'Usual Suspects: Experience, Reflection, and the (En)gendering of Knowledge', *International Journal of Lifelong Education*, Vol. 15, No. 6, pp. 438–54.

Middleton, S. (1992), 'Developing a Radical Pedagogy', in I. Goodson (ed.), *Studying Teachers' Lives* (pp. 18–50), London: Routledge.

Moffitt, K. H. and Singer, J. A. (1994), 'Continuity in the Life Story: Self-Defining Memories, Affect, and Approach/Avoidance Personal Strivings', *Journal of Personality*, Vol. 62, pp. 21–43.

Monk, R. (2012), *Inside the Centre: The Life of J Robert Oppenheimer by Ray Monk*, London: Jonathan Cape.

Moses, R. (1991), 'On Dehumanizing the Enemy', in V. Volkan, J. Montville and D. Julius (eds), *The Psychodynamics of International Relations* Vol. II, (pp. 111–8), Lanham, MD: Lexington Books.

Mullen, M. K. (1994), 'Earliest Recollections of Childhood: A Demographic Analysis', *Cognition*, Vol. 52, pp. 55–79.

Murray, H. A. (1938), *Explorations in Personality*, New York: Oxford University Press.

Myerhoff, B. (1992), *Remembered Lives: The Work of Ritual, Storytelling, and Growing Older*, Ann Abor: University of Michigan Press.

Narvaez, L. (ed.) (2010), *The Political Culture of Forgiveness and Reconciliation*, Bogota: Fondacion para la Reconciliacion.

Nasby, W. and Read, N. (1997), 'The Life Voyage of a Solo
Circumnavigator: Theory and Methodological Perspectives', *The Journal
of Personality*, Vol. 65, No. 4, pp. 785–1068.

Neimeyer, R. and Tschudi, F. (2003), 'Community and Coherence:
Narrative Contributions to the Psychology of Conflict and Loss',
in G. Fineman, T. McVay and O. Flanagan (eds), *Narrative and
Consciousness: Literature, Psychology, and the Brain* (pp. 166–91), New
York: Oxford University Press.

Neisser, U. and Winograd, E. (eds) (1988), *Remembering Reconsidered:
Ecological Approaches to the Study of Memory*, New York: Cambridge
University Press.

Nelson, M. (2000), *The Unburdened Heart: 5 Keys to Forgiveness and
Freedom*, New York: Harper San Francisco.

Noddings, N. (1992), *The Challenge to Care in the Schools*, New York:
Teachers College Press.

———. (2003), *Happiness and Education*, New York: Cambridge University
Press.

———. (2007), *Philosophy of Education* (2nd edn), Boulder, CO: Westview
Press.

Northrup, T. (1989), 'The Dynamic of Identity in Personal and Social
Conflict', in L. Kriesberg, T. Northrup and S. Thorson (eds), *Intractable
Conflicts and their Transformation* (pp. 55–82), Syracuse: Syracuse
University Press.

Palmer, P. (1998), *The Courage to Teach*, San Francisco: Josey-Bass.

Piaget, J. (1951), *Psychology of Intelligence*, London: Routledge and Kegan
Paul.

———. (1953), *The Origins of Intelligence in Children*, London: Routledge
and Kegan Paul.

Pillemer, D. B. (1998), *Momentous Events, Vivid Memories*, Cambridge,
MA: Harvard University Press.

Polkinghorne, D. (1988), *Narrative Knowing and the Human Sciences*,
Albany: SUNY Press.

Pollack, D. (2000), 'Physician Autobiography: Narrative and the Social
History of Medicine', in C. Mattingly and L. C. Garro (eds), *Narrative
and the Cultural Construction of Illness and Healing* (pp. 108–24),
Berkeley: University of California Press.

Pring, R. (2001), 'The Virtues and Vices of an Educational Researcher',
Journal of Philosophy of Education, Vol. 35, pp. 407–21.

Proust, M. (2006), *Remembrance of Things Past*, Vol. 2, Ware: Wordsworth.

Reiser, B. J. (1983), *Contexts and Indices in Autobiographical Memory*, New Haven, CT: Cognitive Science Program, Yale University.

Reiser, B. J., Black, J. B. and Kalamarides, P. (1986), 'Strategic Memory Search Processes', in D. C. Rubin (ed.), *Autobiographical Memory* (pp. 100–21), New York: Cambridge University Press.

Ricoeur, P. (1988), *Time and Narrative* (K. Blamey and D. Pellauer, trans.), Chicago: University of Chicago Press.

———. (1992), *Oneself as Another* (Kathleen Blamey, trans.), Chicago: University of Chicago Press.

Riessman, C. (1997), 'A Short Story About Long Stories', *Journal of Narrative and Life History*, Vol. 7, Nos. 1–4, pp. 155–9.

Riessman, C. and Quinney, L. (2005), 'Narrative in Social Work: A Critical Review', *Qualitative Social Work*, Vol. 4, pp. 391–412.

Robinson, J. A. (1992), 'First Experience Memories: Contexts and Function in Personal Histories', in M. A. Conway, D. C. Rubin, H. Spinnler, and W. A. Wagenaar (eds), *Theoretical Perspectives on Autobiographical Memory* (pp. 223–39), Dordrecht, the Netherlands: Kluwer Academic.

Robinson, J. A. and Taylor, L. R. (1998), 'Autobiographical Memory and Self-Narrative: A Tale of Two Stories', in C. P. Thompson, D. J. Herrman, D. Bruce, J. D. Read, D. G. Payne, and M. P. Toglia (eds), *Autobiographical Memory: Theoretical and Applied Perspectives* (pp. 125–44), Mahwah, NJ: Erlbaum.

Rogers, C. (1961), *On Becoming a Person: A Therapist's View of Psychotherapy*, Boston, MA: Houghton Mifflin.

———. (1969), *Freedom to Learn: A Provocative Signpost Pointing Toward What Education Might Become*, Columbus, OH: Charles E. Merrill Publishing.

Rosland, S. (2009), 'Victimhood, Identity, and Agency in the Early Phase of the Troubles in Northern Ireland', *Identities: Global Studies in Culture and Power*, Vol. 16, No. 3, pp. 294–320.

Ross, A. (2006), 'Coming in from the Cold: Constructivism and Emotions', *European Journal of International Relations*, Vol. 12, No. 2, pp. 197–222.

Rossiter, M. and Clark, M. (2007), *Narrative and the Practice of Adult Education*, Malabar, FL: Krieger.

Rotberg, R. and Thompson, D. (eds) (2000), *Truth v. Justice: The Morality of Truth Commissions*, Princeton: Princeton University Press.

Rowson, J. (2011), 'G. Sorros Quoted', in J. Rowson (ed.), *Transforming Behaviour Change: Beyond Nudge and Neuromania*, London: RSA.

Rubin, D. C. (ed.) (1986), *Autobiographical Memory*, New York: Cambridge University Press.

————. (ed.) (1996), *Remembering Our Past: Studies in Autobiographical Memory*, New York: Cambridge University Press.

————. (1998), 'Beginnings of a Theory of Autobiographical Remembering', in C. P. Thompson, D. J. Herrmann, D. Bruce, J. D. Read, D. G. Payne, and M. P. Toglia (eds), *Autobiographical Memory: Theoretical and Applied Perspectives* (pp. 47–67), Mahwah, NJ: Erlbaum.

Sammel, A. (2003), 'An Invitation to Dialogue: Gadamer, Hermeneutic Phenomenology, and Critical Environmental Education', *Canadian Journal of Environmental Education*, Vol. 8, pp. 155–68.

Schank, R. C. (1982), *Dynamic Memory: A Theory of Reminding and Learning in Computers and People*, New York: Cambridge University Press.

Schank, R. C. and Abelson, R. P. (1977), *Scripts, Plans, Goals, and Understanding*, Hillsdale, NJ: Erlbaum.

Schuller, T. (2009), *Crime and Lifelong Learning, Inquiry into the Future of Lifelong Learning (IFLL)*, Thematic Paper 5, Leicester: National Institute for Adult and Continuing Learning (NIACE).

Shapin, S. (2012), 'Now, I am Becoming Death', *A Review of Inside the Centre: The life of J Robert Oppenheimer* by Ray Monk, London: Jonathan Cape, *Guardian*, 17 November 2012.

Sherman, L. (2003), 'Reason for Emotion: Reinventing Justice with Theories, Innovations, and Research', The American Society of Criminology, 2002 Presidential Address, *Criminology*, Vol. 41, pp. 1–38.

Siegel, H. (1988), *Educating Reason: Rationality, Critical Thinking, and Education*, New York: Routledge.

Singer, J. A. (1990), 'Affective Responses to Autobiographical Memories and their Relationship to Long-Term Goals', *Journal of Personality*, Vol. 58, pp. 535–63.

Singer, J. A. and Salovey, P. (1993), *The Remembered Self*, New York: The Free Press.

Smyth, M. (1998), 'Remembering in Northern Ireland: victims, perpetrators and hierarchies of pain and responsibility', in B. Hamber (ed.), *Past Imperfect: Dealing with in Northern Ireland and South Africa* (pp. 31–49), Derry: Incore.

Standish, P. (1995), 'Post-Modernism and the Education of the Whole Person', *Journal of Philosophy of Education*, Vol. 29, No. 1, pp. 121–35.

Staub, E. (1989), *The Roots of Evil: The Origins of Genocide and Other Group Violence*, New York: Cambridge University Press.

Staub, R. and Bar-Tal, D. (2003), 'Genocide, Mass Killing, and Intractable Conflict: Roots, Evolution, Prevention, and Reconciliation', in D. Sears, L. Huddy and R. Jervis (eds), *The Oxford Handbook of Political Psychology* (pp. 710–55), Oxford: Oxford University Press.

Strauman, T. J. (1990), 'Self-Guides and Emotionally Significant Childhood Memories: A Study of Retrieval Efficiency and Incidental Negative Emotional Content', *Journal of Personality and Social Psychology*, Vol. 59, pp. 869–80.

———. (1996), 'Stability Within the Self: A Longitudinal Study of the Structural Implications of Self-Discrepancy Theory', *Journal of Personality and Social Psychology*, Vol. 71, pp. 1142–53.

Taylor, C. (1985), 'Interpretation and the Sciences of Man', *Philosophy and the Human Sciences: Philosophical Papers*, Vol. 2, pp. 15–57.

———. (1989), *Sources of the Self*, Cambridge: Cambridge University Press.

Taylor, E. (1997), 'Building Upon the Theoretical Debate: A Critical Review of the Empirical Studies of Mezirow's Transformative Learning Theory', *Adult Education Quarterly*, Vol. 48, pp. 34–59.

Taylor P. (2012), *The Independent*, July 2012.

Tedder, M. and Biesta, G. (2009), 'Biography, Transition and Learning in the Lifecourse: The Role of Narrative', in J. Field, J. Gallacher and R. Ingram (eds) *Researching Transitions in Lifelong Learning* (pp. 76–90), Abingdon: Routledge.

Thesiger, W. (2002), 'Wild at Heart', *Guardian*, 29 June.

Thomas, W. and Znaniecki, F. (1918), *The Polish Peasant in Europe and America: Monograph of an Immigrant Group*, Chicago: University of Chicago Press.

Thorne, A. (1995), 'Developmental Truths in Memories of Childhood and Adolescence', *Journal of Personality*, Vol. 63, pp. 138–63.

———. (2000), 'Personal Memory Telling and Personality Development', *Personality and Social Psychology Review*, Vol. 4, pp. 45–56.

Tisdell, E., Hanley, M. and Taylor, F. (2000), 'Different Perspectives on Teaching for Critical Consciousness', in A. Wilson and E. Hayes (eds), *Handbook of Adult and Continuing Education* (pp. 132–46), San Francisco: Jossey-Bass.

Tóibín, C. (2012), 'Ghosts in the Room', *Guardian*, 18 February.

Van Evera, S. (1994), 'Hypotheses on Nationalism and War', *International Security*, Vol. 18, No. 4, pp. 5–39.

Volkan, V. (1996), *The Need to Have Enemies and Allies: From Clinical Practice to International Relationships*, Northvale, NJ: Jason Aronson.

——. (2006), *Killing in the Name of Identity: A Study of Bloody Conflicts*, Charlottesville, VA: Pitchstone Publishing.

Wang, Q., Leichtman, M. D. and Davies, K. (2000), 'Sharing Memories and Telling Stories: American and Chinese Mothers and their 3-Year-Olds', *Memory*, Vol. 8, pp. 159–77.

Watson, J. (2010), 'The Theory of Human Caring: Retrospective and Prospective', *Nursing Science Quarterly*, Vol. 1, pp. 49–52.

White, M. and Epston, D. (1990), *Narrative Means to Therapeutic Ends*, New York: Norton.

Williams, B. (2009), 'Life as Narrative', *European Journal of Philosophy*, Vol. 17, No. 2, pp. 305–14.

Winders, J. (1993), 'Narratime: Post-Modern Temporality and Narrative', *Journal of Issues in Integrative Studies*, Vol. 11, pp. 27–43.

Wink, J. (2005), *Critical Pedagogy: Notes from the Real World* (3rd edn), Boston, MA: Allyn and Bacon.

Woike, B. A. (1995), 'Most-Memorable Experiences: Evidence for a Link Between Implicit and Explicit Motives and Social Cognitive Processes in Everyday Life', *Journal of Personality and Social Psychology*, Vol. 68, pp. 1081–91.

Yentob, A. (1991), Dennis Potter Interview on 'Writers Revealed', BBC Radio 4, June 4.

Yorks, L. and Kasl, E. (2002), 'Toward a Theory and Practice for Whole-Person Learning: Reconceptualizing Experience and the Role of Affect', *Adult Education Quarterly*, Vol. 52, No. 2, pp. 176–92.

——. (2006), 'I Know More than I can Say: A Taxonomy for Using Expressive Ways of Knowing to Foster Transformative Learning', *Journal of Transformative Education*, Vol. 4, No. 1, pp. 43–64.

Zehr, H. (2008), 'Doing Justice, Healing Trauma—The Role of Rrestorative Justice,' *Peace-building, Peace Prints: South Asian Journal of Peacebuilding*, Vol. 1, No. 1, pp. 1–16.

Index

Note: The letter 'n' following locators refers to notes